ASSET BUILDING & COMMUNITY DEVELOPMENT

Gary Paul Green
University of Wisconsin — Madison-Extension

Anna Haines
University of Wisconsin — Stevens Point-Extension

Sage Publications
International Educational and Professional Publisher
Thousand Oaks ▪ London ▪ New Delhi

For information:

 Sage Publications, Inc.
2455 Teller Road
Thousand Oaks, California 91320
E-mail: order@sagepub.com

Sage Publications Ltd.
6 Bonhill Street
London EC2A 4PU
United Kingdom

Sage Publications India Pvt. Ltd.
M-32 Market
Greater Kailash I
New Delhi 110 048 India

Printed in the United States of America

Library of Congress Cataloging-in-Publication Data

Green, Gary Paul.
    Asset building and community development / by Gary Paul Green and Anna Haines.
        p. cm.
    Includes bibliographical references and index.
        ISBN 0-7619-2464-7 (cloth: acid-free paper) — ISBN 0-7619-2263-6 (pbk.: acid-free paper)
    1. Community development—United States. 2. Community development corporations. 3. Community development. I. Haines, Anna. II. Title.
    HN90.C6 G724 2000
    307.1′4—dc21

                                                        2001001274

02   03   04   05   06   07   7   6   5   4   3   2   1

Acquiring Editor:	Marquita Flemming
Editorial Assistant:	Mary Ann Vail
Production Editor:	Diane S. Foster
Editorial Assistant:	Candice Crosetti
Typesetter/Designer:	Rebecca Evans
Indexer:	Monica Smersh
Cover Designer:	Michelle Lee

CONTENTS

PREFACE

C an residents work together to develop their community? There are numerous examples where residents have improved their quality of life by providing affordable housing, job training, and financing for local businesses. Yet there continues to be skepticism about the ability of communities to overcome problems of concentrated poverty in the inner city, underdevelopment in rural areas (e.g., Appalachia and American Indian reservations), and social isolation in many of our communities today. In this book, we examine the promise, and limits, of community development.

Community development is defined as a planned effort to produce assets that increase the capacity of residents to improve their quality of life. These assets may include several forms of community capital: physical, human, social, financial, and environmental. For each type of community capital, we examine why community-based organizations (CBOs), as opposed to governments or markets, are better able to produce these assets, the strategies that communities can use to develop these assets, and the institutions and organizations that are involved in the community development process. We contend that these assets will not generate as many local benefits if communities rely on either markets or state and federal governments to guide their development. Development that is controlled through CBOs provides a better match between the assets and needs of the communities, whether we are talking about job skills, housing, or banking capital.

We should note that we define community development in fairly broad terms. Many people today limit their definition of community development to the activities of community development corporations (CDCs). Although these organizations have become key actors in the nonprofit sector that provide affordable housing, many other organizations and institutions are actively involved in promoting locality development. We focus a great deal on CDCs, but we will also explore other organizations outside the "industry." In particular, we look at local economic development organizations and neighborhood associations. But there are many other informal organizations, such as neighborhood watches, building-level tenant associations, block clubs, and voluntary groups of youth doing community service, that serve as the foundation for community development work. We also consider the role of fairly specialized organizations, such as microenterprise loan funds, land trusts, and training consortia.

Most people use the term *community* to refer to residents of a geographical area, such as a neighborhood. Our book is directed primarily at "communities of place," although the material is relevant for "communities of interest," such as organizations and associations, as well. We also discuss many innovative regional programs that go beyond traditional place-based community development efforts. Although most of the literature on community development focuses on urban issues, we address rural communities and their concerns too. Discussions of community development also are frequently limited to low-income neighborhoods. Again, we take a broader perspective here and examine how middle-class communities are relying increasingly on CBOs to address problems of urban sprawl and environmental concerns. Many of the lessons learned about working in low-income neighborhoods can be applied to a variety of community problems.

We do not intend this book to be a "cookbook" on how to mobilize communities. Instead, we provide students and practitioners with several basic elements of community development: (a) the basic concepts and theories; (b) a map of the institutions, organizations, and actors involved in various arenas of community development; (c) common strategies and tactics used by communities; (d) case studies of successful (and unsuccessful) communities; and (e) resources available on various topics related to community development.

Part 1 of this book (Chapters 1-4) presents the history and organizational context of community development. In Chapter 1, we discuss the major concepts, issues, and theories used in the field of community development. Although community development draws from a variety of disciplines, a growing number of concepts and theories help define community development in theory and in practice.

In Chapter 2, we present a brief overview of the history of community development in the United States. We move from a discussion of early attempts at community development with the rise of settlement houses, through the New Deal and the War on Poverty, to contemporary efforts of community development corporations (CDCs), community development finance institutions (CDFIs), and comprehensive community initiatives (CCIs). A critical assessment of the history of the movement will help us identify the strengths and weaknesses of contemporary community development efforts.

In Chapter 3, we analyze the process of community development, with a focus on four stages of the process: community organizing, visioning, planning, and implementation/evaluation. Many academics and practitioners have debated the importance of process (development *of* community) versus outcomes (development *in* the community). Most community development programs today involve both elements. In this chapter, we focus on various strategies for developing a process that will engage residents in the strategic decisions affecting their localities.

In Chapter 4, we describe how CDCs are structured and review some of their strengths and weaknesses. We examine some of the constraints and limitations that CDCs face in promoting neighborhood development. We also look at other CBOs, such as local development organizations and neighborhood organizations.

CDCs are the most prevalent form of institution responsible for community and neighborhood development. There continues to be a debate over the effectiveness of CDCs in accomplishing a variety of issues. Critics charge that CDCs have lost their capacity to mobilize communities and have become simply technical assistance providers. We examine these debates and assess the future of CDCs.

In Part 2 (Chapters 5-9), we examine five forms of community capital: human, social, physical, financial, and environmental capital. We refer to these attributes as *capital* because investments in them will yield greater returns in the quality of community life. Each chapter follows a similar structure: limits to individual or government solutions to these problems, history of community development efforts in these areas, theoretical basis for community intervention, key actors and institutions involved, and strategies.

Human capital theory examines the relationship between a worker's education, skills, and experience and the individual's labor market experiences. According to the theory, workers with lower-level skills tend to be less productive and therefore are rewarded less in the labor market. A major focus of many community-based development organizations is training, which is assumed to increase the level of human capital and ultimately the quality of life in the community.

In our chapter on human capital (Chapter 5), we focus on workforce development and the role of CBOs in providing training and linking workers to jobs. We discuss how federal and state efforts are placing increasing emphasis on comprehensive approaches to workforce development that rely on CBOs. These workforce development strategies help overcome some of the obstacles that workers face in obtaining training and that employers encounter in providing job training.

Social capital can be defined as the norms, shared understandings, trust, and other factors that make collective action feasible and productive. Social capital enables members of a neighborhood or social network to help one another, especially in terms of education, economic opportunity, and social mobility. In our chapter on social capital (Chapter 6), we focus on community networks (both individual and organizational) that influence local development. These social ties and networks can serve as both resources and constraints in the community's effort to promote collective action. In many ways, social capital is at the center of asset building for all the forms of community capital we discuss. It is an essential feature of community action.

Physical capital refers to buildings, tools, and infrastructure. In Chapter 7, we focus on housing, primarily affordability issues. The federal government has had a large role in physical capital, as evidenced by the variety of programs for housing and other forms of physical capital, such as roads and other infrastructure, since the Depression. Due to federal devolution to lower levels of government and other organizations, communities have an opportunity to pursue innovative affordable housing solutions. In this chapter, we examine the variety of ways in which communities can address affordable housing problems.

Poor and minority communities frequently lack access to capital. Capital markets typically do not solve these problems. Many communities are building community financial institutions, such as revolving loan funds, microenterprise loan funds, and community development banks, to address their credit problems. Chapter 8 explores various strategies for addressing credit problems in communities. We examine how community credit institutions can meet both social and economic needs of their neighborhood.

In Chapter 9, we discuss environmental capital. Many communities are beginning to recognize that wisely managed natural resources, a community's environmental capital, play a major role in community satisfaction, quality of life, and economic development. CBOs can offer an alternative to public sector zoning and regulations that aim to protect a community's environmental capital, especially in places that do not have the broad support necessary for protecting key environmental resources. To demonstrate the role of CBOs in preserving natural resources, we look carefully at the role of land trusts in addressing environmental problems.

In Part 3 (Chapters 10-12), we cover community sustainability, international community development efforts, and the future of community development. Originally a concept from ecology, sustainability has been given many definitions. Essentially, the term refers to the ability of a system to sustain itself without outside intervention.

In Chapter 10, we evaluate how communities are attempting to build sustainability into their development strategies and the types of indicators that communities are using to assess their progress toward the goal of achieving sustainability.

Community development is rooted largely in the U.S. experience. Most other developed and underdeveloped countries tend to be much more centralized in their development programs and have less history with CBOs and locality development. Yet there has been tremendous growth in nongovernmental organizations (NGOs) and grassroots efforts in developing countries. One example is the Grameen Bank in Bangladesh, which successfully used microenterprise loan funds for community development. Chapter 11 explores community-based efforts in international settings, especially in underdeveloped countries.

Globalization and technological change are presenting new challenges and obstacles to community development and to the organizations that pursue it. As financial capital becomes more mobile, it may be increasingly difficult to establish bonds among other forms of capital to create a sense of place in a community. In Chapter 12, we look at how communities attempt to link up with global markets and the broader society without sacrificing control over their future. We also consider how technological changes are presenting new obstacles, and possibly new opportunities, to the development of community.

Acknowledgments

Several people contributed to this book. Pat Walsh and Dave Sprehn provided support early on in the project. They convinced us of the need for basic materials for community development practitioners. Steve Halebsky helped us identify community visioning efforts across the United States and made important contributions to the chapter on community development processes. Several people, both practitioners and researchers, reviewed individual chapters for us, including Elaine Andrews, Bo Beaulieu, Terry Besser, Calvin Brutus, Tim Carlisle, Steve Deller, Dan Diaz, Roger Hammer, Steve Malpezzi, Dave Marcouiller, John Merrill, Dave Neuendorf, Ron Shaffer, Jeff Sharp, Daniel Sullivan, Greg Wise, and Ann Ziebarth. The manuscript has benefited immensely from all of their comments and suggestions. Valeria Galetto was an outstanding research assistant and helped us take care of all of the loose ends. Jill Lucht assisted with much of the library work. Adam Dunn contributed to some of the computer analysis that we needed. Karen Morgan helped with many of the figures and tables in the text. Marquita Flemming, at Sage Publications, was a joy to work with throughout the project.

Finally, we would like to thank the students and practitioners we have worked with over the years. Community development is an exciting field, partially because it can bring together academics and practitioners. Not only have we learned from our interaction with students and practitioners, but we continue to be influenced by their enthusiasm for the potential of community development.

Gary Green
Anna Haines

History and Organizational Context of Community Development

CHAPTER 1

The Role of Assets in Community-Based Development

Community development has its roots in several academic disciplines, including sociology, economics, urban and regional planning, social work, and even architecture. The interdisciplinary approach of community development offers several advantages, such as providing a holistic view of communities, but it also presents problems. Among the major weaknesses are the lack of a common language, conceptual framework, and set of agreed-on issues and problems. There also is considerable debate among practitioners about whether community development is primarily a process or an outcome. In addition, community development has always had a diverse set of objectives: solving local problems (e.g., unemployment), addressing inequalities of wealth and power, promoting democratic values and practice, improving the potential of individual residents, and building a sense of community (Rubin & Rubin, 1992). As a result, community development has been defined in a variety of ways, including local economic development, political empowerment, integrated service provision, housing programs, comprehensive planning, and job-training programs. We are not going to be able to overcome this ambiguity in this book, but we will define some of the major concepts and issues on which there is considerable agreement in the community development field. We believe that the asset approach offers some possibility of providing a common conceptual field for community development theory and for practitioners. We begin with one of the most slippery terms—*community*.

Whither Community?

Community is one of the simplest concepts in the social sciences, yet it frequently lacks a precise definition. In a review of the literature many years ago, George Hillery (1955) found more than 94 separate definitions. The problem of defining community has been confused even more in recent years because it has been used interchangeably with neighborhood. In this section, we provide working definitions of *community* and *neighborhood* and discuss some of the implications of these definitions for community development.

- In 1990, 3,417 census tracts (or 5.7%) had poverty rates of 40% or higher.

- The number of high-poverty census tracts more than doubled from 1970 to 1990.

- Hispanics experienced the most rapid increase in the number of persons living in high-poverty areas from 1970 to 1990.

- Only 12% of all poor persons in the United States in 1990 lived in a high-poverty neighborhood.

SOURCE: Jargowsky (1997).

Following Kenneth Wilkinson (1991), we define community as including three elements: (a) territory or place, (b) social organizations or institutions that provide regular interaction among residents, and (c) social interaction on matters concerning a common interest. This definition excludes communities of interest, such as professional organizations or religious groups. Although many people continue to use the concept of community of interest, we will focus on communities of place in this book. Communities of place can vary considerably in terms of size and density. Areas with very low densities of population present some very difficult obstacles to the development of community. Low density may reduce the opportunities for interaction, which may ultimately make it more difficult to develop a sense of community. We also consider the existence of local institutions, such as a school or even a restaurant, as important in facilitating the development of a sense of community. These local organizations and institutions are important for a couple of reasons. They provide residents with opportunities for interaction, and they frequently represent the common interests of those in the area, such as a school district. Finally, this definition suggests that community is a contingent phenomenon, dependent on a number of conditions to achieve social interactions in pursuit of mutual interests. Action promoting a common interest is not necessarily a result of objective conditions, participation in local organizations and institutions, or even the realization that individual well-being is linked to the quality of life in the community. Thus, living in a place with local institutions does not necessarily lead to a sense of community. We will discuss some of the factors that can contribute to community later in the book.

Probably the easiest way to distinguish between community and neighborhood is to use the latter in reference exclusively to a specific geography and the former to refer to social interaction on matters concerning a common interest. By this distinction, a community may be place based or not. A community can be defined, for example, as a group of residents acting on a common interest, such as a school or road issue. Or it can be defined as a group sharing a common interest that is not necessarily place based, such as religious beliefs, professions, or ethnicity. In most cases, the development of community involves the existence of social institutions or organizations that provide the opportunity for regular social interaction among members. For our purposes in this book, we will limit our discussion of community to placed-based communities. The term neighborhood usually refers to a specific geographical area, such as a residential area demarcated by major streets or other physical barriers. It does not assume, however, that there is any social interaction or efforts to address common needs in the area, as is the case in the definition of community.

This simple distinction between *neighborhood* and *community* does not resolve some of the conceptual problems involved in using these terms. One of the perennial problems is that individuals in neighborhoods and communities of place, especially people who live in metropolitan areas, do not limit their social relationships to people in the same locality. Sociologists have shown that most individuals have extensive social ties with other people outside their neighborhood (Gans, 1962; Suttles, 1972). Thus, the boundaries of the neighborhood or community are difficult to define. Many researchers use official areas such as census tracts (Jargowsky, 1997) or counties (Lobao, 1990) to define neighborhoods or communities. These designations, however, do not necessarily correspond to bounded areas of social relationships, although the census bureau does consider things such as natural barriers in their process of defining census tracts. One result of the growing tendency to maintain contacts outside one's neighborhood is that it may be increasingly difficult to develop a sense of common interest with people in one's neighborhood.

This problem of defining the boundaries of neighborhoods and communities, however, does not mean that individuals do not maintain social relationships and ties with their neighbors. There is ample evidence that neighborhood ties and relationships continue to be important sources of support for many people (Campbell & Lee, 1992). Thus, communities of place should not be considered bounded entities that contain most of the social ties and relationships that residents have. As individuals now tend to work, live, and consume in different places, it is more likely that they will develop social relationships in these different settings. The rise of the Internet and improved transportation systems also have increased the likelihood that people will have social ties and relationships beyond their immediate area. The liberation of community ties from place does not make the development of communities of place impossible to achieve, but it does make such development more difficult in some settings. Although local crises, such as a plant closing or an environmental threat, may lead to short-term actions based on common interest, they may not be sustained over the long run.

Growth Versus Development

Growth and development are often considered to be synonymous, and the two concepts are seen increasingly by community residents in negative terms, especially by those who assume that growth and development automatically lead to more people, traffic, congestion, and environmental degradation. There are some important differences, however, between the two concepts that we should consider. Growth usually refers to increased quantities of specific phenomena, such as jobs, population, and income, but it also can be used to refer to changes in quality, such as better jobs or more secure sources of income. Development involves structural change in the community, especially in (a) how resources are used, (b) the functioning of institutions, and (c) the distribution of resources in the community. One of the primary goals of community development is to make the local economy less vulnerable to shifts in production technology and in the market environment. Thus, in most cases, when people refer to growth as a goal, the term *development* would be more appropriate.

On the basis of these definitions, we can see that growth may or may not lead to development. A few examples of changes that would be considered growth rather than development may help to illustrate these differences:

- A community experiences an increase in wealth, but most of it is concentrated in the hands of a few families.

- A community attracts a new employer that provides 100 new jobs, but 90 of the jobs are taken by people outside the community (and those 90 workers do not purchase goods and services locally).

- A community locates a fast-food chain in the neighborhood, but most of the profits from the operation are drained from the local area.

- A forest-dependent community attracts a paper mill that exploits the natural resources of the area in an unsustainable manner. (Destruction of the resources for future economic activity cannot lead to additional development.)

Development may lead to a more efficient use of resources, reduce the community's dependency on external resources and decision making, and create a better system of managing markets (financial, housing, labor, etc.) to satisfy local (societal) needs. A key element of the process is the allocation of development decisions to the local level, where relationships between economic development, the environment, and social needs are most visible.

People Versus Place

One of the continuing debates in community development is whether policies and programs should emphasize place or people. Supporters of people-based policies contend that there is not much evidence that place-based programs really work (Lemann, 1994). They point out that it is very difficult to attract businesses to poor communities or to help new businesses start there. There also is a tendency for workers to leave the community if the programs are successful. The dilemma for most communities is that increasing the skills and education of their existing workforce may not have any payoff if workers cannot find jobs in the area.

Place-based approaches have been at the core of community development efforts over the past 40 years. Advocates of placebased programs argue that an emphasis on people rather than places ultimately leads to more problems, as those who are successful leave their community. There are a variety of place-based strategies. Communities may choose to attract outside capital through tax and financial incentives. The Clinton administration has established Empowerment Zones (EZs) and Enterprise Communities (ECs) in several poor communities in the United States in an effort to promote development. These communities can offer a variety of incentives for businesses locating in these areas.

Other place-based approaches may focus less on outside investments and more on ways of increasing the quality of life through establishing new institutions, improving the physical infrastructure, or building on existing resources in the community. The assumption behind most of these approaches is that the existing institutional structure undermines the viability of most poor and minority communities. Institutional change is required to improve the quality of life and to capture the resources leaving the community. Most of these efforts attempt to leverage local resources (i.e., land, labor, and capital) to promote local ownership and control of resources. In other words, community-based strategies frequently generate demand among extralocal actors that produces benefits and returns the created surplus to the community (Gunn & Gunn, 1991).

The Challenge of Regionalism

Aside from the criticism that it is too difficult to create development in poor neighborhoods and communities, two other critiques are frequently made regarding place-based community development efforts. The first is that the focus on community and neighborhoods ignores the regional nature of development, especially at the metropolitan level. For example, Orfield (1997) argued that we need to take a regional approach to addressing the problems of concentrated poverty in the central city. He contended that racial segregation of housing, the lack of resources in ghettos, and incentives for migration to the suburbs make traditional community development efforts inadequate unless they address these social and economic forces. Among Orfield's policy recommendations are property tax base sharing across cities and suburbs, deconcentration of affordable housing across suburban areas, and land use policies that discourage sprawl. Other regionalists such as Rusk (1993) have emphasized the importance of cities' ability to expand their boundaries to capture the benefits of the movement of people and jobs to the suburbs.

A second critique is that a regional approach to promoting community stability helps us avoid making the false choice between people and place that is often presented in the community development literature. One example is the so-called mobility strategy (Hughes, 1991), which attempts to help city residents commute to suburban jobs rather than trying to bring employers to the city or move workers to where the jobs are. This approach has the advantage of solving the labor market and income problems of the poor while still keeping them in their neighborhoods. This strategy can be carried out in a few different ways. The most common tactic is to develop transportation systems that assist workers in finding and obtaining jobs in other parts of the region. Many cities are now providing transportation from the inner city to jobs in the suburbs. Another approach, however, might be to bring work (rather than the entire business) from employers in the suburbs into the inner city. This tactic helps develop the experience of the workforce in the inner city and often gives employers some confidence that these workers have the needed skills.

These regional strategies are not necessarily an alternative to traditional place-based community development strategies, but they represent a recognition of the linkages between communities and their regions. Recommendations for the mobility strategy are still based on the assumption that it is important to build the community or neighborhood.

CASE STUDY 1.1

The Dudley Street Neighborhood Initiative

Probably one of the most widely acclaimed success stories in the community development field over the past decade is the Dudley Street Neighborhood Initiative (DSNI). The philosophy behind DSNI was to build on the local assets rather than to focus on the needs of residents. Dudley Street is located in Boston's Roxbury District, one of the poorest areas in Massachusetts. Approximately 35% of the families lived below the poverty line, the neighborhood contained many abandoned buildings and a large number of vacant lots (20% of the lots), and there was a persistent drug problem in the community.

DSNI began in 1984 when the Riley Foundation, a Boston area community foundation, decided to make an investment in the neighborhood. The plan presented by the Riley Foundation was challenged by local residents because it was not "their" plan. In response to this initiative, residents established DSNI, which had a 31-member board of directors, with the majority being local residents. There are more than 2,500 voting members of DSNI, and the organization employs approximately 16 full-time staff.

The organization launched several projects that were immediately successful, including removing the illegal dumps on Dudley Street and even providing affordable housing for residents. Part of DSNI's success was due to its combining the role of developer of low-income housing and provider of social services with the role of community organizer. The most controversial project of DSNI was its program to take eminent domain of 30 acres of vacant land and develop it as a land trust. DSNI had strong support from the city government for this project.

To date, DSNI has been able to construct 77 single-family and cooperative homes for low- and middle-income residents. It has organized a youth committee to address their concerns, such as recreation and educational opportunities. DSNI has been especially concerned about recognizing the various cultures in the neighborhood and has sponsored several multicultural festivals. The organization has begun to move into the area of economic development but has had less success with these efforts.

For more information on DSNI, see Medoff and Sklar (1994). The video *Holding Ground: The Rebirth of Dudley Street* (Lipman & Mahan, 1996) documents the efforts of DSNI as well.

Asset Building

We have defined community development as a planned effort to build assets that increase the capacity of residents to improve their quality of life. John Kretzmann and

FIGURE 1.1
Community Needs
Map

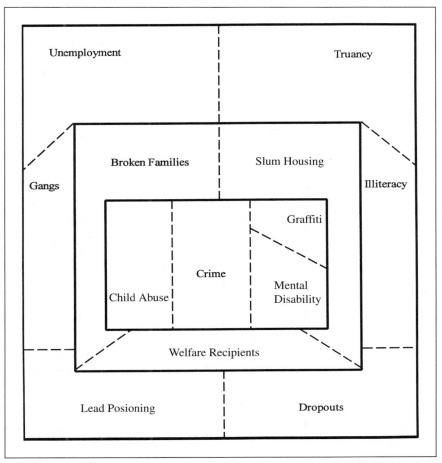

SOURCE: From J. Kretzmann and J. McKnight (1993). *Building Communities From the Inside Out.* Evanston, IL: Institute for Policy Research, Northwestern University. Reprinted with permission.

John McKnight (1993) defined assets as the "gifts, skills and capacities" of "individuals, associations and institutions" within a community (p. 25). This focus on the assets of communities, rather than the needs, represents a major shift in how community development practitioners have approached their work in recent years (see Case Study 1.1). In the past, community development practitioners began their efforts by conducting a "needs assessment" that examined the problems and weaknesses of the community (Johnson, Meiller, Miller, & Summers, 1987). Figures 1.1 and 1.2 provide comparisons of the typical needs and assets available in a community.

Asset mapping is a process of learning what resources are available in your community. Examples of assets mapping might be:

- The identification of economic development opportunities through the mapping of available skills and work experience

- The identification of natural resource assets that may serve as an important source of economic development by drawing tourists or increasing the value of homes

FIGURE 1.2
Community Assets
Map

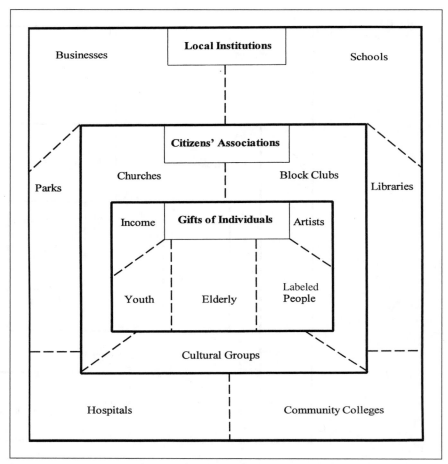

SOURCE: From J. Kretzmann and J. McKnight (1993). *Building Communities From the Inside Out.* Evanston, IL: Institute for Policy Research, Northwestern University. Reprinted with permission.

- An assessment of consumer spending practices to identify the potential for new businesses in the neighborhood

- A community resources inventory to identify the suitability of residents for providing services, such as child care, so as to identify the potential for having more providers in the community

This definition does not explicitly consider the built environment: the homes, businesses, and parks that are part of a community or neighborhood. In this book, we expand the definition of community assets to include five types: physical, human, social, financial, and environmental. There are obviously other assets that we might consider, but most community development activities focus on these five forms.

We use the term *community assets* here for a few reasons. First, the term suggests that there are resources in the area that are underused (Kretzmann & McKnight, 1993). Individuals may have jobs skills or experiences that do not match what is demanded locally. Individuals and families may have savings that are being invested outside the community. The community may have natural resources that could be of value as amenities. Community development efforts typically try to mobilize these resources to better meet the needs of residents.

The asset approach also implies that the community development effort is directed toward the locality or place. Rather than providing training for jobs that workers must take elsewhere, there is an attempt to match training efforts to jobs that can be created locally. Similarly, if a community's natural resources are processed by an absentee-owned firm, many of the benefits will flow outside the community. The same thing may occur if families place their savings in banks and other financial institutions that invest these resources in other localities.

Finally, the asset approach assumes that many institutional obstacles to the development of places cannot be overcome through individual action but instead must be addressed through the activities of community-based organizations (CBOs). These organizations can overcome many of the collective action and economy-of-scale problems associated with community development. For example, though individual employers in a community may lack skilled workers, and though they all have an interest in having a skilled workforce, individual businesses may be reluctant to invest in training because they may lose these workers after they receive the training. Community development offers collective solutions to these problems by building on the existing resources within the community.

In his analysis of community-based development organizations (CBDOs), Herbert Rubin (2000) found that asset building is the real objective of these organizations:

> It matters less what is built than that projects introduce assets, both material and social, for those in neighborhoods of deprivation. These assets create an economic stake in society, for both recipients and the CBDO, as well as a set of obligations—paying rent, maintaining property, concern with the quality of the neighborhood—that is socially empowering. (p. 162)

Public Participation

Community development requires the involvement and participation of local residents in identifying the strategies they wish to use to improve the quality of life. Most people use the term citizen participation to characterize this process. We prefer to use the term public participation in this book. Stuart Langton (1978) defined citizen participation as "purposeful activities in which citizens take part in relation to government" (p. 17). This concept is too restrictive for our purposes for a couple of reasons. First, this definition is limited to citizens—legal residents. By using the term public participation, we also include people who do not have all the rights and obligations of citizenship. Given the high rates of immigration in many American cities, and in rural areas as well, and the disproportionate number of poor communities with a large number of immigrants, excluding them does not make sense today. Second, the term citizen participation includes only activities related to the government. Public participation refers to activities in any public institution of society or the government, which includes organizations and institutions other than government. Although many community development activities, such as improving social service provision or transportation systems, either collaborate with or are directed at governments, many more activities do not involve government at any level.

Having differentiated between citizen and public participation, we should comment that much of the public's participation in the past has been in relation to local, state, and federal governments. It is useful to distinguish between two types of participation here. First, there is community action that results from activities initiated and controlled by CBOs and that is frequently directed at changing government services and policies. Second, there is community action that is public involvement initiated and controlled by the government.

There has been a rapid growth in the number of programs initiated by the government to promote public involvement. Almost all federal or state programs contain some element of public participation. Some examples are federal requirements for public participation in the Coastal Zone Management Act, the Federal Water Pollution Control Act, the Airport and Airways Development Act, and, more recently, the Intermodal Surface Transportation Efficiency Act (ISTEA). The primary purpose of these programs is to gain support for decisions, programs, and services. Of course, many of these programs have been criticized for not allowing the public to make these decisions but rather simply giving them an opportunity to comment on decisions that have already been made. We will examine these issues in more detail later when we discuss the community development process (Chapter 3).

Why is there so much emphasis on public participation in community development? The key assumption is that local residents will be much more supportive of the project, and therefore increase the likelihood of success, if they have some input into the decision-making process. Also, local residents probably have much better knowledge about the assets and needs in the community. Finally, public participation is considered the centerpiece of the democratic process. This emphasis on public participation, however, has not always been accepted by local officials. As we will see in Chapter 3, public participation among the poor during the 1960s was an especially controversial topic.

The Role of Community-Based Organizations

One of the distinguishing characteristics of community development, as opposed to community organizing, is that it involves the creation of local organizations to help build assets. Throughout this text, we place a great deal of emphasis on the role of CBOs. CBOs offer several advantages compared to nonlocal organizations for carrying out place-based programs. They are rooted in place and have extensive contacts and information about the neighborhood. Their primary mission is in the community; they emphasize the importance of place over other goals. CBOs also are, ideally, controlled by local residents. Typically, control is characterized by representation on the board and input regarding the organization's policy and programs.

One of the principal vehicles for carrying out community development activities in the United States today is the *community development corporation (CDC)*. Because CDCs are so important to the community development movement, we devote almost an

TABLE 1.1
Comparison of Three
Themes of Community
Development

Themes	Role	Task/Process Orientation
Self-help	Facilitator/educator	Process
Technical	Adviser/consultant	Task
Conflict	Organizer/advocate	Process and task

SOURCE: From "Themes of Community Development," by J. A. Christenson, in *Community Development in Perspective*, edited by J. A. Christenson and J. Robinson, Jr., 1989 (pp. 26-47). Ames: Iowa State University Press. Copyright 1989 by Iowa State University Press. Reprinted with permission.

entire chapter to discussing their activities (see Chapter 4). Community development, however, can occur in a variety of other CBOs.

Throughout the text, we will discuss some of the different types of CBOs that are emerging today. For example, we also examine *local development corporations*, which are responsible for coordinating economic development activities in many communities and regions. We pay special attention to the role of *neighborhood associations*, which play an important role in addressing issues such as real estate development and social service provision.

A wide variety of other community-based development organizations are active in the field. *Community foundations* are nonprofit organizations that provide long-term funds for organizations and activities in a defined geographic area. There are more than 400 community foundations, with total assets exceeding $8 billion (Mayer, 1994). *Religious organizations* have played an increasingly important role in providing services to the poor and are more involved in job training and housing issues than they were in the past, largely due to welfare reform. There are a large number of non-*religious nonprofit organizations*, such as homeless shelters, neighborhood clinics, and child care centers, that typically play a more specialized function in communities. Throughout this book, we will discuss other specialized CBOs, such as loan funds and training organizations, that may or may not be related to broader organizations.

The organizations discussed above tend to have paid staff that serve residents. Many nonprofit organizations, without staff, also play a critical role in community development. Examples of these organizations are parent-teacher organizations, tenant associations, block clubs, recreational clubs, and other smaller organizations. These organizations play a critical role in community development efforts but probably receive very little attention in the literature.

Models of Community Development

Although there are some common issues and problems in the field of community development, there is still wide variation in how practitioners approach their work. One of the ways of conceptualizing these differences is the typology developed by James Christenson (1989). Christenson identified three different community development themes or approaches: self-help, technical assistance, and conflict (see Table 1.1). Although many community development efforts do not fall neatly into one of these three categories, the typology is useful for understanding some of the different ways practitioners may approach their work.

Self-Help Approach

At the heart of the self-help approach is the belief that community development is primarily about helping people help themselves. Practitioners who adopt this model tend to define their role as that of facilitator, helping the community identify its goals and increasing the community's capacity to participate in the solution of collective problems. The facilitator generally adopts a neutral position in the change process and is much more concerned about the process of community development than the specific outcomes (e.g., jobs, houses, services). The self-help approach assumes that increasing the capacity of residents to address their problems will result in improvements in the quality of life and the ability of residents to help themselves in the future.

The self-help approach requires several conditions to be effective. Individuals must have the necessary democratic skills. Participants must have a reasonable expectation that their efforts will have some impact. They also must identify their shared interests to develop a common set of goals. Community development efforts using the self-help approach tend to have a more long-lasting effect than some of the other approaches because residents have greater ownership in the process.

Technical Assistance Approach

Practitioners who adopt the technical assistance approach assume that the most important obstacle communities face is technical assistance and information. This model is firmly rooted in the rational planning approach to development. Thus, the appropriate role for the community development practitioner is that of consultant. Those who advocate the technical assistance model are much more concerned with the eventual outcome of the community development effort than they are with the capacity of residents. Technical assistance also can be provided in a variety of ways, from ongoing local assistance to short-term consulting.

A variety of issues should be considered in the technical assistance approach to community development. Whose values are being served by the assistance? How have the goals been established? Are there other alternatives that should be considered? Will the assistance help participants address community problems better in the future?

Technical assistance to neighborhoods and communities can be provided through several different institutional arrangements: a centralized location, a regional provider, or local assistance. Technical assistance offered through a centralized location is the most cost efficient but often lacks the follow-up that is frequently necessary. An alternative is to provide technical assistance through local or regional providers. This approach has several advantages. The consultant usually has much more knowledge about local or regional conditions. He or she also is available for follow-up consultation once the project has been initiated. Of course, this type of technical assistance is usually much more costly than the traditional consultant model.

Conflict Approach

Probably one of the most established traditions in community development is the conflict approach, which is most often identified with Saul Alinsky (1969). The practitioner's approach in this model is one of organizer or advocate. Practitioners who adopt this approach assume that the fundamental source of most community problems is that community members lack power. This approach often begins with an assessment of the local power structure.

According to Alinsky, the community organizer then needs to choose a problem to address and to organize the community around this problem. The conflict should be small and winnable. The goal is to demonstrate to residents that they can be successful. Alinsky's approach is based on the assumption that community organizations should not directly confront the power structure. Instead, they should use a variety of tactics to embarrass local political leaders and to demonstrate the value of power to residents. Although this approach has proven to be successful in low-income neighborhoods, it is unclear how successful these tactics would be in middle-class neighborhoods. More important, community organizers using this approach frequently have difficulty in maintaining momentum in the community development process once residents have had some successes.

Summary and Conclusions

Community development defies many of the standard assumptions we make about community and development in America today. Its emphasis on CBOs rather than the power of markets or government programs challenges the policy prescriptions of both political conservatives and liberals. The requirement that residents participate in the solutions to common problems contradicts the accepted view today that "community" no longer exists. Emphasis on place rather than people also puts community development squarely in opposition to the individualistic nature of our culture and society. Because of the focus on the local level, community development fails to capture much of the attention of the media, the public, or policy makers.

Yet community development is consistent with some of the ideals we hold to be extremely important, such as democratic control and local autonomy. The political system may be driven by financial interests, and individuals may have little control over bureaucratic institutions (e.g., the corporation, educational system, the government), but the community offers a place for people to learn the value of cooperation and civic virtue. Participation, like any other skill, must be learned through experience. The promise of community development is that these skills can be transferred to other walks of life.

KEY CONCEPTS

Assets	Development	Self-help
Citizen participation	Growth	Technical assistance
Community	Neighborhood	
Conflict approach	Public participation	

QUESTIONS

1. Compare and contrast the three models of community development described by James Christenson.

2. What are the three necessary elements in the definition of community? Why is community such a difficult concept to define?

3. What is the difference between growth and development? Provide some examples.

4. Identify three key differences between the assets approach and the needs assessments approach to community development.

5. What are the basic strengths and weaknesses of place- versus people-oriented approaches to development?

EXERCISES

1. Identify a CBO where you live. Interview several members of the organization, and identify which model of community development the organization appears to use in its work. Look at some specific successes and failures of the organization to examine these issues. What are the strengths and weaknesses of this organization?

2. Ask several of your neighbors to draw a map of your community or neighborhood. Are their maps similar, with similar boundaries and other identifying features, or different? How many neighbors do they know in this area? How often do they have contact with these people? Do they belong to any clubs, organizations, or associations in this neighborhood?

3. Identify all the CBOs (both nonprofit and profit) in your neighborhood or community. Assess the overlap in their mission and the networks that exist between these organizations.

REFERENCES

Alinsky, S. D. (1969). *Reveille for radicals.* New York: Random House.

Campbell, K., & Lee, B. (1992). Sources of personal neighbor networks: Social integration, need, or time? *Social Forces, 70,* 1077-1100.

Christenson, J. A. (1989). Themes of community development. In J. A. Christenson & J. Robinson (Eds.), *Community development in perspective* (pp. 26-47). Ames: Iowa State University Press.

Gans, H. J. (1962). *The urban villagers: Group and class in the life of Italian-Americans.* New York: Free Press of Glencoe.

Gunn, C., & Gunn, H. (1991). *Reclaiming capital: Democratic initiatives and community development.* Ithaca, NY: Cornell University Press.

Hillery, G. A., Jr. (1955). Definitions of community: Areas of agreement. *Rural Sociology, 20*(2), 111-123.

Hughes, M. (1991). Employment decentralization and accessibility: A strategy for stimulating regional mobility. *Journal of the American Planning Association, 57,* 288-298.

Jargowsky, P. A. (1997). *Poverty and place: Ghettos, barrios, and the American city.* New York: Russell Sage.

Johnson, D. E., Meiller, L. R., Miller, L. C., & Summers, G. F. (Eds.). (1987). *Needs assessment: Theory and methods.* Ames: Iowa State University Press.

Kretzmann, J., & McKnight, J. (1993). *Building communities from the inside out: A path toward finding and mobilizing a community's assets.* Evanston, IL: Northwestern University, Center for Urban Affairs and Policy Research.

Langton, S. (Ed.). (1978). *Citizen participation in America.* Lexington, MA: Lexington.

Lemann, N. (1994, January 9). The myth of community development. *New York Times Magazine,* pp. 27-31.

Lipman, M., & Mahan, L. (Producers & Directors). (1996). *Holding ground: The rebirth of Dudley Street* [Video]. (Available from New Day Films, 22nd Hollywood Avenue, Ho-Ho-Kus, NJ 07423)

Lobao, L. M. (1990). *Locality and inequality: Farm and industry structure and socioeconomic conditions.* Albany: State University of New York Press.

Mayer, S. E. (1994). *Building community capacity: The potential of community foundations.* Minneapolis, MN: Rainbow Research.

Medoff, P., & Sklar, H. (1994). *Streets of hope: The fall and rise of an urban neighborhood.* Boston: South End.

Orfield, M. (1997). *Metropolitics: A regional agenda for community and stability.* Washington, DC: Brookings Institution.

Rubin, H. J. (2000). *Renewing hope within neighborhoods of despair: The community-based development model.* Albany: State University of New York Press.

Rubin, H. J., & Rubin, I. S. (1992). *Community organizing and development* (2nd ed.). Boston: Allyn & Bacon.

Rusk, D. (1993). *Cities without suburbs.* Washington, DC: Woodrow Wilson Center.

Suttles, G. D. (1972). *The social construction of communities.* Chicago: University of Chicago Press.

Wilkinson, K. P. (1991). *The community in rural America.* New York: Greenwood.

ADDITIONAL SUGGESTED READINGS

Readings ■

Boyte, H. C. (1984). *Community is possible: Repairing America's roots.* New York: Harper & Row.

Brophy, P. C., & Shabecoff, A. (2000). *A guide to careers in community development.* Washington, DC: Island. This book is an excellent reference for anyone considering working in the community development field. The authors include information on jobs; universities and colleges offering community development curricula; training programs; and other resources on community development.

Bruyn, S., & Meehan, J. (Eds.). (1987). *Beyond the market and the state: New directions in community development.* Philadelphia: Temple University Press.

Downs, A. (1994). *New visions for metropolitan America.* Washington, DC: Brookings Institution.

Ferguson, R. F., & Dickens, W. T. (Eds.). (1999). *Urban problems and community development.* Washington, DC: Brookings Institution.

Gottlieb, P. D. (1997). Neighborhood development in the metropolitan economy: A policy review. *Journal of Urban Affairs, 19*(2), 163-182.

Peterman, W. (2000). *Neighborhood planning and community-based development: The potential and limits of grassroots action.* Thousand Oaks, CA: Sage.

Web Sites ■

National Community Development Policy Analysis Network (NCDPAN). <www.brook. edu/es/ncdpan>. NCDPAN's goal is to stimulate policy research on the development of low- to moderate-income communities, including, but not limited to, the work of CDCs. Research that concerns "people" and "places" simultaneously is their focus.

Community Development Society. <www.comm-dev.org>. The international Community Development Society is a professional association of community development practitioners. The society represents a variety of fields, including health care, social services, economic development, and education.

Comm-Org: The On-Line Conference on Community Organizing and Development. <comm-org.utoledo.edu>. This site has a wealth of references, data, syllabi, and other resources on community organizing and development.

Videos ■

Mobilizing Community Assets (1995), produced by Civic Network Television, directed by Steve Crane. Video training program for *Building Communities From the Inside Out,* by John Kretzmann and John McKnight. Available from ACTA Publications, 4848 N. Clark South, Chicago, IL 60640, phone (800) 397-2282.

Periodicals ■

Community Development Digest. This publication provides an excellent summary of legislation pending on community development issues.

Urban Research Monitor. A useful reference tool developed by HUD USER. The publication makes it easy for researchers, policy makers, academicians, and other professionals to keep up with the literature on housing and community development. Each issue contains a listing of recent books, articles, reports, dissertations, and other publications related to housing and community development.

CHAPTER 2

A History of Community Development in America

C ommunity development emerged in the United States in the 1960s with the rise of place-based policies (mostly antipoverty programs), professional training programs and degrees, and formal organizations with community development as their primary mission. Many of the ideas behind community self-reliance, however, have their roots in earlier intellectual sources, such as Alexis de Tocqueville (1961) and John Dewey (1916). Some of the first intentional efforts at promoting community development occurred at the turn of the century.

In this chapter, we outline the evolution of community development in America. We begin our analysis at the turn of the century, with the Progressive Era and some of the efforts to construct community programs to address poverty and other social problems. We examine the programs of the New Deal and the Great Society, which placed the federal government in a central role in community development. Finally, we examine some of the current efforts to promote development in poor and minority neighborhoods in the United States. Because of some key differences between rural and urban communities at the turn of the century, we discuss the different origins of community development efforts in these two settings.

The Evolution of Community Development

Although there continues to be much debate about the best approach to promote community development or the effectiveness of community self-reliance, the public generally supports the ideas of local control and the importance of community in our social life. The idea of the role of community and its role relative to the government has evolved considerably over this century. In this brief review, we identify the main currents of thought in the community development field over the past century.

The Progressive Era

Many people trace the origins of community development to the Progressive Era, especially to the ideas of social scientists and reformers at the time. The most distinguishing characteristic of Progressives was that they resisted individualistic explanations for poverty and social disorganization (e.g., juvenile delinquency, crime, and the breakup of the family). Instead, they explained poverty and deviant behavior by focusing on how social conditions in communities produce such behavior. Such behavior was seen as a result of the subcultures of these neighborhoods. Progressives saw local conditions as an obstacle to integration into the larger society. They argued that to improve local conditions, social intervention should have three important characteristics (O'Connor, 1999). First, it should be comprehensive, focusing on the integration of education, services, jobs, and physical conditions in a locality. Second, it should promote collaborations between experts and citizens in addressing local problems. The growth of comprehensive city planning during the period is one example of this model. Finally, Progressives placed a great deal of emphasis on citizen participation. As we will see, in the 1960s this element of the community development program was highly controversial, especially during the War on Poverty.

The Chicago School of sociology, especially Robert Park's (1915) interpretation of urban development, provided much of the intellectual basis for intervention in urban neighborhoods. Park insisted that the problems of cities, such as juvenile delinquency and crime, rather than being the result of social disorganization, reflected the gradual assimilation of immigrants into the mainstream society. There was more social order in these settings than observers recognized. A certain level of neighborhood disorganization was necessary because it meant that immigrants were shedding their cultural influences. Park argued that this process was necessary for immigrants to eventually be integrated into the social life of cities. It was necessary, however, to provide stability at the neighborhood level—for example, through the provision of services to facilitate immigrants' social integration.

One of the most visible efforts to promote community development in urban areas at the time was the settlement house movement. The objective of the settlement house movement was to help immigrants to the cities adjust to their new environment. The programs provided adult education (especially English language lessons), day care centers, libraries, recreational facilities, and other services that would integrate these residents into the larger society. Probably the most famous of the settlement houses was Hull House in Chicago, which was established by Jane Addams and Ellen Gates Starr.

Whereas the problems of concern in urban America at the time were poverty and social disorganization, the problems in rural areas were different: a lack of technical information on agricultural conditions, poor educational opportunities, monopolization of forest land, inadequate roads, the lack of credit, poor health services, soil depletion, and the limited role of women. The major impetus to improving rural life at the time was President Theodore Roosevelt's 1908 Country Life Commission. One of the major outcomes of this movement was the establishment of the Cooperative Extension Service, as provided by the Smith-Lever Act of 1914. The Cooperative Extension Service provided at least one educator in each agricultural county who was responsible for programs related to the social, economic, and financial well-being of rural residents. The system had the same emphasis as the Progressive movement in urban reforms on collaboration between experts and citizens in solving local problems. The Cooperative Extension Service was able to draw on the research and expertise of the land grant system and build its program on the basis of the involvement of local residents in identifying community needs. In many states, it also focused on comprehensive solutions that acknowledged the importance of recreation and social activities in the community.

Community development efforts during the Progressive Era focused on community-level intervention that was intended to integrate residents into the larger society. The philosophy behind the movement was that professional expertise could be linked with participation by the poor in solving these problems. The goal was to help residents become full citizens by either improving the services available to them or providing them with the scientific information they would need to improve their quality of life. In both rural and urban areas, there was an interest in helping residents develop their own organizations to more adequately serve their needs.

The New Deal

President Franklin Roosevelt's New Deal programs constructed a new approach to the problems of depressed communities. During the 1930s, these programs dealt with a wide array of problems, including job creation, land ownership, housing, physical infrastructure, and social welfare. These programs provided federal support for community intervention, and they became the foundation for community development programs for the next 40 years. One of the chief characteristics of community development efforts during this period was the strong role of the federal government in helping communities address their needs.

Probably the most influential piece of legislation directly affecting depressed communities during the New Deal was the Housing Act of 1937. The Housing Act provided the basis for public housing. Like many of the other New Deal programs, it established a decentralized system of market subsidy and local control. Local authorities were responsible for issuing bonds, purchasing land, and contracting with local builders (O'Connor, 1999). The housing programs were used primarily for slum clearance, which was beneficial to the many real estate developers involved in opening up efforts to revitalize downtown areas. Local control also meant that almost all public housing built at the time was concentrated in central cities.

Many of the New Deal programs (the Home Ownership Loan Corporation and the Federal Housing Administration) had objectives that worked against the goals of addressing the problems of urban poverty. The primary objective of the New Deal housing programs was to promote home ownership. There were several elements to these programs, but some of the most important were the home mortgage loans that were made available to middle- and working-class residents and the loan guarantees to private lenders. These programs provided incentives for people to move to the suburbs, leaving the central cities with a higher rate of unemployment, poverty, and social problems. The federal programs to build interstate highways also exacerbated many of these problems.

The New Deal programs made some important strides in helping distressed communities. The programs, however, also faced other basic problems that have plagued community development programs over the years. In particular, the programs that might have benefited tenant farmers and African Americans in the South were bitterly fought by southern legislators and businesses. Many of the social assistance programs were administered through local welfare offices, where the local elite could influence access to and levels of support for the poor (Piven & Cloward, 1971). This was the trade-off that President Roosevelt made for getting the support of southern Democrats for the New

Deal. This tension between local control and federal support continued through several decades of programs related to community development. The New Deal, however, did represent a major shift in the role of the federal government in attempting to address the problems of poor communities.

Urban Renewal and Area Redevelopment

During much of the 1940s and 1950s, population and employment decentralization contributed to the growth of suburbs and the rise in poverty and blight in central cities. The response to these problems by the federal government was the Housing Act of 1949, which came to be known as urban renewal. The primary objective of urban renewal was to clear the slums, so as to revitalize downtowns and attract middle-class residents back to cities. The Housing Act permitted local redevelopment authorities to use eminent domain to reclaim land for commercial purposes. Urban renewal came to be known as "Negro removal" and was criticized for bulldozing low-income neighborhoods.

The Area Redevelopment Act (ARA) of 1961 focused on a different set of issues at the time—joblessness in areas affected by economic modernization. The program provided low-interest loans to businesses willing to locate or expand in the designated depressed areas. The ARA was eliminated after a relatively brief period (4 years). Among the major criticisms were that the ARA was recruiting nonunion businesses and that it was largely ineffective. The program was transformed eventually into the Economic Development Administration (EDA) and focused on rural infrastructure and regional planning.

The War on Poverty

Three programs during the mid-1960s provided the foundation for President Lyndon Johnson's War on Poverty: the Community Action Program (CAP), Model Cities, and the Special Impact Program (SIP). Many people see these programs as a logical extension of the New Deal policies, but they actually represented something qualitatively different from the previous programs.

CAP became one of the most controversial programs of the War on Poverty (Moynihan, 1969). In Title II-A, Section 202(a)(3), of the Economic Opportunity Act of 1964, CAPs were authorized to be "developed, conducted and administered with the maximum feasible participation of residents of the areas and members of the groups served." There was considerable disagreement among activists, bureaucrats, and policy makers about the involvement of the poor in CAP policy making and program development. Some people thought of this requirement as simply involvement but not decision-making responsibilities. Others interpreted it as requiring some form of social action among the poor.

The most serious criticisms of the program were that it promoted conflict and violence in the inner city, that the government adopted this idea without any understanding of community participation, that bureaucrats had perverted the congressional intent of the program, and that the poor were not ready to assume power in their communities. Daniel Moynihan's (1969) principal concern was that the program led to rising expectations on which it could not deliver.

The requirement for citizen participation was considered a threat by many local politicians. In particular, many city mayors were accustomed to working with established neighborhood organizations and leaders representing minority groups and the poor. CAPs were demanding changes in services and resources allocated to poor neighborhoods. In reality, however, most CAPs were never very representative of the poor. The boards did not have many poor people on them, and the CAPs were required to work through the system to achieve any results.

There appears to be a consensus that most of the citizen participation programs of the 1960s did not work. Several factors operated against them. The federal and local governments never really trusted the CAPs. As a result, many local government officials were able to minimize the level of real community control in the organizations. Resources for the War on Poverty were limited and not sufficient to deal with the magnitude of the problems. The Vietnam War siphoned off money that could have been devoted to the poverty programs. Thus, it is not clear at all that Community Action was a failed idea, but it was never given the chance to demonstrate how effective it could have been.

The second major program directed at concentrations of poor minorities was the Model Cities program. This program was established through the Demonstration and Metropolitan Development Act of 1966. The act provided grants to city agencies to improve housing, the physical environment, and social services in low-income neighborhoods. In many respects, it was a diluted version of Community Action because it placed less emphasis on citizen participation. The major difference was that Community Action worked around local government officials, whereas Model Cities worked with them.

The third major program that was initiated during this period was SIP. SIP provided funds to community development corporations (CDCs) to finance comprehensive development strategies. The program was an outcome of Senator Robert Kennedy's visit to Brooklyn's Bedford-Stuyvestant neighborhood in 1965, which formed the nation's first CDC.

The community development programs of the 1960s placed considerably more emphasis on local control than any previous attempts to address the problems of poor communities had done. Most assessments of the programs have concluded that these efforts to increase the level of participation by the poor in decision making were relatively unsuccessful. These programs also emphasized the need for neighborhood organizations to address local problems. The continued growth of CDCs today suggests that this may have been one of the most successful long-term elements of these programs.

Retrenchment During the Nixon and Reagan Administrations

The Nixon administration's New Federalism fundamentally altered the role of the federal government in community development. The administration attempted to dismantle many of the programs that were created in the 1960s by giving states and localities more authority in influencing how public funds were spent. Probably the best example of this shift was the creation of Community Development Block Grants (CDBGs) in 1974, which replaced many (seven) of the categorical grants to localities for specific purposes to address poverty. The Nixon administration replaced these categorical grants with a form of revenue sharing that would have given localities much more autonomy in their decisions in how to spend these dollars. The CDBGs fall in between these two extremes.

CDBGs have three major objectives: (a) to benefit low- and moderate-income families (defined as families earning no more than 80% of the area median income), (b) to eliminate or prevent slums, and (c) to meet urgent community needs. Communities must use at least 70% of the CDBG funds to principally benefit low- and moderate-income persons. The CDBG program is one of the largest of the federal grant programs. In Fiscal Year 1999, approximately $4.75 billion was allocated to the CDBG program. Over the past 25 years, CDBG has been allocated almost $87 billion.

Communities that receive funds directly from the federal government today are referred to as entitlement communities. These metropolitan cities and urban counties (842 cities and 147 counties) receive direct grants that can be used to revitalize neighborhoods, expand affordable housing and economic development efforts, and improve community facilities and services. A separate CDBG program allocates funds to the states. States in turn provide grants to localities not covered under the entitlement funds, referred to as nonentitlement communities.

To receive its CDBG entitlement grant, a community must have a plan approved that describes how it will use its funds. Throughout most of the 1980s and 1990s, housing has been the most important use of CDBG in localities. There has been a gradual shift in priorities, however, toward other projects, such as economic development activities. Jobs created through CDBG-funded programs must meet several tests for quality. A recent study by the Urban Institute, funded through the U.S. Department of Housing and Urban Development (HUD, 1995), found that 96% of the jobs created through CDBG funds were full-time jobs, 89% remained after 4 years, 90% paid more than minimum wage, and 32% were held by neighborhood residents where the business was located (HUD, 1995). CDBG funds are supposed to be targeted to needy communities through a formula allocation system that considers population size, poverty, overcrowded housing, and age of housing.

How do communities use their CDBG funds? Communities may acquire real property for public purposes, such as purchasing abandoned houses for rehabilitation. Many localities have used the funds to build public facilities, such as streets, sidewalks, water and sewer systems, and recreational facilities. Increasingly, communities are using CDBG funds to help for-profit businesses by establishing revolving loan funds, assembling land for new industry, or helping existing businesses expand so as to hire low-income workers. In 1998, entitlement communities spent the largest share of their funding for housing and public facilities and improvements (see Case Studies 2.1 and 2.2).

During the Reagan administration, the CDBG program was changed to allow states to administer the grants to small cities. Governors maintained that they could direct the resources better to distressed communities than could the federal government. The evidence suggests that states and localities vary considerably in their capacity and their will to target these funds to the most distressed communities (Rich, 1993). When states target the funds, they tend to distribute the funds to a broader set of communities and are less likely to target the most distressed communities.

Many local officials like CDBG funds because they are a predictable source of funding for community development. Besides, the funds are relatively flexible, although

---

CASE STUDY 2.1

CDBG Funds: Direct Assistance to Low- and Moderate-Income Home Buyers, Waukesha County, Wisconsin

Waukesha County is located in the suburbs of Milwaukee and is one of the fastest growing areas in Wisconsin. Rapid growth and a high median family income mean that housing costs are out of range for most low- and moderate-income families, with only a few homes for sale under $100,000. To respond to these needs, the county used CDBG funds to underwrite low- and moderate-income buyers in three new subdivisions, as well as using CDBG funds in other innovative ways to promote home ownership. The county is also using $350,000 "float loan" financing for buyers' land write-downs in another development.

SOURCE: Gunther (2000).

CASE STUDY 2.2

CDBG Funds: Neighborhood Strategic Plans, Milwaukee, Wisconsin

The city of Milwaukee wanted to obtain more neighborhood-level representation in the development of its consolidated plan. The city trained neighborhood residents to develop strategic plans regarding what their needs and resources were and what activities should be funded. Each neighborhood is provided $10,000 in CDBG funds to develop its strategy. The city bases its funding allocations on the priorities established by the 17 neighborhoods that were involved in the process.

SOURCE: Gunther (2000).

---

there has been some controversy over the years regarding how flexible these funds should be. The funds also can be used to leverage private funds (and other public funds) for community projects.

Probably the most lasting impact of the Reagan administration on community development occurred through the cutbacks that occurred in the federal budget throughout the 1980s. Most of the federal programs that supported community development programs, especially through the HUD, were severely cut. Ironically, these cuts may have strengthened many community-based organizations (CBOs), such as CDCs, which were forced to find new sources of funding, primarily through foundations and other private sources.

The Clinton Years

During the Clinton administration, there have been several programs focusing directly on community development, but the primary effort has been the Empowerment Zone/ Enterprise Community (EZ/EC) initiative. The objective of the program is to "stimulate economic opportunity in America's distressed communities." The program provides tax incentives and performance grants and loans to create jobs and business opportunities. It also focuses on activities to support people looking for work, such as job training, child care, and transportation.

Employers in an EZ are eligible for wage tax credits, worth $3,000 for every employee hired who lives in the EZ. EZ businesses also may write off the expense of the cost of depreciable, tangible property that they purchase up to $37,000. All of the communities are eligible to receive tax-exempt bond financing that offers lower rates than conventional financing to finance business property and land, renovations, or expansion.

Communities are required to submit strategic plans that were developed with the active participation of low-income community residents, and only communities with high rates of poverty are eligible. In the first round, rural EZs received grants of $40 million and rural ECs received about $3 million from the Social Services Block Grant program. Urban EZs received $100 million; urban ECs received the same amount as rural ECs. The first round of empowerment zones included Atlanta, Baltimore, Chicago, Cleveland, Detroit, Los Angeles, New York, Philadelphia, the Kentucky Highlands, Mid-Delta Mississippi, and the Rio Grande Valley, Texas. There also are 95 enterprise communities.

The effectiveness of these programs continues to be debated. HUD reports that by 1998, almost 10,000 jobs were created or saved, 14,000 workers were trained, 25,000 youth were served, and 102 water or waste treatment systems were under construction. Yet critics charge that most of the businesses would have located or stayed in these communities without the tax incentives and that these programs have had only a very limited impact on poverty in these areas. EZ/EC communities also face some of the same opposition by local government officials that the Community Action Program faced in the 1960s.

By the late 1990s, most states have passed their own EZ legislation. States vary widely in what they offer businesses to locate in these zones, including tax incentives (e.g., property tax abatements, investment tax credits, employer and employee tax credits, and lender and investment deductions), financial assistance (e.g., low-interest loans and bond financing), and regulatory changes (e.g., environmental regulations, building permits).

Alongside the promotion of the EZ/EC initiative, the Clinton administration overhauled the welfare system, which had significant implications for poor communities throughout the United States. In 1996, Congress passed the Personal Responsibility and Work Opportunity Reconciliation Act (PRWOR), which ended the program known as Aid to Families with Dependent Children (AFDC). This act had important implications for states and localities because CBOs have become more involved in providing services for welfare recipients and designing programs that will facilitate their entrance into the labor force. These programs have relied heavily on CBOs to coordinate many of the services and training programs that are available to workers.

The Workforce Investment Act of 1998, one of the most ambitious and comprehensive workforce education and training programs ever passed by the U.S. Congress, emphasizes the importance of community building to meet local community workforce needs. This program will place emphasis on local partnerships in designing training programs. The act requires participation of local businesses, government officials, and other local organizations in the program and policy development of workforce development boards. The administration has benefited from the longest period of economic expansion since World War II. This economic growth has meant that many jobs have been created and many regions now suffer from labor shortages. This growth has meant that there have been many job openings for welfare recipients, and the tight labor market has begun to increase the wages for the workers earning the lowest wages. It is unclear what the consequences of welfare reform will be once the economy cools off.

Overall, the Clinton administration has not rebuilt the federal support for community development programs that existed in the 1960s. Instead, the administration has continued the trend begun by the Nixon and Reagan administrations to cut back the role of the federal government in local issues and decentralize much of the decision making to local officials. Probably the best illustration of this trend has been the legislation that reformed the federal government's role in welfare programs. Foundations, such as the Ford Foundation and the Kellogg Foundation, have picked up some of the slack that was left from the declining financial support for community development programs.

Community development, however, does stand on firmer ground than it did 20 years ago. There are more CBOs and nonprofit organizations working in the area of poverty. Although many of these organizations continue to struggle for financial support, they have developed many programs that have been shown to be relatively successful. Similarly, the concept of public participation has become more institutionalized in federal and state programs. Elements of public participation are now included in environmental, health, transportation, housing, and economic development programs. Public participation is now considered an important element of good policy making.

Recurring Issues in Community Development

Throughout the history of the United States, several tensions and issues have plagued community development efforts. Among the most important have been the role of participation and the importance of gender and race in shaping development efforts in poor communities.

Participation

Public participation in programs directed at low- and middle-income neighborhoods has been institutionalized since the 1960s. There continues to be debate over how effective this participation has been. At its worst, public participation has been used to simply legitimate the decisions of government officials. At its best, public participation has brought CBOs to the table in some cities, but it probably has not resulted in community control in most cases.

Unfortunately, most government programs look more like pseudo- than full partic-ipation (Pateman, 1970). That is, they provide residents with an opportunity to partici-pate but really no power to make decisions. Government agencies frequently are required to include some form of public participation but are unwilling to leave the decision-making process to local residents. Instead, they use the opportunity to gain legitimation for their decisions. Similarly, efforts by the federal government to promote public participation have been fought by local government officials who see these efforts as reducing their political patronage or support.

The issue in many cases is that decentralization of federal programs does not mean that local residents will have more control over these programs. In many community development programs, decentralization has contributed to greater control by the local elite. Conversely, centralization of the programs almost always ensures that the poor will have very little control over these programs.

One of the central issues in the debates over public participation is how much infor-mation and knowledge residents need to be effective. On the one hand, advocates of public participation contend that residents hold the most relevant information about their community and that they should be the ones making decisions about issues affect-ing their locality. On the other hand, critics charge that many of the issues affecting communities today are highly technical and that residents should rely on experts to help them make these decisions or should be educated on these issues. There probably is no resolution to this problem, but in recent years the community development field has emphasized the importance of the local knowledge of residents and the significance of their participation, even in highly technical decisions.

Race

Another critique of community development programs is that they are race neutral, ignoring the role of racial discrimination in generating the high poverty rates in minority communities. The high rate of poverty among minorities, especially among African Americans, has been assumed to be a result of low levels of human capital, high crime rates in poor neighborhoods (which deter businesses from locating there), and high levels of unemployment in the metropolitan area. Although these issues are cer-tainly a constraint to place-based policies, other factors that more directly involve racial discrimination are seldom considered.

Racial discrimination is defined as "involving actions that serve to limit the social, political, or economic opportunities of particular groups" (Fredrickson & Knobel, 1982). Racial discrimination may be directed at residents of minority communities in several ways. Redlining by lending institutions and insurance companies may be directed at minority neighborhoods. Similarly, employer discrimination may focus on workers from specific neighborhoods or schools (Kirschenman & Neckerman, 1991).

Quadagno (1994) argued that racial discrimination played an important role in undermining the War on Poverty in the 1960s. She provided several examples in which community development programs failed because of white opposition and the unwill-ingness or inability of the federal government to overcome this opposition. When the CAPs were first formed, many were quickly taken over by civil rights activists, who chal-lenged many big-city mayors and political organizations. The Office of Economic Opportunity (OEO) was very sensitive to the criticism by local government officials that the CAPs had provided the spark to the urban riots of the 1960s. In 1973, President Nixon abolished the OEO.

Training programs devised during the War on Poverty suffered some of the same problems. The goal of many of these programs was to train more skilled workers in poor neighborhoods. Unions, which attempted to restrict the supply of labor so as to maintain a high level of demand, were opposed to these programs. In addition, the unions were unwilling to change their recruiting practices, which often discriminated against minorities. Eventually, training programs became less focused on low-income and minority workers and so became more acceptable to the larger public. Quadagno showed how attempts by the federal government to deal with racial segregation also created a backlash by local governments, developers, and others. Because most of the housing programs focused on rental subsidies for minorities, they were frequently challenged by local governments.

These three cases illustrate how race has played a critical role in affecting the success of community development programs. There continue to be debates over whether community development programs should directly confront the issue of racial discrimination. Critics of race-specific policies suggest that these programs need broad support and that targeting of race-specific policies will cause programs to fail. In her analysis of the War on Poverty, Margaret Weir (1988) argued that "the racial targeting of the War on Poverty helped to create the conditions for a powerful backlash that would severely damage prospects for meaningful cooperation between blacks and labor in support of employment programs" (p. 184). A better solution, according to Weir, would have been to develop strategies that would press for broader solutions, such as full employment.

Wilson (1978, 1987) has probably been the strongest critic of race-specific programs to address the problems of concentrated poverty. Wilson contended that concentrated poverty is the result of the decline of manufacturing jobs in cities (which paid good wages), the suburbanization of employment, and the rise of low-wage service sector jobs, which has reduced the opportunities for employment in most central cities. As a result, the number of communities with high levels of poverty (greater than 40%) has rapidly increased since the 1960s. Wilson argued that programs like affirmative action have benefited minorities who have higher levels of education and training but that they have not helped the underclass. Like Weir, he claimed that creating tight labor markets is in the long run the best way to address the problems of concentrated poverty.

Critics such Massey and Denton (1993) claimed that racial discrimination, primarily in the area of housing, continues to be the root cause of urban poverty. Massey and Denton argued that housing segregation results in higher concentrations of poverty and the deterioration of social and economic conditions in black communities and that it ultimately leads to attitudes and behaviors that make it difficult for residents to obtain employment outside these neighborhoods. They focus on better enforcement of the Fair Housing Act of 1968 and other race-specific policies directed toward poor neighborhoods.

Race has been an underlying issue throughout the history of community development. There continue to be advocates for projects that focus on the importance of race, such as efforts to address lending, housing, and employment discrimination. Although most community development practitioners recognize the importance of these issues, they continue to debate the effects of these programs for helping the poor and gaining assistance from the larger society.

Gender

Most neighborhood and community organizations are dominated by women. Yet this fact is largely ignored in much of the literature on community development. There is good reason to believe that women approach community activism differently than do men. Steven Haeberle (1989) found that gender was the strongest predictor of community activists' perceptions of their neighborhood organization's success. Men and women approach their neighborhood organizations differently. Men are much more likely to define their neighborhoods in material terms, whereas women focus more on the social relationships and bonds. There also are gender differences in whether they emphasize the process or outcomes of community development. Men tend to favor community development projects that focus on physical improvement projects, such as new or better roads and recreational facilities. Women tend to emphasize the importance of organizational participation in the community development process.

There is very little literature on the role of women in community organizing and development. A recent exception is Naples's (1998b) longitudinal study of women community workers hired in the Community Action Programs (CAPs) during the War on Poverty and her edited book on community activism and feminist politics (1998a). Naples found that the War on Poverty provided opportunities for women to receive pay for the work they performed on behalf of communities. Although many of these women were pulled into other jobs, especially into professionalized social service agencies, they continued to work on behalf of their communities.

As in the debates over race-specific policies, there is a growing recognition that women, especially minority women, may have been disadvantaged by the structural changes that have occurred in the economy over the past 30 years. In particular, there may be fewer job opportunities providing a living wage for women in the central city. Thus, strategies for creating jobs in these poor neighborhoods need to recognize the special constraints that women face in the labor market (especially child care) and the role that gender segregation plays in the labor market.

Summary and Conclusions

Community development is largely an American phenomenon, although we discuss some grassroots development efforts in Third World countries in a later chapter. Community development efforts over the past four decades have shared two key aspects. First, they have been place based, with a special emphasis on minority and low-income neighborhoods and communities. Second, they have emphasized public participation and community control. Both elements continue to be controversial. Critics have charged that these programs do not address the larger structural forces affecting these neighborhoods. Looking at the evidence, we would have to agree that the outcomes of these programs have been limited. But many of the problems are due, not to the theory or practice of community development, but to opposition by local officials or federal programs that have undermined these efforts.

This brief review of the evolution of community development also highlights the difficult role the federal government plays in promoting development in poor and minority neighborhoods. It is clear that the federal government can play an important role in funneling resources to local organizations. It is less clear, however, that the federal government can actually build neighborhood organizations or create public participation. As we will see in the chapter on CBOs, there are many institutional obstacles that the federal government may not be able to overcome. Thus, the real hope for community development may rely more on generating grassroots efforts that are initiated at the local level.

KEY CONCEPTS

Community Action
   Program (CAP)
Community Development
   Block Grants (CDBG)
Cooperative Extension
   Service
Country Life Commission

Empowerment Zone/
   Enterprise Community
   (EZ/EC)
Fair Housing Act of 1968
Model Cities
Progressive Era

Racial discrimination
Settlement house movement
Special Impact Program
   (SIP)
Urban renewal
War on Poverty

QUESTIONS

1. Describe the history of community development in the United States. What do you consider to be the most important trends in how community development has been approached?

2. Why was the Community Action Program so controversial? How did these controversies affect poverty programs in the late 1960s?

3. What have been the long-term effects of New Federalism on community development programs?

4. Discuss some of the strengths and weaknesses of the empowerment zone/ enterprise community (EZ/EC) program.

5. What are the arguments for and against race-based programs in community development?

EXERCISES

1. Interview a local government official in your community, and assess how community development programs have affected residents in your area. How many public housing units are there? How many people receive rent subsidies? How are Community Development Block Grants used in your community? Try to obtain some historical information on how your community participated in previous programs to help poor neighborhoods. How has community development changed over the past 30 years in your community?

2. Contact a Fair Housing Association in your community. Meet with representatives of the organization to discuss their recent activities. In what types of projects is the organization involved? What is the primary source of complaints regarding fair housing in your community?

REFERENCES

de Tocqueville, A. (1961). *Democracy in America.* New York: Schocken.

Dewey, J. (1916). *Democracy and education: An introduction to the philosophy of education.* New York: Macmillan.

Fredrickson, G. M., & Knobel, D. T. (1982). A history of discrimination. In S. Thernstrom, A. Orlov, & O. Handlin (Eds.), *Prejudice: Dimensions of ethnicity* (pp. 30-87). Cambridge, MA: Harvard University Press.

Gunther, J. J. (2000). Blue ribbon practices in community development. U.S. Department of Housing and Urban Development. <www.hud.gov/ptw/menu.html>

Haeberle, S. H. (1989). *Planting the grassroots: Structuring citizen participation.* New York: Praeger.

Kirschenman, J., & Neckerman, K. M. (1991). We'd love to hire them, but . . . : The meaning of race for employers. In C. Jencks & P. Peterson (Eds.), *The urban underclass* (pp. 201-235). Washington, DC: Brookings Institution.

Massey, D. S., & Denton, N. A. (1993). *American apartheid: Segregation and the making of the underclass.* Cambridge, MA: Harvard University Press.

Moynihan, D. P. (1969). *Maximum feasible misunderstanding: Community action in the war on poverty.* New York: Free Press.

Naples, N. A. (Ed.). (1998a). *Community activism and feminist politics: Organizing across race, class and gender.* New York: Routledge.

Naples, N. A. (1998b). *Grassroots warriors: Activist mothering, community work, and the war on poverty.* New York: Routledge.

O'Connor, A. (1999). Swimming against the tide: A brief history of federal policy in poor communities. In R. F. Ferguson & W. T. Dickens (Eds.), *Urban problems and community development* (pp. 77-137). Washington, DC: Brookings Institution.

Park, R. E. (1915). The city: Suggestions for the investigation of human behavior in the city. *American Journal of Sociology, 20,* 577-612.

Pateman, C. (1970). *Participation and democratic theory.* Cambridge, UK: Cambridge University Press.

Piven, F., & Cloward, R. A. (1971). *Regulating the poor: The functions of public welfare.* New York: Vintage.

Quadagno, J. (1994). *The color of welfare: How racism undermined the War on Poverty.* New York: Oxford University Press.

Rich, M. J. (1993). *Federal policymaking and the poor: National goals, local choices, and distributional outcomes.* Princeton, NJ: Princeton University Press.

U.S. Department of Housing and Urban Development. (1995). *Federal funds, local choices: An evaluation of the Community Development Block Grant Program.* Washington, DC: Author.

Weir, M. (1988). The federal government and unemployment: The frustration of policy innovation from the New Deal to the Great Society. In M. Weir, A. S. Orloff, &

T. Skocpol (Eds.), *The politics of social policy in the United States* (pp. 149-197). Princeton, NJ: Princeton University Press.

Wilson, W. J. (1978). *The declining significance of race: Blacks and changing American institutions.* Chicago: University of Chicago Press.

Wilson, W. J. (1987). *The truly disadvantaged: The inner city, the underclass, and public policy.* Chicago: University of Chicago Press.

ADDITIONAL SUGGESTED READINGS

Readings ■

Berry, J. M., Portney, K. E., & Thomson, K. (1993). *The rebirth of urban democracy.* Washington, DC: Brookings Institution.

Lemann, N. (1994, January 9). The myth of community development. *New York Times Magazine,* pp. 27-31.

Levitan, S. A. (1969). *The Great Society's poor law: A new approach to poverty.* Baltimore, MD: Johns Hopkins Press.

Web Sites ■

U.S. Department of Housing and Urban Development (HUD). <www.hud.org>. This site provides information on HUD programs, especially related to housing. Under this site, <www.hud.gov/cpd/cpdalloc.html> provides data on the CDBG allocations—how much each entitlement community has received, and <www.hud.gov/ptw/docs> provides case studies of award-winning CDBG programs.

CHAPTER 3

The Process of Community Development

The process of community development can be a difficult, time-consuming, and costly job. Community residents often are more concerned with daily tasks than thinking about, and coming up with, a vision of their community's future. Residents want their children to go to good schools, they want decent jobs, and they want a safe and clean environment in which to live. Without a vision, however, communities have a limited ability to make decisions about these issues. It is analogous to driving across the country without a map.

Who should determine a community's future other than the community residents? A consultant hired by the local government to develop a plan, a state or federal agency making decisions about highway bypasses or wetlands preservation, or a private developer constructing a shopping mall or a residential subdivision could make a large impact on a community's future. Residents of a community need to participate in and actively envision the future of their community; otherwise, other groups and individuals will determine their future for them.

The process of community development can be as important as its products. The process we present in this chapter follows the model in Figure 3.1. The model shows a linear process that begins with community organizing and moves on to visioning, planning, and finally implementation and evaluation.

There continues to be some debate over the importance of process versus outcomes in community development. Some people argue that the goal of community development is increasing public participation and that it does not matter if their efforts are successful. Others contend that the ultimate goal is to improve the quality of life in the community and that public participation is simply a means to an end. Our position is closer to the latter one. We focus in this chapter on the process of community development, with an ultimate goal of building the assets in communities. It is difficult to maintain interest and commitment to the effort if participants cannot point to successes. In the long run, both process and outcomes are essential parts of community development.

In this chapter, we focus on three areas: (a) community organizing, (b) community visioning and planning, and (c) evaluation and monitoring. In the first section of this chapter, we focus on public participation. We are especially interested in identifying various forms and techniques for encouraging public participation.

FIGURE 3.1
A Community
Development Process

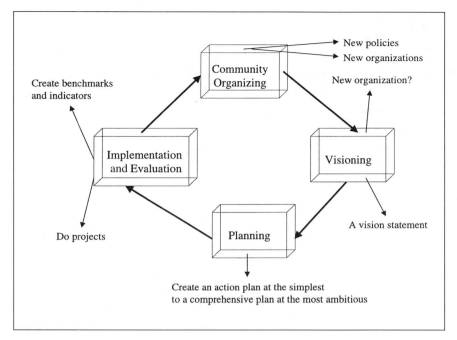

Public Participation

Over 100 years ago, Alexis de Tocqueville (1835/1945) remarked on the extent of civil society in the United States, with its remarkable number and mix of voluntary organizations and associations—the types of organizations that are likely to rely on public action. Although this number and mix have shifted since he made his observations, voluntary organizations and associations are still an important part of the fabric of civil society. Although many lament that public participation has declined in the United States, at the same time there has been an enormous increase in the number of community-based organizations (CBOs) involved in development over the past two decades.

In most cases, community development practitioners grapple with the issue of participation. How is a community motivated to effect change? How does a community maintain momentum? Who in the community should get involved? To begin the discussion, we address some conceptual issues surrounding public participation.

There are at least four types of public participation: public action, public involvement, electoral participation, and obligatory participation. Table 3.1 provides an overview of the differences among these types of public participation. By understanding the differences, we can better understand the community development process and its relationship to and use by CBOs and local governments. It is clear from this comparison that public action fits closest to the community development process model. In this type of public participation, the activities are initiated and controlled by citizens, with the intent of influencing government officials and others. Public involvement and obligatory participation, on the other hand, are initiated and controlled by government officials. Yet this type of public participation is growing; it can have a meaningful impact on the quality of life and may ultimately lead to a community-initiated effort.

TABLE 3.1

Categories of Public Participation

	Public Action	**Public Involvement**	**Electoral Participation**	**Obligatory Participation**
Major distinguishing feature	Refers to activities initiated and controlled by citizens for some purpose	Refers to activities initiated and controlled by government for administrative purposes	Refers to activities to nominate and elect representatives or to vote on pertinent issues on a regularly scheduled basis established by law	Refers to activities in which participation is compulsory according to law
Major purpose	To influence decisions of government officials or voters	To improve decision making and services and develop consensus and support for decisions	To provide stability, continuity of leadership, and a workable consensus for government	To provide sufficient support for government to perform its legal functions
Examples of activities	Lobbying; public education; protest; public advocacy; civil disobedience; class-action suits	Advisory committees; public hearings; goals programs; surveys; hot lines; volunteer programs	Voting; running for office; working for a candidate; volunteering to help a political party	Paying taxes; jury duty
Dominant concerns	Organizing effectively; obtaining appropriate information; developing support; raising funds; making maximum political and public impact	Involving more citizens; informing citizens better; broadening the range of representation; maintaining interest; effectively using public involvement in decision making; obtaining necessary funds	Increasing voter turnout; raising funds for a party or candidate	Increasing public understanding of the obligations of citizenship; attracting and retaining capable jurors
Typically interested groups	Neighborhood and community groups; public interest and consumer groups; community agencies; individual citizens	Legislative committees; administrative agencies; regulatory agencies	Elected officials; political parties; political candidates	Judges; court officers; tax officials

SOURCE: From "What Is Citizen Participation?" by S. Langton, in *Citizen Participation in America: Essays on the State of the Art,* edited by S. Langton, 1978 (pp. 13-24). Lexington, MA: Lexington Books. Copyright 1978 by Lexington Books. Reprinted with permission.

In the community development process model (Figure 3.1), the role of public participation may start with public action and shift to public involvement, depending on the organizational context and "ownership" of the process. Generally, public action is the category of public participation on which CBOs focus.

Sherry Arnstein's (1969) "ladder of public participation" is a useful framework for understanding the role of CBOs in public participation (see Figure 3.2). This "ladder" has eight "rungs" divided into three sections that illustrate degrees of participation and public power. Arnstein argued that power and control over decisions are necessary

FIGURE 3.2
Ladder of Public
Participation

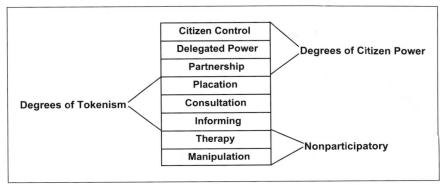

SOURCE: From "A Ladder of Citizen Participation," by S. R. Arnstein, 1969. Reprinted by permission of the *Journal of the American Planning Association, 35*(4), 1969.

ingredients to "real" public participation. The lower two rungs are nonparticipatory participation and are called manipulation and therapy. Examples include public or neighborhood advisory committees or boards that have no authority or power in controlling projects or programs but simply represent a way to vent frustration.

The next three rungs illustrate "degrees of tokenism": informing, consultation, and placation. Methods include simple communication tools, such as posters, and more sophisticated tools, such as surveys, meetings, public hearings, and placement of citizens on powerful boards.

The final three rungs represent "degrees of citizen power": partnership, delegated power, and citizen control. Here, planning and decision making can have three degrees of power in relation to a citizens' group, board, or corporation: shared power between citizens' group(s) and the public authority, authorized power to prepare and implement a plan or program, or empowerment to essentially act as a decentralized local government with full control over particular programs (Arnstein, 1969, pp. 223-224).

Ideally, CBOs attempt to place themselves in the top rungs of the ladder, whereas many local governments conduct their participation efforts at the lower rungs of the ladder. Especially when CBOs are newly established, the original catalyst was often public action, and the desire to maintain public input on a regular basis is strong. In the day-to-day work of CBOs, however, public participation is difficult to maintain for several reasons. First, it increases the complexity of decision making. Second, it is time consuming and thus can be seen as inefficient. Third, reaction time is slowed, a disadvantage when the organization needs to act quickly to take advantage of a funding deadline. Finally, the demands for funding and reporting require a professional staff (see Chapter 4). Thus, reality can fall short of the ideal. CBOs can encounter two pitfalls in relation to public participation: (a) With professionalization, they can lose sight of their community base and at worst become unrepresentative of the community, and (b) due to the funding requirements, their agenda—goals and programs—can become coopted by external forces.

So far, we have discussed conceptual models and types of public participation that CBOs would fall under, given their purpose. We have yet to ask why people participate. The natural tendency is to think that people get involved because of the importance of the issue—it directly affects them, and they have an interest in finding solutions to the problem. Many organizers assume that they can increase the level of participation by educating people on the issue and encouraging them to get involved with the effort to address the issue.

Although this approach may work for some people and in some cases, we must recognize that there are a variety of other reasons why people may become involved in a local organization. Many people may become involved in neighborhood/community organizations because of social relationships. Participation is a way to meet new people and develop new friendships. Similarly, people may become involved because a friend or a neighbor is participating in the project. Thus, these social relationships can be a valuable mechanism for encouraging others to participate.

People also may become involved because of the kind of activities offered through the organization. Although many residents do not have much time for community activities, others may be looking for new activities. Getting involved in fund-raising or planning may provide opportunities for which some people are searching.

Although time is frequently cited as the primary reason for lack of participation, it is rarely the real issue. A variety of other constraints may limit participation. Among the most important barriers are lack of child care, transportation, accessibility to the disabled, interpreters, and advance information. Local organizations need to provide these types of services if they want to have residents participate in meetings and activities.

Communication is another reason why residents may not participate. This issue may be especially important in a neighborhood or community where there are no newspapers, radio stations, or television stations specific to that area. Even in communities where there are adequate communication systems, it may be difficult to reach the people in the community.

Residents also need to see real, direct benefits to participation. This is why it is important for community organizers to identify small projects where they can demonstrate success to the community. Residents typically need to see that their actions are having some impact.

Understanding why people do and do not participate in a community development process can help us to further identify techniques of public participation. There are many techniques, each with varying functions. Depending on what a CBO is trying to accomplish, it will need to choose the appropriate technique for the purpose it is trying to achieve. In Table 3.2, we identify a wide variety of public participation techniques and their objectives. The table is not exhaustive, but it provides a range of techniques that can be and are used by CBOs and other organizations to achieve different purposes. The choice of the appropriate technique depends on several issues, such as the context for the process, the number of people participating, the resources available, and the level of interest among participants.

Because the choice of issue can affect the level of participation and the likelihood that participants will stay with the organization, the techniques need to focus on accomplishing something. They cannot be seen as meaningless exercises. The technique should be one that helps unite, rather than divide, people. Most community organizers begin with small, simple techniques that have a clear outcome. The techniques need to be explained clearly to participants so that they understand clearly the process they will use to make decisions.

TABLE 3.2 Public Participation Techniques and Their Function

Technique	Identify Attitudes and Opinions	Identify Affected Groups	Solicit Affected Groups	Facilitate Participation	Clarify Planning Process	Answer Citizen Questions	Disseminate Information	Generate New Ideas and Alternatives	Facilitate Advocacy	Promote Interaction Between Interest Groups	Resolve Conflict	Plan Program and Policy Review	Change Attitudes Toward Government	Develop Support/ Minimize Opposition
Arbitration and mediation planning	X						X		X	X				
Charrette[a]	X			X	X	X	X	X	X	X	X	X		
Citizen's advisory board	X			X	X	X	X	X			X	X	X	X
Citizen referendum	X			X						X	X	X		
Citizen representatives on policy-making bodies	X		X	X			X					X	X	
Citizen review board				X							X		X	
Community surveys	X		X											
Community training				X	X			X				X		
Community technical assistance	X		X	X			X	X						
Computer-based techniques	Depends on specific technique chosen, such as Geographic Information Systems													
Drop-in centers		X	X	X	X	X	X				X	X	X	
Focus group	X	X	X	X	X	X				X				
Meetings—community sponsored	X		X	X	X	X	X	X			X		X	
Meetings—neighborhood	X		X	X	X	X	X	X				X	X	
Meetings—open informational			X		X	X	X				X			

(continued)

TABLE 3.2 Continued

Technique	Identify Attitudes and Opinions	Identify Affected Groups	Solicit Affected Groups	Facilitate Participation	Clarify Planning Process	Answer Citizen Questions	Disseminate Information	Generate New Ideas and Alternatives	Facilitate Advocacy	Promote Interaction Between Interest Groups	Resolve Conflict	Plan Program and Policy Review	Change Attitudes Toward Government	Develop Support/ Minimize Opposition
Neighborhood planning council	X		X				X	X			X			
Ombudsperson		X			X	X	X				X	X		
Open-door policy		X	X	X	X	X					X	X		
Policy delphi[b]	X						X							
Public hearing		X	X	X		X	X					X		
Public information programs				X		X				X	X			
Short conference	X		X	X	X	X	X		X	X	X	X		
Task forces			X					X	X		X	X	X	
Web sites—issue balloting	X	X	X	X										
Workshops	X	X	X	X	X	X		X	X	X	X	X	X	

SOURCE: From "Matching Method to Purpose: The Challenges of Planning Citizen-Participation Activities," by J. Rosener, in *Citizen Participation in America: Essays on the State of the Art*, edited by S. Langton, 1978 (pp. 109-122). Lexington, MA: Lexington Books. Copyright 1978 by Lexington Books. Reprinted with permission.

NOTES: a. Process that convenes interest groups (governmental and nongovernmental) in intensive interactive meetings lasting from several days to several weeks.

b. A technique for developing and expressing the views of a panel of individuals on a particular subject. The process is initiated with the solicitation of written views on a subject; successive rounds of presented arguments and counterarguments work toward consensus or clearly established positions and supporting arguments.

Community Organizing

To many, organizing can sound like a daunting task. How does one individual or a small group organize people to change something? As Kahn (1991), a leading authority on community organizing, reminded us, "Organizing doesn't need to be big to be successful" (p. 19). Organizing begins with one person wanting to change one thing. It is a way for people to work together to solve a problem.

Organizing has various forms. Union organizing addresses people who work in the same place. Constituency organizing involves group characteristics such as gender, race, language, or sexual orientation. Issue organizing addresses a particular concern, such as school, taxes, or housing. Neighborhood or community organizing focuses on place and addresses people who live in the same place (Kahn, 1991, p. 70). Community organizing, therefore, is distinct from other forms of organizing because it focuses on mobilizing people in a specific area.

There are three approaches to problem solving in communities: service, advocacy, and mobilizing. The first two approaches do not involve community residents in problem solving. In fact, residents may never be consulted. Service focuses on the individual, trying to address an individual's problems, such as unemployment, poverty, lack of health insurance, or mobility limitations. Service programs address problems one at a time, not comprehensively, and do not examine or challenge the root causes of those problems. Advocacy is a process in which one person or a group of individuals speaks for another person or group of individuals. Advocates can effect change in organizations and institutions on behalf of others. Mobilizing involves community residents' taking direct action—for example, to protest property tax increases—or writing a letter to the editor. There are many tactics in organizing; we will discuss some of these later. Mobilizing is important because it gets people involved in direct action on a problem (Kahn, 1991, pp. 50-51).

CBOs use two different strategies to mobilize residents: social action campaigns and the development model. *Social action campaigns* are efforts by CBOs that aim to change decisions, societal structures, and cultural beliefs. Efforts at change can be small and immediate, such as getting a pothole filled, or large and long-term, such as promoting civil rights or fair trade practices. Tactics used in social action campaigns include, but are not limited to, appeals, petitions, picketing, boycotts, strikes, and sit-ins (see Case Study 3.1). Some tactics are nonviolent yet illegal and represent a form of civil disobedience (Rubin & Rubin, 1992).

The development model is more prevalent at the community level. Community development corporations (CDCs) represent a type of community organization that uses the development model to achieve community development goals (see Chapter 4 for a discussion of CDCs and other types of CBOs). These organizations focus on providing economic and social services in disenfranchised neighborhoods and communities (Rubin & Rubin, 1992).

Rubin and Rubin (1992) identified several different community organizing models that are used across the United States. Probably the most popular model has been the Alinsky model. The Alinsky model involves a professional organizer, who tends to work with existing organizations to identify issues of common interest in the neighborhood.

Community Organizing

There are many examples of community organizing. Two are briefly related here. In New York City, Asians organized to protest a federally funded project in their community in 1974. They established a volunteer organization, now called Asian Americans for Equality (AAFE), a CDC. The group organized pickets, demonstrations, and marches because the builder of the project, called Confucius Plaza, had not hired any minority workers, particularly Chinese from the neighborhood. Through their actions, the group demanded a change in the builder's employment policy. Their actions resulted in a change of policy, and minority workers were hired. After that success, the group turned to other areas of concern.

Another CDC that has its roots in organizing, Chicanos Por La Causa (CPLC), was started in the 1960s by a group of Mexican American university students who were attempting to build Chicano pride and address problems in their community. One organizer brought the university students and neighborhood residents together to expand the reach of the movement. By 1969, when the group officially incorporated, it had become an advocate for Chicano causes.

SOURCE: From "Community Development Corporation Oral History Project," <www.picced.org/advocacy/bldghope.htm>, February 1997. Pratt Institute Center for Community and Environmental Development, Brooklyn, NY. Copyright 1997 by the Pratt Institute Center for Community and Environmental Development. Reprinted with permission.

The Boston model takes a different approach by contacting welfare clients individually at their residences and relies heavily on appeals to the self-interest of each person. In recent years, the Association of Community Organizations for Reform Now (ACORN) has mixed these two models. The ACORN model is based on developing multi-issue organizations that are much more political than the other two models. Another model that has received a great deal of attention in the literature is the Industrial Areas Foundation (IAF) model, which emphasizes the importance of intensive training of organizers. Although this model is a direct descendent of the Alinsky model, it emphasizes the importance of maintaining close ties with existing community organizations as the neighborhood is organized. Each of the models has advantages and disadvantages. The choice of which model to use is based largely on the context, the resources, and the circumstances.

In the next section, we describe a specific process—visioning—that many communities are adopting to help them define the future. Visioning is not the only process that practitioners use, but it represents one of the most important new approaches in the community development field. We will show how visioning is making community planning models more open and accessible to the entire community and establishing a more open and democratic process for envisioning a future at the outset of a process.

| BOX 3.1 | **Visioning Defined** |

Visioning is a *process* by which a *community* envisions the *future* it wants and *plans* how to achieve it. Through *public* involvement, communities identify their *purpose,* core *values,* and *vision* of the future, which are then transformed into a manageable and feasible set of community *goals* and an *action plan.*

SOURCE: Green, Haines, and Halebsky (2000, p. 1.2).

Community Visioning

Community visioning has become an accepted planning technique. By the late 1990s, many communities had used this technique to promote broad public participation on the direction in which a community should move in the future (Shipley & Newkirk, 1998). A visioning process establishes a desired end state for a community, a vision of the future to strive toward. Shipley and Newkirk (1998) saw vision as "a metaphor that describes social, cultural, and perhaps emotional attributes" (p. 410). They further considered visioning as a way to return to the roots of planning, when individuals, such as Le Corbusier, Daniel Burnham, John Nolen, and Frank Lloyd Wright, had visions of place. The visioning technique, however, strives to establish a vision of place through broad public participation rather than one individual's view. In theory, a community vision occurs through a group process that tries to arrive at a consensus about the future of place. The visioning process can be done by a neighborhood, a whole city, or by an organization.

Over the past decade, a growing number of neighborhoods and communities in the United States have been engaged in a formal process to develop an overall image of what their neighborhood or community should be and how it should look at some point in the future—what we refer to here as community visioning. In this section, we briefly describe the visioning process, how the process differs from other planning efforts, and how visioning is used by communities.

The basic advantage of visioning is that it allows for an expansive, innovative, and proactive future orientation. Visioning focuses on what strengths must be developed to reach a desired end state. It expands the notion of public participation beyond the other models and suggests that the community can design and create its own future.

The Roots of Visioning: Context and History

With the advent of public participation beginning with the Housing Act of 1954 (Glass, 1979), a debate was opened about the purpose of public participation and how it was to be included in decision-making processes of local governments and higher levels of government and in CBOs (Howe, 1992; Meyerson & Banfield, 1955; Rabinovitz, 1969). The acceptance of public participation in government decision-making processes occurred during the turbulence of the 1960s and, in many instances, was mandated as part of the policy-making process.

Especially in professions where public participation was a routine event, such as in urban planning, the idea of grassroots participation, community organizing, and planning from the bottom up was much discussed. The dominant planning model transformed over time as ideas about public participation and how it should work were appended to the base model. In this next section, we describe this model and two other planning models that have influenced the process of neighborhood, town, and urban development. Community visioning represents the latest transformation of a general process that ideally strives to involve residents in creating and deciding on their mutual future.

Comprehensive-Rational Planning

Comprehensive-rational planning has been the most common form of planning used in cities, villages, and towns to address their future. The comprehensive-rational model is focused on the production of a plan that is to guide development and growth. The plan aims at comprehensiveness and implies focusing on the elements/functions of a place (Rittel & Webber, 1973; Wildavsky, 1973). Critics have leveled several different criticisms of the model. Among the most important criticisms are that it is impossible to analyze everything at once; "wicked" problems cannot be addressed (Rittel & Webber, 1973); it cannot react swiftly; it is based on assumptions of growth and thus cannot deal effectively with decline or stagnation (Beauregard, 1978); it is based on past trends and forecasting that prove to be inaccurate; and it is ineffective because the plans rarely reach the implementation stage (Hudson, 1979). More radical critiques argue that it supports the accumulation and legitimation functions of the state (Beauregard, 1978; Fainstein & Fainstein, 1982) and is elitist and centralizing (Grabow & Heskin, 1973).

Advocacy Planning

Paul Davidoff (1973) promoted a new model of planning in the 1960s. It was based on the idea of Legal Aid to establish "Planning Aid." The process of advocacy planning involved advocate planners, representing community groups, presenting alternative plans to a city council, which decided on the plan or plan elements that were politically feasible, appropriate, and doable. The product of the process would be plural plans offering different, alternative visions of a community. Advocacy planning promoted a level of public participation and community involvement unheard of under the comprehensive-rational planning model.

There are several strengths to this model: It focuses on one issue or geographic area; plans are not comprehensive (which makes it less daunting for residents); and the model attempts to bring equality into the planning process by giving poor and disadvantaged groups a voice. The advocacy approach has several weaknesses, however, including the risk of conflicting plans. If plans conflict, who will mediate? Politicians? Or planners? There also is a risk of being co-opted by a local bureaucracy and/or more powerful interest groups. How likely is it for a planner in a public planning office to act as an advocate? If planners are outside the system—for example, if they work in a CDC or another CBO—they can be ignored or frozen out of the process, and they risk having their plans co-opted by political and/or bureaucratic forces.

Strategic Planning

Another model, strategic planning, originated in the military and moved into the corporate world, where it was limited to budgeting and financial control. By the 1980s, strategic planning was applied to local governments and nonprofit organizations. Bryson (1995) offered the following general definition: Strategic planning is a

> disciplined effort to produce fundamental decisions and actions that shape what an organization is, what it does, and why it does it. . . . [This effort] requires broad yet effective information gathering, development and exploration of strategic alternatives, and an emphasis on future implications of present decisions. (pp. 4-5)

There are many corporate-style strategic planning approaches, but the most well-known and used model in the public sector and in CBOs is the Harvard policy model. This model has been around since the Harvard Business School developed it in the 1920s. "SWOT" analysis, a systematic assessment of a community's or organization's strengths, weaknesses, opportunities, and threats (Bryson & Roering, 1987), comes from this model.

There are several strengths to strategic planning. The process aims to build agreement in an organization or community. It forces the community to ask and answer the questions "What are our goals and aims?" and "What do we want to accomplish?" These questions encourage communities to think and act strategically, maximizing effectiveness; identify their comparative advantage; focus on critical issues; and turn liabilities into assets.

There also are several weaknesses to strategic planning. The process is not always well suited to the public sector or to CBOs that have multiple objectives. The process may have difficulty satisfying competing and often conflicting demands. In addition, it is internal to the organization, so involving the public may be difficult. Because the process relies heavily on analyses of the status quo, it makes demands for information and data that many communities find overwhelming. It also embraces competitive rather than cooperative behavior.

Visioning

Visioning is used as an accepted step in many strategic planning processes. Community strategic planning efforts usually begin with a scan of where the community is headed, which may involve some assessment of demographic, economic, social, and fiscal trends in the area. The next logical step is to develop a common view of where the community should be headed, which usually involves some form of visioning process. The process may be considered so important that it is given its own event. A community may convene a special meeting, or series of meetings, to develop a community vision. The primary product of such an event is a guide for subsequent planning or, in the case of a CBO, program development. Usually, the vision is followed by the development of specific strategies and of an action plan that the community wishes to follow.

The visioning process focuses on possibilities rather than on the problems of the community. It begins with identifying an overall community vision, then develops

TABLE 3.3
A Visioning Process

Step	Component	Component Explanation
1	Getting started	The coordinating committee forms and begins planning for the first workshop.
2	Community visioning workshop	The coordinating committee facilitates the process of preparing a general vision statement and identifies key areas.
3	Establishment of task forces	At the workshop, task forces assemble by key area and meet to set action plan.
4	Key area visioning workshops	Each key area task force convenes a community workshop to facilitate a process for preparing a key area vision statement and identifying key subareas.
5	Review of plans and/ or programs, etc.	Task forces review all relevant existing plans and zoning and subdivision regulations.
6	Data gathering and analysis	Each task force gathers and analyzes pertinent data and prepares strategies. Larger task force evaluates data and strategies against general and key area visions.
7	Goal and strategy development	Task forces develop goals and strategies based on data and vision statements.
8	Community feedback workshop	The coordinating committee plans on a community-wide workshop to present the general and key area visions and broad strategies.
9	Development of action plans	Each task force prepares action plans based on agreed-on strategies and goals.
10	Implementation	Action plans are undertaken.
11	Monitoring, evaluation, and revision	The coordinating committee plans a meeting that reviews the activities and accomplishments to date and the activities that will be implemented the following year.

SOURCE: From *Building Our Future: A Guide to Community Visioning* (Report No. G3708), by Gary Green, Anna Haines, and Stephen Halebsky. University of Wisconsin Extension, Cooperative Extension, Madison, WI, 2000. Reprinted with permission.

visions in strategic areas (such as housing, land use, education, and workforce development). Action plans (identifying specific projects, deadlines, and who is responsible for completing tasks) are created on the basis of these visions (see Table 3.3). The process requires a substantial commitment by local residents and an ongoing role for facilitation. This role of ongoing facilitation can be provided by a group of individuals trained in facilitation processes. CBOs, because of their connection to communities and their experience with different forms of public participation, can play an active and helpful role in a visioning process. Visioning differs from some of the other planning techniques because it usually does not begin with a detailed analysis of trends or rely heavily on data to identify needs. Instead, it begins with the values of residents and the visions they have for their community.

Over the past decade, many community development practitioners have turned away from strategic planning and comprehensive planning to visioning methods. One of the reasons for this shift is that visioning does not rely as much on data as the other planning methods. The heavy emphasis of, for example, comprehensive-rational and strategic planning on providing basic data on the trends and structure of the community frequently overwhelms participants at the beginning of the process and sometimes diverts attention away from the important issues the community is facing. Visioning may involve data collection and analysis, but these usually come after there is some agreement on the direction the community should take and the issues the community is facing.

Timing and Momentum

One of the issues that communities may face is the question of whether they are ready to begin a visioning process. Should they focus on developing new leaders in the community before engaging in this process? Should they develop new and existing organizations that may be needed to implement the community's action plans instead? Timing and preparedness certainly should be considered before moving ahead with a community visioning process. At the same time, organizational and leadership development are frequent results of visioning efforts. By successfully completing projects that have been identified in the process, communities can develop the capacity to address bigger and more complex issues. Participants may discover along the way that what they really need are more leaders in their community and may decide to invest in a leadership training program. Without initiating the process, they might not have come to this realization.

Keeping the process on track and moving forward can be a challenging task. It is also one of the chief criticisms of this kind of process. Most guidebooks on visioning provide pointers on how to maintain initiative (see Green, Haines, & Halebsky, 2000).

Workshops

To guide the process, three questions can be asked to drive the workshop forward and should shape the way in which participants think about their community:

1. What do people want to *preserve* in the community?

2. What do people want to *create* in the community?

3. What do people want to *change* in the community?

One way to help the community develop their vision is to ask them to complete the sentence "In the year 20XX in our community, we would like to see _____ _____." It is useful to look beyond the immediate future and develop the vision for at least a 15-year period. To go beyond 25 years, however, may be difficult for the group to work with in such a session. Case Study 3.2 shows a sample agenda used in a community in Wisconsin.

CASE STUDY 3.2

Lodi, Wisconsin

VISION FOR OUR COMMUNITY: LODI 2025

In 2025, Lodi is a community that links the future with the past by recognizing the importance of history in growth and development. The center of our small town is a pedestrian-friendly main street that celebrates historic architecture, while our waterways and surrounding vistas nourish the health and beauty of the valley.

- *Land Use and Growth Management*—Our community is committed to planning and community involvement in directing its future growth to meet the needs of our residents. Our community encompasses a mix of distinct neighborhoods and districts, and by encouraging compatible land uses within those districts, we are maintaining our unique small-town character, protecting natural resources, and promoting sustainable development and growth.

- *Downtown Revitalization*—Our revitalized downtown promotes a pedestrian-friendly retail and government center that maintains and enhances our city's historic and architectural integrity.

- *Business Retention and Expansion*—Our community fosters business development and recognizes the importance of a balanced business district with retail shops, services, facilities, and light industries.

- *Housing and Historic Preservation*—Our exemplary community is committed to historic preservation, conservation of neighborhood character, beautification of residential settings, and provision of housing that meets the needs of diversified social and economic groups. Our historic homes provide a bridge from the past to the future and enhance the beauty and warmth of the community. There is widespread public awareness of historic preservation programs and ongoing restoration of Lodi's historic homes, businesses, parks, and transportation systems. Every home in the historic districts has been restored to its original condition. New residential development is carefully designed with the preservation of natural settings and resources—woods, creeks, and wetlands. Neighborhoods are picturesque, with period lighting, fencing, and walkways. Our long-range planning has thwarted sprawl by providing development that is sympathetic to, and respectful of, the topography, the environment, and changing societal demographics. Ample housing is available to meet the needs of different economic groups and the desires and requirements of residents across the life span.

- *Community Services and Public Works*—Our community services and facilities maintain their functionality, address the needs of our diverse population, and adapt and change as the community grows. Services include programs that promote a neighborly atmosphere that reflects the concerns of individuals and families in our community.

- *Natural Resources*—Our community is situated in scenic Lodi Valley, surrounded by tree-covered bluffs and bisected by the pristine, trout-filled Spring Creek, which travels through Lodi Marsh, known across the state as home to abundant wildlife. An enlightened community advocates for watershed and shoreline preservation; maintenance and improvement of its existing vistas, parks, trees, and green spaces; and managed growth in areas suitable for development. Much of the above can be attributed to the fact that the Lodi school system is a national model for environmental education in the tradition of Aldo Leopold's concept of community and John Muir's principles of living in harmony with the environment.

SOURCE: Department of Urban and Regional Planning (2000).

SAMPLE COMMUNITY WORKSHOP AGENDA

Lodi's Community Visioning Workshop

Lodi Elementary School, Lodi, WI

Saturday, February 5, 2000

Supplies Needed: 100+ name tags in 10 different colors, thin markers, safety pins, tape, colored paper to match the name tags (to identify tables), flip charts, colored stickers (small circles) or Post-its for the group vote, and 15 to 20 fat colored markers.

Facilitators hand out name tags, in 10 different colors, at registration. Ask attendees to provide contact information (name, address, phone number) so they can be contacted when the task forces meet. Direct attendees to the appropriate tables (where their color will be displayed).

WELCOME AND INTRODUCTIONS (30 MINUTES)

Facilitators ask each person in the small groups to share his or her earliest fond memory of Lodi. Write these down on flip charts or on a pad of paper (they might be useful later).

(continued)

CASE STUDY 3.2

Continued

IDENTIFICATION OF WHAT TO PRESERVE,
CREATE, CHANGE (1 ½ HOURS)

What would the lodi community like to preserve?

1. Ask each individual in the small groups to write down on a piece of paper (20 minutes):

   ■ Three places in Lodi where you like to take out-of-town visitors, and a sentence for each that explains why

   ■ Three words or short phrases that describe Lodi, the place/space (facilitators ask individuals to be specific: Something like "good place" will not count—descriptors like "pretty river" or "compact downtown" are more appropriate)

   ■ Three areas or places that should be protected and preserved (these can be the same or can overlap with the places where you like to take visitors)

   Facilitators should be prepared to help people who get stuck by asking questions to draw them out.

2. Group discussion (20 minutes):

   ■ Facilitators divide flip chart pages into three columns, based on the exercise above, so that the flip chart looks like this:

   Places for Visitors   Phrases About Lodi   Places to Protect

   ■ Facilitators have each person list off what he or she wrote down, and put the responses in the appropriate columns. Put a check mark by repeat responses.

   ■ Some discussion follows about why people chose the places they did.

   ■ Groups pick the top five places out of the two lists (places for visitors and places to protect) that they would like to see preserved in the community and the top five phrases that describe Lodi. This will help with the group vote later on. These top five places and top five phrases are written on two separate flip chart sheets in preparation for the group vote.

   ■ At the end of the session, facilitators collect the individual sheets of paper—these might help with writing the vision statement or report.

What would the Lodi community like to change and/or create?

Brainstorming exercise (30 minutes):

1. Individuals in small groups brainstorm about what they would like to change and/or create in Lodi.

2. On one flip chart sheet, facilitators write down individuals' ideas about what existing areas of Lodi should be developed or changed in the future.

3. On a second flip chart sheet, facilitators write down individuals' ideas about what types of buildings, parks, spaces, etc., should be added to Lodi in the future (individuals are asked to think about what they will need in the future if they get stuck).

4. Then facilitators ask the group to look at the two flip charts and pick the top five ideas about what should be developed, added, or changed in the future.

5. These top five ideas are placed on a separate flip chart sheet in preparation for the group vote.

Group vote (20 minutes)

By now, every small group should have three flip chart sheets, listing

1. The group's top five places to be preserved

2. The group's top five phrases that describe Lodi

3. The top five ideas about what should be developed, added, or changed in Lodi in the future

Facilitators should take these three sheets and place them with other small groups' sheets. So, for example, all the sheets on the top five places to be preserved should be put next to each other on one wall, all the sheets on the top five phrases should be put next to each other on another wall, etc. Facilitators should then give every person in the group six colored stickers (or Post-its). Each person gets two votes per category. So each person places a sticker next to the two top places to be preserved out of all the lists, the two top phrases, etc.

Break (10 minutes)

Facilitators compile a list of the top places, phrases, and additions/changes for the vision statement session.

(continued)

CASE STUDY 3.2

Continued

DEVELOPMENT OF A VISION STATEMENT (1 ½ HOURS)

1. Small groups write vision statements (30 minutes).
   - Each of the 10 groups writes its vision for Lodi in two or three paragraphs.
   - Facilitators put one sentence on a separate sheet of flip chart paper.

2. Small groups present to large group (20 minutes).
   - Large group assembles, and each small group presents its vision.
   - Facilitators divide the large group into three small groups.

3. Small groups rewrite vision statements (20 minutes).

4. Large group assembles again and synthesizes the statements into one vision statement (20 minutes).

RECOGNIZING THEMES AND WRAP-UP (20 MINUTES)

1. Relate vision statement to themes (10 minutes).
   - Facilitators assist large group in categorizing vision statement into themes.
   - Facilitators list the themes on flip charts.

2. Conduct sign-up for task forces (10 minutes).
   - Limit numbers to keep them effective, and ensure that there are people in all groups.

In Table 3.4, we provide a list of the types of participants who should be involved in a visioning process. Some communities have sought to gain some support for their vision by getting it formally adopted by a local government. Formal adoption has several benefits, such as broad dissemination of the vision, increased legitimacy in the community, and possible influence in getting local government officials involved in the implementation stage.

Goals and Strategy Development

Participants in a visioning process usually want to jump immediately into identifying specific projects that could be undertaken by the group. Visioning processes require that participants identify broad goals and strategies first before moving too quickly to developing specific projects. These goals and strategies can be introduced to the group or

TABLE 3.4
Types of Participants

Economic Sectors	Organiza-tions	Government	Personal Factors	Political Views
Agriculture, forestry, fishing	Art and culture	Elected officials	Age	Conservative/ liberal/ moderate/etc.
Wholesaling	Education	Planning department	Ethnicity/race	
Retailing	Churches	Police, fire	Sex	Progrowth/ antigrowth
Construction	Civic (e.g., Rotary)	Natural resources/ water	Income level	
Manufacturing	Unions		Home owners/ renters	
Transportation/ utilities	Business	Transportation	Blue/white collar	
Finance, insurance, real estate	Youth	Housing	Have children/ don't have children	
Services	Neighborhood	Education		
Tourism	Social service agencies	Economic development	Geographic location	
Local media	Health care	Workforce development	Long-time resident/newer resident	
Business type (size; locally owned)	Environmental	Regional planning		
	Recreational			

SOURCE: From *Building Our Future: A Guide to Community Visioning* (Report No. G3708), by Gary Green, Anna Haines, and Stephen Halebsky. University of Wisconsin Extension, Cooperative Extension, Madison, WI, 2000. Reprinted with permission.

developed within the group itself. This step in the process helps provide a tighter linkage between the vision and the action plan that will be developed. Without developing a set of goals and strategies, communities may identify specific projects that are not related to the vision established earlier in the process.

Developing Action Plans

An action plan is a description of the activities needed to be done to move the community toward its vision. For each project that is identified, there should be a detailed plan of what needs to be done, who can do it, when it will be done, what information is needed, and what resources are necessary to implement the strategy. Action plans should be prepared that are based on agreed-on strategies and goals. In Box 3.2, we provide a description of the types of information that are needed to prepare an action plan.

BOX 3.2 **Action Planning: Basis for Worksheet**

Below is a list of the categories and questions that should be asked for each identified project. The purpose of using a worksheet for action planning is to help the CBO or other group to thoroughly analyze and assess how it can start and complete a project. An important facet of this analysis is a political assessment. A formal acknowledgment and assessment of the local political situation can help move projects forward. This assessment will help the CBO or group to decide whether it is feasible to move forward on any particular project.

1. *Assess fit of vision and project.* What is your vision theme? What is your project? Why are you doing this project (purpose or desired outcome)? Who will potentially benefit from this project? Who will potentially be harmed by this project?

2. *Analyze the situation.* Where does this project fit into current community priorities? Are there any groups working on related projects? Have there been past attempts on this or similar projects? Whom does it affect positively (individuals and groups)? Whom does it affect negatively (individuals and groups)?

3. *Assess helping and hindering forces.* Who are the decision makers (formal and informal, individuals and organizations, internal and external)? Who can help or hinder this project? Who makes the contacts? What strategies will you use to influence the decision makers? Who is likely to support the project in the community, and who should contact them? What do the contacted people think of the vision and project, what would they like to see as an outcome, and how would they carry out the project? How will you enlist their support? Who is likely to oppose the project, and who should contact them? What do the contacted people think of the vision and project, and what are their specific objections? What would they like to see as an outcome, and how would they carry out the project?

4. *Decide who is going to do it and how.* Were any new individuals identified who would be valuable resources for your task force? Are some task force members ready to move on to other projects, or do they feel that they have made their contribution? Who will coordinate the task force? How often will the task force meet? What subgroups, if any, are needed? How will you keep each other informed? How will you keep the community informed? How will you keep people outside the community informed?

5. *Create a community resource inventory.* What skills, knowledge, linkages (networks), representation, or resources are
needed for the CBO or group at this stage of the project? The
inventory should cover the following categories of needs: skills
and expertise, physical (facilities, equipment), information,
finances, and other.

Monitor, Evaluate, and Revise

Communities engaged in development are seldom interested in monitoring their progress and evaluating their efforts. They are primarily concerned with getting things
done. But there are several reasons why it is useful for a community to measure its program and evaluate its efforts:

- To keep people involved in the community development process by showing them
  tangible results of their efforts

- To show foundations, local governments, and other financial supporters that their
  resources are well spent

- To improve the community's efforts by establishing a reliable system of monitoring
  progress

- To gain support of the community at large for development efforts by having an
  effective evaluation system in place

Monitoring is an assessment of the planning process itself. The purpose of monitoring is to provide indications of whether corrections need to take place in the action plan.
For each element of the action plan, communities should ask such questions as: Are the
time deadlines being met? Is the budget appropriate? Is the staffing appropriate? Is the
amount of work realistic? Are priorities receiving the appropriate amount of attention?
How are we working as a group? Are we learning something important to share? What
else do we need?

Evaluation focuses on the specific accomplishments of the process. A distinction
should be made between measuring outputs and outcomes. Outputs are usually things
that can be counted that result from the action plan. They are "intermediary" measures. Examples of outputs would include number of jobs created, number of houses
built, and the number of programs developed. Outcomes, however, are usually much
more long-term and are more difficult to link to the specific elements of the action
plan. They are more closely linked to the ultimate objectives identified in the visioning
process. Examples of outcomes would be decreased levels of poverty or increased levels
of personal income, more people's acceptance of leadership roles, or improved social
networks among residents. Specifically, participants in the visioning process should ask
how a community is better off as a result and then try to measure success in terms of
goals stated in the action plan.

To monitor or evaluate a community's actions, it is useful to assess the change in the outputs and outcomes over time. It is important to collect information on the value of the measure at the starting point, often referred to as the *baseline*. When evaluating the change, a community should identify the *unit of analysis*. The *unit of analysis* is the basic unit whose properties you choose to measure and analyze. For most communities, the unit of analysis will be the neighborhood, the city, or possibly, the county. The decision of what unit of analysis to use may be determined by who is involved in the effort or by data availability. The length of time used to assess change also may vary. The length of time should be based on a reasonable expectation of how long it should take for the actions to have an effect. So if your goal is to create new jobs, you may be able to see the effects of your actions in a few years. Improvement in environmental quality, however, may take a longer period. Thus, the period to be studied may vary by the specific outcomes and impacts that the community wishes to examine.

A written action plan, containing benchmarks or performance indicators and describing the points of success along the way when possible, is essential in monitoring results. Benchmarks are especially useful for long-term projects. For instance, a community may have a long-term vision that involves high-quality health care. Reaching this vision may involve a set of goals and strategies that span several years. Knowing the number of people without access to health care or the number of physicians in the community at the start of the project helps local leaders track their progress.

The benchmarks should be reasonable in terms of what can be accomplished in a specified period of time but, at the same time, should keep efforts focused on the ultimate goal(s) in the strategic visioning document. In this regard, photographs of the community when the visioning process started can be useful in making "before" and "after" presentations to show that benchmarks, such as improvements in buildings or streets, have been met. In designing benchmarks or performance indicators, however, community leaders must recognize that community development is not limited to job and/or income creation; rather, it should include sustainability, historic preservation, health care, education, recreation, and other essential characteristics of a healthy and vibrant community.

Linking benchmarks to each goal provides residents with information on progress in each section of the plan. When one part of the overall effort is not performing well, adjustments can be made to bring it in line without substantially changing the entire approach. Regular reviews of the action plan and comparisons with benchmarks can be very useful. Showing progress on small projects can build confidence and encourage more involvement by residents and businesses.

Evaluation of Visioning Processes

Several studies have examined the experience of visioning programs. Each study identified factors for success. Klein, Benson, Anderson, and Herr (1993) identified ten factors as important to successful visioning projects: (a) There is a front-end emphasis; (b) one size does not fit all; (c) the project is inclusive (with involvement of individuals from various parts of the community); (d) leadership is impartial; (e) the project shows attention to detail; (f) risks are taken; (g) projections are made; (h) the project gets media attention; (i) the project shows long-range thinking; and (j) results are validated.

Two studies examined the public participation process undertaken in a visioning exercise. Woodmansee (1994) examined the techniques used by six communities to encourage public participation in the visioning process. He identified nine factors that contribute to public participation in visioning programs: connections, personal context, coherence, room for ambivalence, emotion, authenticity, sense of possibility, catalysts, and mediating institutions. Helling (1998b), in a study of Atlanta's metropolitan region visioning project, found that two types of participants—employee sponsored and self-sponsored—differed in their motivation, levels of satisfaction, and attendance. Self-sponsored individuals experienced higher net personal costs and were less motivated and satisfied with the process. This finding may have implications for CBOs that want to pursue a visioning process.

In another article on Atlanta's visioning project, Helling (1998a) reported that the project yielded few significant, immediate results, despite a $4.4 million budget and a program of community participation. The general ineffectiveness of this program was caused by three factors:

> setting process rather than outcome objectives, requiring consensus without having the means to spur compromise, and de-emphasizing the importance of substantive planning expertise and information without reference to an alternative standard of accuracy or source of public credibility. (p. 349)

Helling's assessment, however, should consider the fact that the Atlanta project was initiated outside local neighborhoods. Although there was a great deal of outside support for the process, there was very little capacity or self-initiated effort in the project. The failure of the Atlanta project may have been due more to how the process was initiated than to the emphasis on process or the lack of expertise or information in the process.

The objective is to take these vision statements and convert them into action items. Did the communities that conducted a visioning process and successfully came up with a vision statement go any further in trying to move the community toward that vision? Or was the vision statement the end of the process? If the vision statement was acted upon, did different organizations take ownership of various parts of the vision? What were the outcomes of the visioning process? What were the impacts of the visioning process?

Summary and Conclusions

In this chapter, we have focused on the role of public participation in the community development process and presented visioning as a particular process used by communities to guide their futures. The visioning process lends itself well to using a variety of public participation techniques, as well as including aspects of community organizing. Visioning exercises have become part of general planning processes at the local government level but also are used by voluntary groups and CBOs to guide them in their work in communities and neighborhoods.

There continues to be some debate over the importance of process and outcomes in community development. Some practitioners believe that the process is the key and that the eventual outcomes of the process do not matter. Others believe that visible outcomes are all that matter and that the process is relatively unimportant. Probably the most reasonable position to take regarding this debate is that most community development efforts require both a meaningful process that involves residents and tangible products that participants can point to as the result of their effort.

KEY CONCEPTS

ACORN model	Electoral participation	Public action
Advocacy planning	Evaluation	Public involvement
Alinsky model	IAF model	Strategic planning
Boston model	Monitoring	Visioning
Community organizing	Obligatory participation	
Comprehensive- rational planning	Outcomes	
	Outputs	

QUESTIONS

1. Why is public participation important in a community development effort?

2. What are the four forms of public participation? What are some differences between these forms?

3. How do the forms of public participation relate to the ladder of public participation?

4. What are the different organizing models, and how do they differ?

5. What is visioning?

6. How do public participation and visioning relate to the future growth and development of communities?

7. What is community organizing?

8. Define evaluation and monitoring.

9. What are the differences between outcomes and outputs? Give some examples of each.

EXERCISES

1. Contact a CBO to evaluate its community development process. Ask the following kinds of questions: What kind of public participation techniques did the CBO use? Did the CBO develop a plan? What kind of process was used to create that plan? What kinds of outcomes have occurred? Are any impacts claimed due to the process? Has the CBO developed any indicators to monitor progress? Discuss the advantages and limitations of the CBO's public participation

techniques and its planning process and action plan. Discuss the limitations of claiming outcomes and outputs. Discuss how the CBO can make its process broader and more participatory in the future.

2. Identify a federal, state, or local agency that has recently conducted a public participation process in your community. An example might be a transportation plan for a city. Evaluate its effort to involve the public in the decision-making process. What were the strengths of the process? What were the weaknesses of the process? How could the process be improved in the future?

REFERENCES

Arnstein, S. R. (1969). A ladder of citizen participation. *Journal of the American Planning Association, 35,* 216-224.

Beauregard, R. A. (1978). Planning in an advanced capitalist state. In R. Burchell & G. Sternlieb (Eds.), *Planning theory in the 1980's: A search for future directions* (pp. 235-254). New Brunswick, NJ: Rutgers University, Center for Urban Policy Research.

Bryson, J. M. (1995). *Strategic planning for public and nonprofit organizations: A guide to strengthening and sustaining organizational achievement.* San Francisco: Jossey-Bass.

Bryson, J. M., & Roering, W. D. (1987). Applying private-sector strategic planning in the public sector. *Journal of the American Planning Association, 53*(1), 9-22.

Davidoff, P. (1973). Advocacy and pluralism in planning. In A. Faludi (Ed.), *A reader in planning theory* (pp. 277-296). New York: Pergamon.

Department of Urban and Regional Planning. (2000). *Lodi 2025: Envisioning the future through the year 2025.* Madison, WI: Author.

de Tocqueville, A. (1945). *Democracy in America.* New York: Vintage. (Original work published 1835)

Fainstein, N., & Fainstein, S. (1982). New debates in urban planning: The impact of Marxist theory within the United States. In C. Paris (Ed.), *Critical readings in planning theory* (pp. 147-173). New York: Pergamon.

Glass, J. J. (1979). Citizen participation in planning: The relationship between objectives and techniques. *Journal of the American Planning Association, 45,* 180-189.

Grabow, S., & Heskin, A. (1973). Foundations for a radical concept of planning. *Journal of the American Institute of Planners, 39*(2), 106-114.

Green, G., Haines, A., & Halebsky, S. (2000). *Building our future: A guide to community visioning* (Report No. G3708). Madison: University of Wisconsin Extension.

Helling, A. (1998a). Collaborative visioning: Proceed with caution! Results from evaluating Atlanta's Vision 2020 project. *Journal of the American Planning Association, 64,* 335-349.

Helling, A. (1998b). Employer-sponsored and self-sponsored participation in collaborative visioning: Theory, evidence and implications. *Journal of Applied Behavioral Science, 34,* 222-240.

Howe, E. (1992). Professional roles and the public interest in planning. *Journal of Planning Literature, 6,* 230-248.

Hudson, B. (1979). Comparison of current planning theories: Counterparts and contradictions. *Journal of the American Planning Association, 45,* 387-398.

Kahn, S. (1991). *Organizing: A guide for grassroots leaders.* Silver Springs, MD: National Association of Social Workers.

Klein, W. R., Benson, V. L., Anderson, J., & Herr, P. B. (1993). Visions of things to come. *Planning, 59*(5), 10-19.

Langton, S. (1978). What is citizen participation? In S. Langton (Ed.), *Citizen participation in America: Essays on the state of the art* (pp. 13-24). Lexington, MA: Lexington.

Meyerson, M., & Banfield, E. (1955). *Politics, planning and the public interest: The case of public housing in Chicago.* Glencoe, IL: Free Press.

Rabinovitz, F. (1969). *City politics and planning.* New York: Atherton.

Rittel, H., & Webber, M. (1973). Dilemmas in a general theory of planning. *Policy Sciences, 4*(2), 155-169.

Rosener, J. (1978). Matching method to purpose: The challenges of planning citizen-participation activities. In S. Langton (Ed.), *Citizen participation in America: Essays on the state of the art* (pp. 109-122). Lexington, MA: Lexington.

Rubin, H. J., & Rubin, I. S. (1992). *Community organizing and development* (2nd ed.). Boston: Allyn & Bacon.

Shipley, R., & Newkirk, R. (1998). Visioning: Did anybody see where it came from? *Journal of Planning Literature, 12,* 407-416.

Wildavsky, A. (1973). If planning is everything, maybe it's nothing. *Policy Sciences, 4*(2), 127-153.

Woodmansee, J. (1994). *Community visioning: Citizen participation in strategic planning* (MIS Report, Vol. 26, No. 3). Washington, DC: International City Management Association.

ADDITIONAL SUGGESTED READINGS

Readings ■

Aspen Institute, Rural Economic Policy Program. (1996). *Measuring community capacity building: A workbook-in-progress for rural communities.* Washington, DC: Author.

Bunker, B. B., & Alban, B. T. (1997). *Large group interventions: Engaging the whole system for rapid change.* San Francisco: Jossey-Bass.

Carlson, C. (1990). Creating a strategic vision. *Western City, 66*(5), 10-44.

Christenson, J. A., & Robinson, J., Jr. (Eds.). (1989). *Community development in perspective.* Ames: Iowa State University Press.

Daniels, T. L., & Keller, J. W. (1988). *The small town planning handbook.* Washington, DC: Planners Press.

Darling, D. L., Rahman, M. H., & Pillarisetti, J. R. (1994). Measuring and monitoring change with a community life cycle model. *Journal of Community Development Society, 25*(1), 62-78.

Emery, M., & Purser, R. E. (1996). *The search conference: A powerful method for planning organizational change and community action.* San Francisco: Jossey-Bass.

Kretzmann, J. P., & McKnight, J. L. (1993). *Building communities from the inside out: A path toward finding and mobilizing a community's assets.* Evanston, IL: Northwestern University, Center for Urban Affairs and Policy Research.

Lewis, J. A. (1996). Visioning for tangible results. In B. McClendon & A. Catanese (Eds.), *Planners on planning: Leading planners offer real-life lessons on what works, what doesn't, and why* (pp. 163-180). San Francisco: Jossey-Bass.

Littrell, D. W., & Hobbs, D. (1989). The self-help approach. In J. Christenson & J. Robinson, Jr. (Eds.), *Community development in perspective* (pp. 48-68). Ames: Iowa State University Press.

North Central Regional Center for Rural Development. (2000). *Take charge: Participatory action planning for communities and organizations.* Ames, IA: Author.

Walzer, N. (Ed.). (1996). *Community strategic visioning programs.* Westport, CT: Praeger.

Weisbord, M. R., & Janoff, S. (1995). *Future search: An action guide to finding common ground in organizations and communities.* San Francisco: Berrett-Koehler.

Web Sites ■

Aspen Institute Policy Programs. <www.aspeninstitute.org/csg/csg_ccb.asp>. The Aspen Institute has a Web site that describes various issues around measuring community capacity. It also has a workbook titled *Measuring Community Capacity Building: A Workbook in Progress* that is very useful.

Axelrod Group. <www.AxelrodGroup.com/>. Information regarding the conference model (an approach that includes use of Future Search and follow-up conferences designed to develop an action plan).

Future Search. <www.ctarrce.org>. This Web site provides information on Future Search, an organizational development technique of collaborative inquiry that focuses on the future of an organization, a network of people, or a community.

Videos ■

Collaborative Planning (1990), produced by the American Planning Association, directed by Edith Nettle. This video "shows how citizens can work together in their communities to plan for the future." Available from Community Services—Washington, 915 15th St. NW, Suite 601, Washington, DC 20005.

CHAPTER 4

Community-Based Organizations

For many people, *community development* is synonymous with community development corporations (CDCs). CDCs have become the primary organizations for carrying out local development activities in many urban neighborhoods and rural communities. Other community-based organizations (CBOs), such as local development corporations (LDCs) and neighborhood associations, also are involved in development activities. In this chapter, we review the basic structure and mission of CDCs, LDCs, and neighborhood associations. We are especially interested in examining how these organizations operate, how they balance community organizing and development activities, and their effectiveness in generating valuable outcomes and impacts in their neighborhoods and localities. There are other types of CBOs, but they often have a more narrow focus and will be discussed in the following chapters on community assets.

We focus on CBOs because they play an especially important role in the community development process. Rubin and Rubin (1992) suggested that organizations make community action more effective for several different reasons (pp. 96-97). First, organizations create power. Government officials and other large organizations (such as foundations) are more likely to respond to demands when an organization represents a large number of people. At the same time, individuals are more likely to participate in a project because they are no longer acting alone. Second, organizations provide continuity. The membership may change, but the organization can continue to sustain its activities. Continuity also is important for attracting resources, especially from foundations, and for developing ties with local government officials. Third, organizations help develop expertise, either through collective or accumulated experiences or through obtaining resources to hire experts when needed. Finally, organizations enable residents to respond to problems more quickly. Without organizations, residents would have to organize and mobilize around new issues each time a problem developed.

The organizations we discuss below all struggle with some of the major issues affecting community development efforts: how to encourage pubic participation; how to avoid becoming too bureaucratic; how to obtain external resources without losing control over the process; how to address multiple objectives (e.g., economic, social, and environmental) at once; and how to build the capacity of local residents. Most of these organizations began as nonprofit organizations, but many evolved into for-profit entities as they became established and were able to maintain their financial base.

BOX 4.1   **CDC Facts**

- As of 1990, there were more than 2,000 CDCs in the United States.

- Two thirds of the CDCs served one neighborhood or a multineighborhood area smaller than a city.

- Almost all CDCs were involved in housing; a smaller number were involved in other activities, such as economic development and community building.

- Approximately 70% of the CDCs developed fewer than 25 housing units per year; 6% produced more than 100 units per year.

SOURCE: Stoutland (1999).

Community Development Corporations

The origins of CDCs can be traced back to Community Action Programs (CAPs) of the 1960s, although most CDCs have been organized more recently. There are more than 2,000 CDCs in the United States today. The National Congress for Community Economic Development (NCCED, 1995) defined a CDC as a private nonprofit entity, serving a low-income community, governed by a community-based board, and serving as an ongoing producer in housing, commercial-industrial development, or business development. CDCs' primary goals are to serve low-income communities and to empower residents. These dual-purpose goals have been the source of much debate in the 1990s.

CDCs are intended to be community-controlled organizations. For most people, this means that the board of directors is drawn from community residents, especially low-income residents. There are some reasons to question whether having a representative board really constitutes "community control" (see discussion in Chapter 3 regarding the "ladder of public participation"). For example, the board may not exercise much power and may defer to professional and technical staff to make decisions. Because of the increasingly technical nature of development projects, many board members may feel that they do not have the expertise to make independent judgments. There is little evidence that neighborhood residents are able to directly control CDC activities in most neighborhoods.

Although CDCs are involved in a wide variety of activities, their affordable housing activities have been most successful and visible. Surveys of CDCs show that more than 90% report that they are engaged in housing and that almost one half have produced more than 100 units (NCCED, 1995). Between 1960 and 1990, CDCs and other nonprofit developers produced about 736,000 units of federally assisted housing. Production of housing appears to be the preferred activity for several reasons. For many poor neighborhoods, residents are in dire need of affordable housing. Adequate housing, and the stable resident population it encourages, is a foundation for stimulating business and commercial development in a neighborhood. There are relatively more funding sources for housing in poor neighborhoods than for other types of activities, partially due to the perceived lower risk of housing activities. Most CDCs are able to tap into resources from federal and local governments for financing housing projects. In particular, Community Development Black Grants (CDBGs) (since 1974) and more recently the HOME programs (since 1990) have provided steady sources of federal funding for CDCs. The HOME program, for example, mandates that at least 15% of each participating jurisdiction's funds be earmarked for nonprofit housing producers. Recently, CDCs have moved increasingly beyond housing into areas such as business development and have been criticized for not proving to be as successful, at least initially (Lemann, 1994).

CDCs claim to provide several advantages in leading the community development effort in localities. First, many CDCs view themselves as involved in comprehensive development—a variety of activities, from physical and economic development to provision of social services and promotion of cultural activities and the arts. Second, they have the technical expertise to address community problems. Third, CDCs are more entrepreneurial, more efficient, and less bureaucratic than the local, state, and federal government agencies involved in community development. And fourth, CDCs are more equipped to shape the development process by the community's vision and needs.

Three Generations of CDCs

Many people trace the origin of CDCs to Robert Kennedy's tour of Bedford-Stuyvesant and the Special Impact Amendment to the Economic Opportunity Act. The Bedford-Stuyvesant Restoration Corporation is considered the first CDC in the country (see Case Study 4.1). Most of the early CDCs emerged from neighborhood-based political activities and attempted to empower residents. Over time, they began to rely more heavily on paid staff and to be a major source of technical assistance in low-income neighborhoods. Below, we briefly discuss the historical development of CDCs in the United States.

The 1960s: Activist Organizations

The first CDCs were engaged in housing projects, but their primary focus tended to be on business and workforce development. The CDCs that were established during the 1960s (fewer than 100) were founded primarily by community activists. The first major source of federal funding for CDCs was the Special Impact Program (SIP). This program established block grants to CBOs that would design and implement their own development strategies. The program faced serious opposition within the Johnson administration, and it has been moved from several different agencies (O'Connor, 1999). Eventually, the program was considered a success and was seen as a key element of the place-based development strategies of the War on Poverty. During a 20-year period from 1968 to 1986, the federal government allocated more than $75 million in this program to CDCs.

The 1970s: Specialization

During the 1970s, the number of CDCs increased to several hundred. Their focus shifted, primarily to housing projects. Many of the CDCs that were created during this period were organized by groups involved in redlining issues and problems related to urban renewal (Vidal, 1992). At about the same time, foundations began investing

CASE STUDY 4.1

Bedford Stuyvesant Restoration Corporation (BSRC)

In 1966, New York Senator Robert F. Kennedy visited the Bedford Stuyvesant neighborhood in Brooklyn. From the 1940s to 1960, the population had shifted from 75% white to 85% African American and Latino. The neighborhood suffered from a loss of jobs, disinvestment of local resources, and inadequate public services. With the assistance of local leaders, Senator Kennedy helped establish the Bedford Stuyvesant Renewal and Rehabilitation Corporation, which eventually became the Bedford Stuyvesant Restoration Corporation. This organization became the nation's first community development corporation (CDC).

At the core of the CDC's strategies was the improvement of the physical conditions of the neighborhood, which, it was hoped, would improve the likelihood of attracting new businesses and other revitalization efforts. The neighborhood turned its attention to improving basic services, such as garbage collection and infrastructure maintenance, as the first step in improving the physical environment.

One of the first projects was a program to help residents weatherize and renovate the exteriors of their homes. This project had the dual purpose of improving the physical conditions of the community (more than 4,200 housing units were rehabilitated) and generating new job opportunities (over 2,000 temporary and permanent jobs) that gave local residents job experience and training.

Probably the most visible project of the BSRC was the redevelopment project at Restoration Plaza. The multipurpose complex was an abandoned milk-bottling factory. Since 1975, the complex has been the home of a variety of businesses, including commercial banks, utility companies, a grocery store, a theater, and several community-based service organizations. The project became the center of the revitalization efforts in the neighborhood.

For more than 30 years now, BSRC has addressed a variety of needs in the Bedford Stuyvesant neighborhood. It has attracted more than $370 million in investments and provided residents with important jobs skills and experiences.

SOURCE: From "Community Development Corporation Oral History Project," <www. picced.org/advocacy/bldghope.htm>, February 1997, Brooklyn, NY. Copyright 1997 by the Pratt Institute Center for Community and Environmental Development. Reprinted with permission.

much more in CDCs. The Ford Foundation's Grey Areas Program was one the largest and most visible efforts during this period. The Grey Areas Program sought to coordinate service programs among local bureaucracies in an effort to integrate low-income residents into urban society.

The 1980s and 1990s: Professionalization

In the 1980s, the number of CDCs expanded to more than 2,000. CDCs became increasingly specialized, concentrating on housing activities. CDC staff generally were more professional and played much less of an activist role than they had in the past. One of the most important changes in the community development field during the 1980s was the rise of national financial intermediaries, which served to support CDCs in the area of housing. Three of the most important intermediaries are the Local Initiatives Support Corporation (LISC), the Enterprise Foundation, and the Neighborhood Reinvestment Corporation (NRC). These intermediaries provide CDCs with the financial resources, technical assistance, and information that made them much more effective in the field of housing. Some analysts have pointed to a growing tension between CDCs and these intermediaries because of the influence that the control of resources generates (Rubin, 2000). Yet there is no question that the CDCs have benefited from the rise of these intermediaries.

Debates Over CDCs

The shift in the CDCs' mission or orientation from activists/organizers to professional/ technical assistance providers has recently been criticized (Stoecker, 1997). Stoecker raised several questions about the ability of CDCs to adequately deal with the limits that capitalism imposes on these nonprofit organizations. He stated that CDCs have evolved into institutions that support the free market instead of challenging it. Because CDCs are so dependent on external sources of financing, they are pressured to ensure that their projects are profitable rather than addressing the social needs of residents (Marquez, 1993). In particular, because CDCs rely so much on federal funding, they are unlikely to challenge government policies. Probably one of the most frequent criticisms of CDCs is that their institutionalization reduces their willingness to push for basic structural change in the way the federal government deals with poor communities (Piven & Cloward, 1977).

CDCs, however, continue to have their defenders. Goetz and Sidney (1995), for example, found that CDCs continue to play a significant role in organizing communities. In their study of CDCs in Minneapolis and St. Paul, they found that many of the CDCs were politically active, in terms of both gaining support for their projects and addressing broad issues affecting their neighborhoods. Many CDCs channel their political activities through broader coalitions or trade associations involved in nonprofit housing development.

Other supporters of CDCs disagree with the distinction between development and empowerment (Rubin, 1994). CDCs may help initiate activist groups in some cases, which essentially buffers them from the politics of the issue (Rubin, 1993).

Stoecker (1997) proposed a new model for CDCs. He argued that community organizing and development functions probably should not, and cannot, occur within the same institutions. Because CDCs may threaten their investors if they take on a confrontational approach in their organizing efforts, they cannot adequately provide financial support and serve an organizing function. Stoecker argued that separating out these functions into different organizations could facilitate local development for several reasons. Community organizing might be more effective when it is loosened from the ties of financial interests. When these functions were no longer tied to one another, community organizing might reflect more accurately the needs of the community than the needs of financial interests. Separating out the functions also might allow the development function to operate more efficiently because it would allow organizations to increase their capital capacity by becoming larger and serving several locations. The degree to which this separation has already occurred through other CBOs, such as neighborhood associations that both support and oppose the local CDC depending on the issue, is not well understood.

Another line of criticism focuses on the tendency for CDCs to specialize in housing projects. Vidal (1997) contended that housing is less of a priority for poor neighborhoods today than in the past. Instead, there are pressures to increase the role of CDCs in other areas, such as workforce development and social service delivery. Lemann (1994), however, contended that CDCs have proven to be relatively successful in the housing arena but that they are very limited in their ability to successfully promote business or commercial development, training, or even social service delivery. Lemann argued that communities have a very limited ability to affect economic development because of larger economic and political forces affecting the fate of localities.

Although CDCs do concentrate on housing, they tend to provide some services that are not easily replaced by other for-profit developers. In particular, they often supplement their real estate activities with tenant or home owner counseling, property management, and crime prevention (Berger & Kasper, 1993).

The most likely scenario is that CDCs will continue to be involved in housing but will probably be forced to move into new areas as well. CBOs are well positioned to contribute to local development through such areas as workforce development and social service delivery. In particular, there is much more emphasis in the field today on community or capacity building. CDCs find themselves in a unique position that enables them to build social relationships among various institutions and organizations in the community, which can serve as assets for future development (Gittell & Vidal, 1998).

Institutional Support for CDCs

Like most development organizations, CDCs must rely on leveraging resources from outside to be successful. CDCs have become dependent on a variety of institutions, especially federal government agencies and banks, to provide the necessary resources for their activities. In this section, we will look at the growth of intermediary institutions that support CDCs.

The oldest of the institutions providing technical assistance to and support for CDCs is the NRC, which was established in 1978 by Congress in the Neighborhood Reinvestment Corporation Act. NRC provides direct financial assistance, technical assistance in developing local lender pools or acquiring low-cost financing, and assistance in starting revolving loan funds.

In 1979, the Ford Foundation established LISC, which has worked with more than 1,000 CDCs to build 53,000 affordable homes and 9 million square feet of commercial and industrial space. LISC provides financial and technical assistance. In 1991, LISC established a demonstration program in three localities (Palm Beach County, Florida; Little Rock, Arkansas; and New Orleans, Louisiana) to test the effectiveness of a "consensus organizing" approach to community development (Gittell & Vidal, 1998). This approach toward consensus organizing was first used in the 1980s in the Monongahela Valley, Pennsylvania. Consensus organizing establishes social capital by building relationships inside the community and new relationships to the larger community.

Another intermediary serving CDCs in the United States is the Enterprise Foundation, which was established in 1981 to develop affordable housing in low-income neighborhoods. The Enterprise Foundation has helped develop more than 36,000 homes. It also has established a financial subsidiary that has raised over $655 million to support low-income housing.

Taken together, these intermediaries have become an important part of the institutional support for community development in this country. They have been especially effective in providing the financial and technical assistance that CDCs need. At the same time, there is a built-in tension between these support organizations and CDCs. Many leaders feel that these intermediary institutions push them to be more concerned with building houses than with community capacity. These intermediaries, however, do allow CDCs to learn from one another, and they provide some of the basic training and skills that CDCs need to be effective.

Local Development Corporations

LDCs can be either profit or nonprofit organizations, although most choose nonprofit status. LDCs can be involved in a wide variety of economic development activities, including leasing and improving real property; acquiring property; making equity investments in small businesses; selling notes to finance projects; borrowing and relending money to assist businesses; receiving grants from federal, state, and local agencies; developing industrial parks; establishing and operating small business resource centers (small business incubators); and undertaking historic preservation activities.

There is no official count of how many LDCs there are in the United States. John Levy (1990) estimated that in the late 1980s about 15,000 organizations were involved in promoting local economic development. As discussed later in this chapter, a large percentage of the active LDCs were created in the 1990s, and probably LDCs are being created at an even higher rate today. In the 1980s and 1990s, economic restructuring, especially in the Northeast and Midwest, provided an incentive for many localities to establish LDCs as a means of institutionalizing their economic development efforts.

LDCs offer several advantages over local governments in conducting economic development activities. First, they can provide a "one-stop" shop for businesses. Many local governments may spread these activities out across several agencies and departments, which makes it difficult for businesses and developers to obtain the information and assistance they need. Second, LDCs provide stronger and more long-lasting relationships between local officials and the business sector. This arrangement, it is argued, will make it more likely that the economic development policies will reflect the community's interests than if either the government or a private development group is responsible for these activities. Critics see public-private partnerships, such as LDCs, as a means of removing economic development decisions from the public realm that primarily benefits realtors, landowners, and developers (Logan & Molotch, 1987). Finally, many communities create LDCs to do things to promote development that some local governments may be prohibited from doing, such as lease property to private businesses. LDCs are simply a legal device to accomplish many of these purposes for communities.

Organizational Structure of LDCs

To evaluate LDC activities and the outcomes of those activities, we draw on a recent national survey of local development organizations (Green, Sullivan, & Dunn, 1999). Most (65%) LDCs indicate they are nonprofit, nontaxable organizations (501c3, c4, and c6). The rest define themselves as either for-profits or technically part of a local government agency, office, commission, authority, or board. Most LDCs (more than two thirds) were established in the 1980s or 1990s. The service area of these organizations is varied, with 44% serving a county, 33% a locality, 17% a region, and the rest a neighborhood.

Most LDCs are relatively small, with a median budget of about $150,000. The average LDC receives more than 60% of its funding from public sources and more than one third from private sources, with the rest coming from grants and loans. The average LDC has one full-time equivalent paid professional and a half-time paid support staff position.

The boards of directors of LDCs appear to be much less representative of their community than boards for CDCs. The average board for an LDC is approximately one third government officials and two thirds individuals from the private sector, primarily the major businesses in the community. Board members are largely white and male. These organizations clearly have a probusiness orientation and typically are not involved with housing, social services, or many of the other activities in which CDCs engage. But there appears to be growing pressure for LDCs to be more directly involved in job training and indirectly involved in affordable housing and child care. Especially in periods of tight labor markets, LDCs will face more pressure to help existing businesses with their workforce needs than to attract more businesses to the community.

LDC Activities

How do LDCs promote economic development? The three most common forms of business incentives are low-cost loans, grants, and free land or land write-downs (Figure 4.1). About 43% of the development organizations offer low-cost loans, 30% provide grants, and 25% provide free land or land write-downs. The average LDC provided loans to about three businesses over the past year, with a total value of more than $350,000.

The popular image of LDCs is that they often provide too many subsidies to businesses to locate in their community and that most of the businesses that locate there would have done so without the subsidies. The survey data suggest, however, that most LDCs are fairly cautious in providing business incentives. About 41% of the organizations always require a performance agreement when providing business incentives. These agreements often include some stipulation for the number of jobs created, the wages paid, the capital investment, and some time period of operation. About one fourth of development organizations always include a "clawback" clause in their performance agreement, which requires a money return if the agreements are not met by a specified time period. One third of the organizations always use a cost-benefit analysis to assess the economic and fiscal impact of offering the incentives.

FIGURE 4.1

Incentives Offered to
Businesses by LDCs

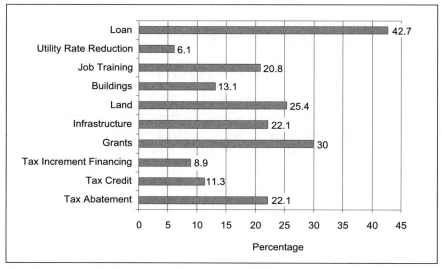

SOURCE: Green et al. (1999).

Outcomes and Impacts of LDC Activities

Throughout this text, we argue that CBOs often can build local assets better than governments or markets. In the following, we present some data that compare the outcomes and impacts of LDCs and local governments. Overall, the information suggests that LDCs are generally more successful than local governments in generating jobs and income in their communities (Table 4.1). More than three quarters of development organizations, compared with less than 60% of the local governments, have had success at business recruitment over the past 3 years. In the last 3 years, the average LDC has attracted more than three firms, bringing a total of 158 jobs, paying an average of $8.88 per hour. Their efforts at job creation are less impressive but still much more likely to be successful than the efforts of local governments. Approximately three firms have been created, providing 35 jobs and paying an average of $7.81 per job. About 74% of the LDCs have been successful at business expansion, with an average of three businesses expanding, providing a little more than 90 jobs at $8.97 per hour. LDCs are generally least successful at business retention. Only 38% of LDCs have had success retaining firms in their communities. An average of less than one firm was retained, saving 76 jobs that paid $8.97 per hour.

In their efforts to promote economic development, many communities have formed public-private development organizations. These organizations are somewhat controversial because they take many activities out of the public realm, although there is public financing behind them. LDCs tend to promote economic development more actively than local governments do, and they are more likely than local governments to create or save jobs and businesses. On the basis of these limited criteria, public-private development organizations appear to have several advantages over local governments. We also find that LDCs tend to help expand or retain businesses that pay higher entry-level wages than do local governments. LDCs may be more selective in whom they assist than local government officials, who are faced with political pressure to create new jobs regardless of the quality of jobs.

TABLE 4.1
Outcomes of Local Development Corporations' and Local Governments' Economic Development Activities

	LDCs		Local Governments	
	Mean	**SD**	**Mean**	**SD**
Business recruitment				
Report success (%)	76.00	0.43	0.59	0.49
No. of firms	3.26	6.03	1.70	2.56
No. of jobs	157.82	347.21	63.33	117.19
Entry-level wages ($)	8.88	2.42	8.51	3.34
Business creation				
Report success (%)	59.00	0.49	0.35	0.48
No. of firms	2.77	6.01	1.01	2.56
No. of jobs	35.33	113.52	13.95	44.05
Entry-level wages ($)	7.81	2.13	7.84	1.97
Business expansion				
Report success (%)	74.00	0.44	0.56	0.50
No. of firms	3.35	6.03	2.08	5.07
No. of jobs	90.89	152.85	48.81	120.15
Entry-level wages ($)	8.97	2.40	7.83	1.81
Business retention				
Report success (%)	38.00	0.49	0.25	0.43
No. of firms	0.69	3.35	0.37	0.90
No. of jobs	76.05	317.38	24.38	111.94
Entry-level wages ($)	8.97	2.45	8.11	1.71
Budget ($)	228,306	395,188	89,029	178,833

SOURCE: Green et al. (1999).

Neighborhood Associations

Logan and Rabrenovic (1990) defined a neighborhood association as "a civic organization oriented toward maintaining or improving the quality of life in a geographically delimited residential area" (p. 68). Like CDCs and LDCs, the 1970s and 1980s were a period of rapid growth for neighborhood associations. In their study of neighborhood organizations in Albany, New York, Logan and Rabrenovic reported that over 70% of them had been established since 1975. Most neighborhood associations are formed as a result of a specific event or issue, with the most common being disputes over commercial or industrial development, typically involving the rezoning of land from residential to nonresidential uses.

Although neighborhood organizations are established as a result of a specific issue, most take on additional issues. Logan and Rabrenovic found that several issues currently dominated the interests of neighborhood organizations but that they could be grouped into four broad categories: safety (e.g., police and fire), collective consumption (e.g., parks, playgrounds, streets, garbage collections), lifestyle (e.g., housing, cleanliness of the area, architectural standards), and development (e.g., residential land use changes, impacts of industrial/commercial development).

Who supports and who opposes neighborhood associations? According to Logan and Rabrenovic's study, local governments were considered to be cooperating organizations about 50% of the time and confrontational organizations about 43% of the time. Businesses and land developers were much more likely to be seen as opponents than as cooperators with neighborhood associations.

Why do residents become involved in neighborhood associations? Research shows that length of residence and interests in protecting the value of the home are strong predictors of membership in neighborhood associations. Having children younger than age 5 also strongly affects membership in these organizations; presumably, interests in safety and education are the motivating factors in this case.

Oropesa (1989) examined the factors related to the success of neighborhood associations. She asked neighborhood association leaders to indicate on a 4-point scale, ranging from *extremely successful* to *not at all successful,* how successful their organization had been in addressing the key problems in their neighborhood. Her study considered several possible influences, including the population characteristics of the community (e.g., poverty level, percentage of families with children, stability), the resources available to the neighborhood association (e.g., number of members, budget, staff, professionalization of leaders), and the political structure of the association (i.e., how decisions are made). Oropesa found that several factors internal and external to associations influenced their effectiveness. Poor neighborhoods were less effective than others, primarily because they were less likely to have professional leaders. Neighborhood associations that faced opposition from the city bureaucracy were less successful than those that did not face opposition. Finally, Oropesa looked at the level of democratic decision making in the neighborhood association and found that organizations promoting public participation were more successful than those that did not.

Overall, neighborhood organizations tend to be less formal and more specialized than the other two types of CBOs examined here. They also tend to emphasize community organizing more than development. Most cities have programs that encourage the development of neighborhood organizations, as they tend to help establish stronger ties between the local government and residents. But there usually is a tension between neighborhood organizations and local governments. Local governments like neighborhood organizations to be active but are usually unwilling to grant too much authority or resources to them. Neighborhood organizations can under certain circumstances exert considerable political power in local elections.

Summary and Conclusions

CBOs play an integral role in the community development process. Successful communities generally have successful organizations representing their interests. Unfortunately, most CBOs pay very little attention to organizational processes because they tend to focus on the community's issues. Yet developing an organization that is fair and effective is undoubtedly an important determinant of the viability of a community development process.

Community-based development organizations do not fit neatly into traditional categories of organizations. They frequently provide services, but they also are activist organizations promoting social change. They are nonprofit organizations, but they increasingly own and manage property. They rely heavily on government support, but they directly challenge government policies at times. These contradictions often produce unique challenges for community-based development organizations.

Probably the biggest challenge that CBOs face is the tension between public participation and leadership. The tension here is that if CBOs are successful at getting the community involved, they may lack the leadership to carry through with their objectives. Conversely, strong leadership may be a deterrent for many people to participate in the organization.

Finally, CBOs typically struggle with the meaning of community control. Does it simply mean that the board of directors (and staff) are representative of the community? Does it mean that the board of directors has the authority to set broad policies and make decisions for the organization? Does it mean that residents have an opportunity to make key decisions for the organization? As we have seen, there appear to be several different answers to these questions.

KEY CONCEPTS

Community development corporation

Enterprise Foundation

Grey Areas Program

HOME

Local development corporation

Local Initiatives Support Corporation

Neighborhood association

Neighborhood Reinvestment Corporation

Special Impact Program

QUESTIONS

1. Describe the major changes that have occurred in the structure and mission of CDCs in the United States over the past 30 years.

2. What have been the major criticisms of CDCs? Do you believe these criticisms are valid? Why or why not?

3. Describe the role that intermediaries play in supporting the activities of CDCs.

4. What are LDCs, and how do they differ from CDCs?

5. In what types of activities do neighborhood organizations get involved? What factors influence their success?

EXERCISES

1. Identify a CDC in your city or region, and evaluate the level of community control in the organization.

   ■ Review the records of the organization to assess how well the community has been represented on the board. What have been the trends in community participation on the board? Have low- and moderate-income residents been well represented on the board?

- Interview the board members and the staff of the CDC to obtain their assessments of community control. Is there agreement or systematic differences between the board and the staff regarding the issue of community control? If there are differences, have there been specific issues where the lack of control has been most apparent?

- Interview community residents to assess their views of how well the CDC is responding to community needs and issues.

2. Identify a neighborhood organization in your community, and interview some members regarding the primary activities of the organization. How has the organization sought to get residents involved in the organization? What were the reasons why the organization was established?

3. Identify an LDC in your area, and interview the staff regarding the economic development activities of the organization. What are the sources of funding for the organization? How does it spend its resources?

REFERENCES

Berger, R. A., & Kasper, G. (1993). An overview of the literature on community development corporations. *Nonprofit Management and Leadership, 4,* 241-255.

Gittell, R., & Vidal, A. (1998). *Community organizing: Building social capital as a development strategy.* Thousand Oaks, CA: Sage.

Goetz, E., & Sidney, M. (1995). Community development corporations as neighborhood advocates: A study of the political activism of nonprofit developers. *Applied Behavioral Science Review, 3*(1), 1-20.

Green, G., Sullivan, D., & Dunn, A. (1999). *Results from the national survey of development organizations.* Unpublished manuscript, University of Wisconsin–Madison, Department of Rural Sociology.

Lemann, N. (1994, January 9). The myth of community development. *New York Times Magazine,* pp. 27-31.

Levy, J. M. (1990). *Economic development programs for cities, counties, and towns.* New York: Praeger.

Logan, J. R., & Molotch, H. L. (1987). *Urban fortunes: The political economy of place.* Berkeley: University of California Press.

Logan, J. R., & Rabrenovic, G. (1990). Neighborhood associations: Their issues, their allies, and their opponents. *Urban Affairs Quarterly, 26*(1), 68-94.

Marquez, B. (1993). Mexican-American community development corporations and the limits of directed capitalism. *Economic Development Quarterly, 7,* 287-295.

National Congress for Community Economic Development. (1995). *Tying it all together: The comprehensive achievements of community-based development organizations.* Washington, DC: Author.

O'Connor, A. (1999). Swimming against the tide: A brief history of federal policy in poor communities. In R. F. Ferguson & W. T. Dickens (Eds.), *Urban problems and community development* (pp. 77-137). Washington, DC: Brookings Institution.

Oropesa, R. S. (1989). The social and political foundations of effective neighborhood improvement associations. *Social Science Quarterly, 70,* 723-743.

Piven, F., & Cloward, R. P. (1977). *Poor people's movements: Why they succeed, how they fail.* New York: Vintage.

Rubin, H. J. (1993). Understanding the ethos of community-based development: Ethnographic description for public administrators. *Public Administration Review, 53,* 428-437.

Rubin, H. J. (1994). There aren't going to be any bakeries here if there is no money to afford jellyrolls: The organic theory of community-based development. *Social Problems, 41,* 401-424.

Rubin, H. J. (2000). *Renewing hope within neighborhoods of despair: The community-based development model.* Albany: State University of New York Press.

Rubin, H. J., & Rubin, I. S. (1992). *Community organizing and development* (2nd ed.). Boston: Allyn & Bacon.

Stoecker, R. (1997). The CDC model of urban redevelopment: A critique and an alternative. *Journal of Urban Affairs, 19*(1), 1-22.

Stoutland, S. E. (1999). Community development corporations: Mission, strategy, and accomplishments. In R. F. Ferguson & W. T. Dickens (Eds.), *Urban problems and community development* (pp. 193-240). Washington, DC: Brookings Institution.

Vidal, A. (1992). *Rebuilding communities: A national study of urban community development corporations.* New York: New School for Social Research, Community Development Research Center, Graduate School of Management and Urban Policy.

Vidal, A. (1997). Can community development re-invent itself? The challenges of strengthening neighborhoods in the 21st century. *Journal of the American Planning Association, 63,* 429-438.

ADDITIONAL SUGGESTED READINGS

Readings ■

Blakely, E. J., & Aparicio, A. (1990). Balancing social and economic objectives: The case of California's community development corporations. *Journal of the Community Development Society, 21*(1), 115-128.

Cowan, S. M., Rohe, W., & Baku, E. (1999). Factors influencing the performance of community development corporations. *Journal of Urban Affairs, 21,* 325-339.

Gittell, R., & Wilder, M. (1999). Community development corporations: Critical factors that influence success. *Journal of Urban Affairs, 21,* 341-361.

Goetz, E. (1993). *Shelter burden: Local politics and progressive housing policy.* Philadelphia: Temple University Press.

Goetz, E., & Sidney, M. (1994). Revenge of the property owners: Community development and the politics of property. *Journal of Urban Affairs, 16,* 319-334.

Goetz, E., & Sidney, M. (1997). Local policy subsystems and issue definition: An analysis of community development policy change. *Urban Affairs Review, 32,* 490-512.

Lenz, T. J. (1988). Neighborhood development: Issues and models. *Social Policy, 18*(4), 24-30.

O'Brien, D. J. (1975). *Neighborhood organization and interest-group politics.* Princeton, NJ: Princeton University Press.

Rohe, W. M. (1998). Do community development corporations live up to their billing? A review and critique of the research findings. In C. T. Koebel (Ed.), *Shelter and society: Theory, research and policy for nonprofit housing* (pp. 177-199). Albany: State University of New York Press.

Stoecker, R. (1994). *Defending community: The struggle for alternative redevelopment in Cedar-Riverside.* Philadelphia: Temple University Press.

Stoecker, R. (1995). Community, movement, organization: The problem of identity convergence in collective action. *Sociological Quarterly, 36*(1), 111-130.

Vidal, A. (1996). CDCs as agents of neighborhood change: The state of the art. In W. D. Keating, N. Krumholz, & P. Star (Eds.), *Revitalizing urban neighborhoods* (pp. 149-163). Lawrence: Kansas University Press.

Web Sites ■

Pratt Institute Center for Community and Environmental Development (PICCED). <www.picced.org>. This Web site includes 15 profiles of CDCs written for the CED Oral History Project.

National Congress for Community Economic Development (NCCED). <www.ncced.org>. NCCED is the trade association and advocate for the community-based development industry. The organization represents over 3,600 CDCs. NCCED serves the community development industry through public policy research and education, special projects, newsletters, publications, training, conferences, and specialized technical assistance.

Neighborhoods Online. <www.libertynet.org/nol/natl.html>. This Web site is an online resource center for people working to build strong communities throughout the United States. It provides information and ideas covering all aspects of neighborhood revitalization.

Rural Local Initiatives Support Corporation. <www.ruralisc.org/index.html>. This organization helps build the capacity of resident-led rural CDCs, increase their production and impact, demonstrate the value of investing in and through rural CDCs, and make the resource and policy environment more supportive of rural CDCs and their work. It provides training, technical, and financial assistance to 70 CDCs and information to more than 1,300 rural CDCs.

Videos ■

Holding Ground: The Rebirth of Dudley Street (1996), produced and directed by Mark Lipman and Leah Mahan (58 minutes). A nice summary of one of the most heralded community development efforts in the United States over the past decade. Available from New Day Films, 22nd Hollywood Avenue, Ho-Ho-Kus, NJ 07423.

Building Hope (1994), produced by Charles Hobson, directed by David Van Taylor (57 minutes). An excellent overview of the history of community development, with special emphasis on the Bedford-Stuyvesant Restoration Corporation. Available from Pratt Institute, Center for Community and Environmental Development, 379 Dekalb Avenue, Brooklyn, NY 11205.

PART II

Forms of Community Capital

CHAPTER 5

Human Capital
Workforce Development Networks

Human capital is the abilities and skills that workers hold that affect their productivity. It may be defined broadly to include labor market skills, leadership skills, general education background, artistic development and appreciation, health, and other skills and experiences. In this chapter, we focus on the labor market skills of individuals, especially the role of workforce development networks in building these skills, which is the main focus of most community development programs. Human capital, however, has benefits beyond simply getting a high-paying job. It is related to other aspects of quality of life as well.

Why do communities engage in workforce development? Many communities have limited information on the changing needs of the workforce and how they can best position themselves to capture the types of jobs that are emerging in the economy. Having an adequate, skilled, and trained workforce is a prerequisite for economic development today. Yet communities face several obstacles in developing their workforce. If the community provides training for jobs that are not available locally, workers may move to where the jobs are, leaving the community with the costs and none of the benefits of the training. If the community attracts new employers requiring skills that are not available locally, the employer may have to hire workers outside the community or face a skills shortage. Training institutions have a difficult time gauging the future needs of employers. Much of the training that employers demand is fairly specific and is too costly for training institutions to provide. Similarly, the availability and cost of child care and housing in the community may not be adequate to support the workforce.

Community-based organizations (CBOs) can address many of the obstacles that workers, employers, and training institutions face in workforce development efforts. By establishing workforce networks, they can improve the flow of information between employers, workers, and institutions involved in the local labor market. They can reduce some of the costs, and risks, of training workers by spreading the costs out across several organizations. This coordination can begin to address some of the obstacles that communities face in building their local labor market.

In this chapter, we review the key concepts and issues surrounding workforce development, the major actors and institutions, and the primary strategies and tactics for building a local workforce. Workforce development efforts have changed dramatically

---

BOX 5.1 **Workforce Development Facts**

- Of the 25 occupations expected to be the fastest growing from 2000 to 2010, 8 require great skills or substantial experience; 9 are in health care.

- Between 1987 and 1995, the average earnings of whites significantly exceeded those of blacks and Hispanics, but blacks increased their earnings more rapidly than whites, and Hispanics lagged even further.

SOURCE: Judy and D'Amico (1997).

---

in recent years due to welfare reform, growth in the economy and the resulting labor shortage in many areas, and the restructuring of the labor force. CBOs are uniquely situated to improve the functioning of local labor markets by providing networks between employers, workers, and trainers. CBOs can be an important source of information for various actors and institutions involved in workforce development. They also can play an important role in informing workers of the other types of programs and services that they may need, such as transportation services and child care. In this chapter, we review some of the strategies and tactics that communities are using to address the changing needs of the workforce.

Workforce Development Issues

Communities face several interrelated challenges regarding workforce development issues. Most of these issues are concerned with the demand for labor, the supply of labor, the matching process between job searchers and job opportunities, or the institutions (e.g., vocational training, child care) involved in supporting employers and workers. Among the issues that might be addressed are:

1. What are the sources of persistent unemployment and underemployment in the community? Are these due to the increased skill requirements of employers and/or the lack of training among workers? Are jobs being created that match the skills of workers?

2. Do workers have sufficient information about the location and skill requirements of jobs? Do employers use the appropriate methods for searching for qualified workers in the community?

3. Is job training being offered by employers? If so, what type? If not, why not, and what obstacles do employers face in obtaining additional training? Do employers invest enough in the training of their workforce? What types of programs are available from training institutions in the region, and how well do they match the needs of employers and workers in the area?

4. What is the current level of job turnover among employers? What are the causes and consequences of this turnover for employers, workers, and the community? What types of programs might reduce the turnover?

5. How many jobs will be created in the area in the next few years, and what are the skills, education, and experience requirements for these jobs? How well does the available demand for labor match the available supply of labor in the region?

6. What are the current levels of wages and benefits available to workers in the region? Do the jobs being created by local employers provide a living wage?

7. How many workers are commuting out of the community, and what are the skills and experience of these workers? Would these out-commuters be willing to work locally if jobs were available that provided similar wages and benefits?

8. To what extent does the availability and/or cost of day care in the community present obstacles to residents entering the labor force? Are employers facing any problems in adding additional shifts because of the costs or availability of day care?

9. Are resources available in the community that are not being used? Do retirees with significant job experience and skills have opportunities to find meaningful work in the area? Are there jobs for the disabled?

10. Are there factors preventing the community from seeking good jobs?

Key Concepts and Debates

Workforce development is a term that is frequently misunderstood; it is often considered as only job training. Harrison and Weiss (1998), however, defined it as the "constellation of activities from orientation to the work world, recruiting, placement, and mentoring to follow-up counseling and crisis intervention" (p. 5). Training is only one component of workforce development.

A growing number of CBOs are responsible for workforce development. Probably one of the most publicized models for workforce development is the Center for Employment Training, which is based in San Jose, California, and now operates throughout the western and southwestern United States (Melendez, 1996). This model has three basic functions: enhancing job-specific skills, assisting with job-search strategies, and facilitating access to jobs by establishing relationships with employers and providing information on job opportunities. Other models may be organized differently, but they provide essentially the same services (see Case Study 5.1).

At the core of workforce programs is the development of human capital. Human capital theory argues that variations in earnings are consequences of differences in worker's abilities and skills (Beaulieu & Mulkey, 1995). Individuals can enhance their future earnings by investing in their labor skills (through education and job training). A basic assumption behind human capital theory is that individuals will be motivated to increase earnings, which means they will be willing to invest in education and training necessary to improve their position in the labor market. Human capital theorists tend to assume that workers are mobile and will move to other locations where there are more job opportunities available. This individualistic view of education and training

---

CASE STUDY 5.1

Milwaukee Jobs Initiative, Inc.

Milwaukee suffers from some of the same problems that affect most major cities—a growing demand for highly skilled workers and a declining demand for unskilled workers. The Milwaukee Jobs Initiative (MJI) was established in 1995 to provide a match between inner-city workers and the broader regional economy, and thus jobs that provide good wages and benefits. The initiative has brought together major businesses, unions, and community organizations to design and implement the project. MJI works on both the demand and supply sides of the regional labor market. The initiative is working primarily with three industry sectors: manufacturing, printing, and construction. In these sectors, MJI establishes intermediary organizations that help to improve employment and training in the sector. Because many of the firms in the sector will have similar training and employment needs, MJI can provide an incentive for employers to participate. The intermediary organizations identify job openings and workforce development needs, and they help with systems to train and retain workers for these sectors. MJI also works with community organizations to recruit low-income individuals for good jobs in the region and provides support for them. Since 1997, MJI has successfully placed 368 individuals in jobs that pay an average of $11.12 per hour with access to health benefits. MJI plans on focusing on establishing clear pathways to high-wage employment for central city residents and coordinating the demand for skilled workers throughout the region.

SOURCE: Center on Wisconsin Strategy (1999).

---

tends to ignore the importance of social networks in providing information on job openings and social support for training. Further, the theory assumes that employers have no responsibility toward their workers for increasing their skills or education. Some employers, however, may see it as being in their interest to provide job training as a way to increase the productivity of their workforce.

Many low-income and minority workers face obstacles in developing their human capital or finding jobs that adequately reward their skills and abilities. In many communities, access to jobs is one of the most important obstacles that minority and poor workers face. Spatial mismatch theory suggests that inner-city minorities experience high unemployment rates because the jobs available in their labor market demand high skills and advanced education, attributes that the inner-city residents lack. The entry-level jobs appropriate for inner-city residents are much more likely to be located in the suburbs. This situation may mean that minorities are paid lower wages or make longer commutes. The poor suffer not only because of physical isolation from the jobs (a lack of transportation to work) but also because of social isolation (a lack of contacts to obtain information about these jobs). Kain (1968) argued that the root cause of spatial mismatch is residential segregation due to racial discrimination in the housing market. The negative effects of housing segregation are magnified by the decentralization of jobs in most cities.

The occupational and industrial structures in the local area shape the demand for labor as well. It is important to distinguish between occupations and industries to understand these forces. An industrial classification identifies what a worker helps to produce, and an occupational classification identifies the kind of work he or she does. An occupation is the group of job-related activities that make up a single economic role directed toward making a living (Hodson & Sullivan, 1990). The Census Bureau has defined more than 500 occupational categories for analyzing these roles. An industry is the branch of economic activity devoted to the production of a good or a service. The Census Bureau uses more than 200 industrial categories.

A local labor market is defined as the social relations between sellers (workers) and buyers (employers) of labor. Within a community, several labor markets may be operating between buyers and sellers, some involving local markets and others constituting regional or national markets. So, for example, professionals, such as computer programmers or attorneys, may be competing in a national labor market, whereas machinists or receptionists may be competing in a local or regional labor market. A local labor market area is difficult to define, especially in rural areas where workers may commute long distances and employers may recruit from surrounding communities.

The labor force participation rate is calculated as the percentage of the population (most government agencies consider only people 16 years or older) in the labor force. Persons not in the labor force consist mainly of students, homemakers, retired workers, inmates of institutions, and others unable or unwilling to seek employment in the reference week (Myers, 1992). The unemployment rate is the percentage of the labor force who are searching for work but are currently unemployed.

Labor markets are frequently portrayed as consisting of individual workers searching for work and employers searching for workers, with no mechanism linking the two together. In many cases, however, workers and employers make use of employment networks or intermediaries. Employment networks are "lines of communication that link many potential occupants of jobs in multiple firms with employers who make decisions to fill those jobs" (Tilly & Tilly, 1998, p. 25).

Theories about how labor markets operate tend to fall into one of three broad categories—supply-oriented, demand-oriented, or institutionally oriented theories—based on which factors are stressed in explaining the functioning of labor markets. Supply-side theories emphasize the numbers of workers with specific skills at various wage levels as the primary determinants of the functioning of labor markets. Supply-side theorists argue that productivity is a function of the skills, knowledge, and experience acquired by workers. Unemployment, underemployment, and poverty are generally explained as a lack of investment by individuals in the types of skills that are demanded in the labor market.

A standard set of issues need to be addressed when analyzing the supply of labor in a community, including sociodemographic characteristics of the population (e.g., race, age, gender, income, and educational background), work experience, training experience and projected needs, job search strategies, commuting behavior, and wages and benefits received. In addition to this basic information, it is useful to assess the availability of other sources of labor. Are there retired workers interested in re-entering the labor market? Are there part-time workers interested in full-time work? Are there workers who are commuting out of the area who might be interested in working locally? Are there workers interested in upgrading their skills to obtain jobs that are available locally? Unfortunately, most communities rarely collect this basic level of information on their workforce.

Demand-side theories emphasize how changes in the structure of occupations, industries, skills, and the location of work shape local opportunities. According to this theory, development depends largely on the creation of new jobs demanding higher skill levels. Demand-side theorists assume that workers have perfect information about the available job opportunities and will seek to obtain the necessary training and education for these jobs.

Most of the information needed to assess the demand for labor can be obtained from surveys of employers. Several methods (such as phone or mail surveys) can be used to collect this information, but face-to-face interviews are preferable if the resources are available. Among the basic questions that need to be asked are the anticipated number of workers to be hired in the next few years; the training, education, and experience required for these positions; the wages and benefits offered to entry-level workers in these positions; and the methods used to search for workers to fill these positions. In addition, it is useful to collect some information on the basic characteristics of the firms, such as number of employees, industry, and organizational structure.

Although it is useful to collect information on the current demand for workers, it also is helpful to obtain data on anticipated demand in order to plan for future training needs. And it may be useful to collect data on training activities among employers to assess what type of training they are providing and how they provide it to workers. This information should provide an understanding of opportunities for mobility within the area and how training institutions can best supplement training efforts that take place in the workplace.

Institutional theories of the labor market recognize the importance of supply and demand factors but emphasize the importance of the organization of work as a mediating factor. These theories emphasize the importance of firm size, industrial sector, and other organizational factors in influencing returns on education, skills, and work experience. For example, workers who are employed in large firms and in industries that are highly unionized may obtain higher returns on their human capital than workers in small firms or industries with low levels of unionization.

In addition, institutionalists may focus on the organizational support for workers and employers in the region. One strategy for obtaining this information is to collect data from training institutions to evaluate the number of people trained in various occupations and the level of training provided to these individuals in order to assess how well the supply matches the current demand among employers. At a minimum, it is necessary for community leaders to have information on the number of graduates from various training programs and the types of programs that are available.

It also may be useful to examine how other institutions in the community are affecting the workforce. How well do the availability and cost of housing match the current and anticipated demand for workers in the area? For example, are employers adding a large number of low-wage positions while few houses are available that would be affordable for these workers? How many positions are there for children in child care centers in the community, and how well does the availability match the local need?

These theories represent different approaches to building local labor markets. Supply-side theory suggests that the way to build the workforce is through development of worker skills and productivity. The availability of a skilled workforce will attract employers to the community, or workers will be more attractive to employers elsewhere and will move to where the job opportunities are. Demand-side theory suggests that it is better to attract, retain, and develop employers that need a skilled workforce. Communities may provide funding for targeted industry, help existing employers modernize, and provide capital for new businesses that will hire a skilled workforce. Of course, the supply of and demand for labor are complementary. It is difficult for trained workers to find work if the employers are not demanding those skills. Conversely, a community may be able to provide incentives for a new business to locate there, but they will need workers who have the required skills and training.

Institutional theory focuses more on how the organizational structure of work may influence the supply of and demand for labor in the community. Here, institutionalists make a distinction between internal and external labor markets. In an internal labor market, an employer hires entry-level workers and trains and recruits workers within the firm. Upward mobility for most workers occurs within the firm. A firm relying on an external labor market tends to hire workers who already have the skills and training needed for these positions. Workers wishing to improve their job skills and move to higher paying jobs may have to obtain the training on their own and take a job with another employer. The trend over the past 30 or so years has been for employers to rely increasingly on external rather than internal labor markets. As we will see below, communities may respond to this problem by identifying the common training needs across groups of employers, so as to ensure an adequate supply of skilled workers for employers, or by re-creating internal labor markets across a set of employers in the community (career ladders).

Community-Based Organizations and Workforce Development

What role can CBOs play in workforce development? Many of the problems that communities face in building their workforce are difficult to address through the actions of individual businesses or workers. They may require efforts by groups of employers and workers, along with public organizations. For example, many employers may be reluctant to invest in the training of their workforce because they fear they will lose their investment if the worker takes a job elsewhere. This dilemma is essentially a collective action problem. It is in the interest of all businesses to have a skilled workforce, but individual firms may be unwilling to take the risk of this investment.

One approach to solving this problem is to build career ladders that link employers in a labor market to create opportunities for mobility across the labor market rather than within firms (Dresser & Rogers, 1997). In Dane County, Wisconsin, an attempt is being made to establish career ladders linking employers that hire largely unskilled/semiskilled workers with those that rely heavily on skilled workers. The system is based on the idea that unskilled workers will stay with employers involved in the career ladder program because the program provides them with opportunities for upward mobility. Employers in the system benefit as well. Employers that rely heavily on low-skilled workers are likely to lower their turnover rate, which can be very costly to these firms. They also are more likely to invest in job training because their workers will be more likely to stay with their employer to get access to better paying jobs. Similarly, employers relying on more skilled workers will benefit from a steady stream of trained workers. CBOs are essential in coordinating these relationships.

There are several other examples of employers' working collectively to solve problems in their labor market. Many communities lack adequate child care facilities. It is probably too expensive for most employers to provide this benefit to workers, but it may be possible for a group of employers to share the costs of child care for their workers. Similarly, employers can share the cost of providing transportation through pooling resources of vans or buses. CBOs can help identify the need, locate resources, and bring employers together to address the need. Currently, there are two different community-based strategies for coordinating these activities. Some communities use a sectoral strategy that brings together employers within an industry, such as banking or health care. This strategy assumes that there are common training needs or issues within the industry that can best be addressed through some collective action. Other communities rely primarily on a place-based strategy that brings together employers that are in close proximity to one another. This approach may work best when the community is addressing problems such as child care that are much more influenced by proximity to employers.

Welfare reform has placed much of the responsibility for assisting the poor on local communities. Many communities are engaged in efforts to prepare former welfare recipients for the workforce, train them, and match them with available jobs. CBOs have strong linkages with local firms, which means they may have a better understanding of the needs of local workers than do state and federal agencies. They are able to provide training programs that better reflect the needs of local employers. In addition, they are able to maintain contact and monitor the progress of individuals. CBOs also may be a better source of job information for workers than more formal mechanisms, such as a state job service. Research suggests, however, that minorities, especially Hispanics, suffer from relying on informal networks to search for jobs (Green, Tigges, & Diaz, 1999). Relying on family or friends to search for jobs means that you do not receive much different information from what you already have. The best job information system would combine the positive aspects of a formal mechanism for accessing job information with the local knowledge and access of informal networks. CBOs can accomplish this by improving the access to job information for employers and workers, while still serving as a formal source of job information in the local labor market.

Most communities are engaged in a variety of activities related to workforce development. For example, many communities have initiated "school-to-work" programs in the past few years. Public-private partnerships are attempting to improve training opportunities. The vision of the local workforce may require the community to establish new programs or provide greater coordination for what is already happening in the community. Or it may lead to identifying the need for new programs. An inventory of current activities may provide useful information on what programs are already in place and how the action plan could build on these activities.

Residents in most communities have a wide range of untapped skills and experiences that could contribute to community development. CBOs are critical institutional mechanisms for identifying these assets, matching them to local needs, and overcoming the obstacles to building human capital. For example, a community that has recently lost a major manufacturing firm in the machine tool industry may have many workers who have a set of skills that would be appropriate and useful for another industry, such as plastics molding. Local knowledge of these assets and experiences is crucial to linking up human capital with employment possibilities.

Context for Workforce Development

The United States relies very heavily on a market approach to matching workers to jobs. Workers obtain education and training based on their interests and their expected outcomes of these investments. Employers move to a region with only a limited amount of information on the labor supply or the skills of the workforce. Workers enter the labor market with imperfect information on available jobs in the region, and often with little idea of the job requirements. In reality, many workers rely heavily on social contacts to find jobs and to obtain information about the nature of those jobs. These social ties also are important for employers, who thereby obtain some information about the worker as well.

The primary purpose of most federal training programs is to assist disadvantaged workers, such as unemployed and dislocated workers. One of the first general training programs was the Comprehensive Employment and Training Act of 1973 (CETA). This program was later replaced by the Job Training Partnership Act of 1982 (JTPA). One of the advantages of JTPA programs was that they were relatively decentralized, giving Private Industry Councils (PICs) greater flexibility in developing programs to meet local needs. PICs were organizations that represented local businesses, unions, and institutions involved in training. These organizations were responsible for designing the public programs that provided resources for training. The PICs had much more business participation than many of the previous training programs. The Workforce Investment Act has established Workforce Investment Boards that now replace PICs.

Recently, there has been interest in programs that provide a much more coordinated approach to linking training with job opportunities at a very early stage. The School-to-Work Opportunities Act of 1994 and the Carl D. Perkins Vocational and Applied Technology Education Act of 1990 provide the basis for school-to-work programs as key labor force strategies. School-to-work programs are designed to increase educational and career opportunities for young people by establishing learning partnerships between employers and schools (Fitzgerald, 1997).

Two recent policy changes at the national level will enhance the role of community-based development organizations in workforce development. First, in 1996, Congress passed the Personal Responsibility and Work Opportunity Reconciliation Act. This legislation ended the program known as Aid to Families with Dependent Children (AFDC) and replaced it with a program called Temporary Assistance to Needy Families (TANF). Under TANF, welfare assistance is no longer an entitlement program. Welfare benefits are time limited and are closely tied to work requirements that are intended to move welfare recipients off welfare and into the labor force.

Second, the Workforce Investment Act of 1998 is one of the most comprehensive workforce education and training programs ever passed by the U.S. Congress. Both of these acts will provide new opportunities for community-based development organizations in addressing the needs of workers.

This brief review of programs suggests a growing recognition that training programs need to be linked closely with employers and workers. The Workforce Investment Act of 1998 places more emphasis on this feature than any previous training program. This emphasis on accountability and local ties places CBOs at the forefront of job training.

Training programs in the United States have been criticized for being isolated from mainstream workers and employers (Osterman, 1988). Most training programs in the United States have been established at the federal level and have fairly standard policies for program implementation. Recently there has been growing criticism of the multitude of federal training programs, which do not appear to be coordinated or focused on specific community needs (Grubb & McDonnell, 1996). High schools still provide some job-specific education, but increasingly vocational schools, community colleges, and postsecondary institutes are responsible for providing vocational education. Although there is a potential for duplication in effort among all these programs, CBOs play a special role in coordinating them (Grubb & McDonnell, 1996). CBOs can provide an informal channel of information between employers, training institutions, and workers that will improve the matching process in the local labor market. Below, we outline different models for organizing these training efforts around CBOs.

Key Actors and Institutions

CBOs are increasingly involved in workforce development networks. Bennett Harrison and Marcus Weiss (1998) identified three prevalent models for these networks: (a) hub-spoke employment training networks, with a focal CBO as the hub; (b) peer-to-peer employment training, with webs of CBOs; and (c) intermediary employment training networks, with intermediaries (e.g., community colleges, public-private authorities, or development finance institutions) at the hub. These models are basically ideal types (there is a lot of variation in how these networks are structured in the real world). Figures 5.1, 5.2, and 5.3 outline these models.

In the hub-spoke employment training network, the CBO is at the center of the network and provides information and ties to providers and resources. In the peer-to-peer model, a group of CBOs serve this function. One of the chief obstacles in this model is providing collaboration and coordination across the various organizations. And in the intermediary employment training model, the CBO is linked with local governments and employers through an intermediary, such as a regional development organization.

Examples of hub-spoke networks include the San Jose-based Center for Employment Training (CET) and Project QUEST in San Antonio. Both of these programs have been replicated around the country. Examples of the peer-to-peer networks are the Chicago Jobs Council, the Pittsburgh Partnership for Neighborhood Development, and the Business Outreach Centers of New York City. Finally, an example of the regional intermediary model is Lawson State, a black community college in Birmingham, Alabama, that is providing technical assistance to small and medium-sized businesses in the region.

FIGURE 5.1
Hub-Spoke Employment Training Networks, With Focal CBO as the Hub

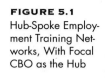

due 10/16

Thao Kabov

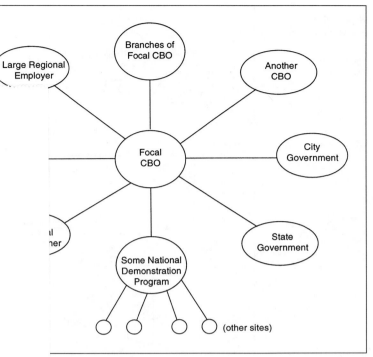

and M. Weiss, *Workforce Development Networks: Community-Based Organiza-
s,* copyright © 1998 by Sage Publications. Reprinted by permission of Sage

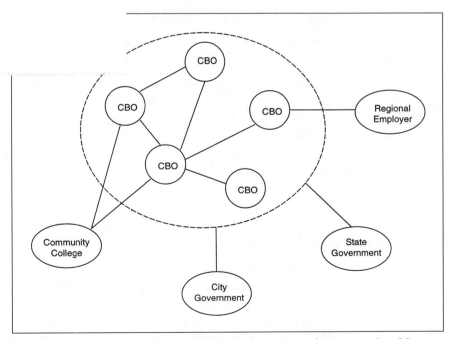

SOURCE: From B. Harrison and M. Weiss, *Workforce Development Networks: Community-Based Organizations and Regional Alliances,* copyright © 1998 by Sage Publications. Reprinted by permission of Sage Publications, Inc.

FIGURE 5.3
Intermediary Employ-
ment Training Net-
works, With Interme-
diaries as the Hub

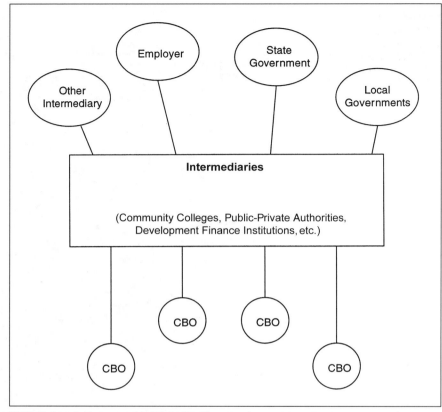

SOURCE: From B. Harrison and M. Weiss, *Workforce Development Networks: Community-Based Organizations and Regional Alliances,* copyright © 1998 by Sage Publications. Reprinted by permission of Sage Publications, Inc.

Probably the most common form of workforce development network is the hub-
spoke network. The San Jose CET model has been widely adopted across the United
States. It requires less coordination than the other types and can more easily link
employers with training. Although these workforce development networks have grown
in popularity, the evidence is unclear at this point whether they can be successful over
time.

Data on Local Labor Markets

A community may decide that it may want to collect information on the local labor
force in order to develop a plan or a vision of its workforce. There exists a wealth of data
on employers and workers. Most of the data is now easily accessible over the Web or
through universities or state agencies (see the list of Web sites at the end of this chapter
for several widely used sources). In addition, the community may decide that it needs to
collect some of its own information on the labor market. Collecting your own data may
be expensive and time-consuming, but it may be the only way to really understand what
is happening in your local labor market area. Also, the data will be more current.

There are four broad issues on which a community might consider gathering and analyzing data:

1. What is the local labor market?

2. What is the current demand for labor in the region, and how is it likely to change in the future?

3. What is the current supply of labor in the region, and how is it likely to change in the future?

4. How are local institutions (e.g., training and educational institutions, temporary agencies, and local job centers) affecting the match between the supply of and demand for labor in the region?

Most communities do not constitute a local labor market area. A local labor market area is difficult to define, especially in rural areas, where workers may commute long distances and employers may recruit from surrounding areas. The size of labor markets may vary by region. Probably the most useful source to help define the local labor market is the Place of Work Data for Municipalities and Counties. These data permit you to evaluate where and how many workers commute to work. By looking at commuting data, you are able to see where local employers draw workers from and where local residents work. Another way to obtain some of this information is to ask local employers to identify the zip code of local workers. On the basis of this information, you may decide to include an adjacent county or region as part of your local labor market area.

In many cases, it is probably sufficient to consider the county as the local labor market area. There are probably a few types of rural areas where this approach would not work. One would be a rural community that is proximate to a metropolitan area. In these counties, a large proportion of workers typically commute into the urban areas, and it would make sense to include this broader region as part of the local labor market. Another exception would be a rural area that is extremely sparse in its settlement pattern and has few local employment opportunities.

It is important for communities to identify what the local labor market is if they are to understand the factors influencing the supply of and demand for labor in the area. By focusing on commuting rates, you also can see how mobile your workforce is in your area. You should recognize that local labor markets do not really exist for some occupations, particularly professional positions. Physicians, for example, are in national or regional labor markets. Most other workers, however, are influenced by the conditions affecting the local labor market area.

Several data sources exist for analyzing the composition of the industrial base, wages, and occupational structure of local labor market areas. Some of the most widely used are the County Business Patterns (CBP), the Bureau of Economic Analysis (BEA), and the Department of Labor. CBP is published by the Department of Commerce and includes employment in business categories (Standard Industrial Codes broken out into two, three, and four digits). The data include employment covered by FICA but not government employment or self-employment. The BEA provides data on county population, personal income, and per capita income.

Developing Goals and Strategies

On the basis of the data that are analyzed through this process, communities can identify the most appropriate strategy for building their local labor force. In the following section, we describe five basic goals and specific strategies that communities can adopt.

Prepare the Future Workforce

To have a productive workforce and employers that are competitive in the global marketplace, it is essential that workers have the basic skills for the workplace today. This goal may require businesses to become much more involved with schools and to forge productive partnerships with school systems. Some younger workers may need basic skills, such as how to interview for jobs and how to plan their careers. Among the specific tactics to be considered are

- *Increasing exposure to issues concerning careers and working in or before high school.* Many communities are accomplishing this goal by asking local employers to visit with students and discuss the types of work available and the training and education required for these jobs.

- *Developing an understanding of all career and postsecondary educational options.* There is increasing concern that students are not being exposed to the variety of postsecondary educational opportunities that are available to them. Several states are beginning to develop programs that better communicate the opportunities to students at an early stage of their educational career.

- *Strengthening career and technical education.* One of the issues here is the need to have a strong educational base to build on for an entire career, with special emphasis on math and reading skills.

Sustaining the Workforce

To attract and retain qualified workers, communities need to address the obstacles that many workers face in obtaining additional training or searching for jobs. Most of the obstacles are related to child care, housing, or transportation, although others may also be important.

Communities can address these obstacles by

- *Developing partnerships for child care availability.* Most employers cannot afford to provide on-site child care for their employees, but there may be opportunities for a group of employers to cooperate and provide more child care opportunities in the community.

- *Creating "family-friendly" work environments.* CBOs can help employers identify ways of making their environment more "family-friendly," such as providing flexible hours or using sick days for children who are sick.

- *Increasing efforts and assistance to employers to retain employees.* Workforce development efforts are increasingly emphasizing programs designed to help employers reduce their turnover. One example of a program that could be offered by communities is an educational program on how to conduct exit interviews, which will help employers better understand why workers leave their firm.

- *Developing partnerships for increased training efforts in the workplace.* As we discussed earlier in this chapter, sectoral and place-based strategies for collaborative efforts to provide training help overcome some of the disincentives for individual employers to provide training.

- *Assessing and providing resources for transportation availability.* Some communities have been able to develop van pools or a busing system to attract workers from other areas or to help local workers commute to jobs outside the local community.

- *Providing affordable housing closer to businesses.* An employer-assisted housing program (discussed in Chapter 7) is one way to accomplish this.

- *Offering postemployment assistance as a way of reducing turnover.* This strategy could involve courses on budgeting/money management assistance, balancing home and work, and so forth.

Upgrading the Workforce

A key to improving the productivity of employers and increasing the earnings of workers is improving the education and training in the community. Several strategies may be necessary to upgrade the workforce. In many cases, it may be in the interest of all employers in the community to upgrade the workforce but not in the interest of any single employer to invest in the training because they may lose their investment. Community strategies need to address this basic problem. Some strategies are

- *Improving success rate for completing education and training.* This goal may be accomplished by linking students up with employers before they have completed their training. These linkages may improve students' motivation for completing the work.

- *Funding and resource shifts to upgrade the workforce.* State governments may be reluctant to provide resources for individual employers, but they may respond to groups of employers that have common training needs and have a major effect on a region's economy.

Expanding the Workforce

In many communities, a major obstacle is the lack of workers, especially workers with the appropriate skills that are demanded by local employers. Communities may consider a variety of tactics to expand the workforce to meet these needs:

- *Developing partnerships that address barriers to expanding the labor pool.* For example, groups of employers (and local governments) may work together to provide a transportation system that helps workers commute from areas in the region that may not be facing such a high demand for workers.

- *Expanding efforts to attract qualified workers needed to meet employer demands.* CBOs can help employers with the screening and matching process to ensure that workers are qualified to meet the demands of the jobs that are available.

- *Increasing efforts to connect education with the world of work.* Apprenticeship and school-to-work programs provide excellent ways of increasing this connection.

Promoting Entrepreneurship

Programs promoting entrepreneurship, especially among women and minorities, have proliferated over the last few decades. Citizens with the vision and ability to start and run a business represent human capital resources that are very important to community welfare. The small business option may be increasingly pursued by women for noneconomic reasons, such as flexibility or accessibility, especially in areas where day care and employment options are more limited (Tigges & Green, 1994). Minorities frequently turn to the small business option because of the obstacles they face in the local labor market. Communities can encourage and support entrepreneurship with a variety of mechanisms, including

- *Establishing loan funds for start-up and working capital.* In Chapter 8, we discuss several different types of loan programs that could be beneficial for small businesses at the start-up stage. In particular, many communities have initiated revolving loan funds as a strategy for this type of development.

- *Providing training programs that build the managerial skills of entrepreneurs.* In particular, communities are becoming involved in helping small businesses with managing their linkages with suppliers and consumers.

- *Providing technical assistance such as information and educational programs for entrepreneurs.* Small business incubators provide an excellent way of providing some of this assistance.

Summary and Conclusions

Most communities face many problems in matching the demand with the supply of labor in their region. In some communities, there may be unemployed or underemployed workers who cannot find any entry-level jobs. In other communities, employers may not find enough workers with the skills and training they need. We have suggested that there are serious limitations to market solutions and government training programs that have addressed these problems. CBOs can play an integral role in solving the training and matching problems in low-income neighborhoods, and we believe that they are critical to implementing an asset-based approach to community development. CBOs have more local knowledge of the skills and experiences of the population and the needs of local employers. They also have a better understanding of the problems that constrain the functioning of the local labor market, such as the lack of child care or transportation.

Federal and state policies are increasingly recognizing the important role of CBOs in workforce development. And increasingly, policies such as TANF emphasize the comprehensive nature of workforce development. It is no longer sufficient just to train workers and expect that they will have access to jobs. Instead, these programs need to be comprehensive and address the housing, transportation, and child care needs of workers. The Workforce Investment Act offers new opportunities for CBOs to become key actors in the workforce development effort.

Finally, federal policy has moved toward involving local actors and institutions much more in the development of training programs. Policy makers recognize that local residents need to be involved in designing these programs and that one standard model will not work in a wide variety of settings.

KEY CONCEPTS

Career ladders	Industry	Occupation
Demand-side theories	Institutional theories	Spatial mismatch theory
Employment network	Internal labor markets	Supply-side theories
External labor markets	Labor force participation	Workforce development
Human capital	rate	
Human capital theory	Local labor market	

QUESTIONS

1. What is the difference between job training and workforce development?

2. Compare and contrast traditional models of workforce development with community-based approaches.

3. Compare and contrast three prevalent models of workforce development networks: hub-spoke employment training networks; peer-to-peer employment training; and intermediary employment training.

4. What are the four main types of information that communities need to assess their labor market situation?

5. What are the broad goals and strategies that are frequently used by community organizations to build their local labor force?

EXERCISE

1. Conduct a local labor market analysis.
   - Define the area of your local labor market. How far do workers commute, and how far do employers recruit in the region?

- Identify the major employers in your community. Conduct an interview with them to assess the following for each job in the firm: wages and benefits; required skills, education, and work experience; current and anticipated openings; and turnover rates.

- Conduct surveys of workers to obtain information on their training, education, and work experience; problems with child care, transportation, and housing; job search strategies; wages and benefits; and commuting behavior.

- Identify local institutions involved in training, and collect information on the types of programs available, the number of graduates in each program, and plans for new programs in the area.

- Obtain information on the number of available positions and costs among day care providers in the community, and provide some assessment of the demand for these positions.

REFERENCES

Beaulieu, L. J., & Mulkey, D. (Eds.). (1995). *Investing in people: The human capital needs of rural America.* Boulder, CO: Westview.

Center on Wisconsin Strategy. (1999). *Milwaukee Jobs Initiative.* Madison, WI: Author. <www.cows.org/projects/mji.html>

Dresser, L., & Rogers, J. (1997). *Rebuilding job access and career advancement systems in the new economy.* Madison: University of Wisconsin–Madison, Center on Wisconsin Strategy.

Fitzgerald, J. (1997). Linking school-to-work programs to community economic development in urban schools. *Urban Education, 32,* 489-511.

Green, G. P., Tigges, L. M., & Diaz, D. (1999). Racial and ethnic differences in job search strategies in Atlanta, Boston and Los Angeles. *Social Science Quarterly, 80,* 263-278.

Grubb, W. N., & McDonnell, L. M. (1996). Combating program fragmentation: Local systems of vocational education and job training. *Journal of Policy Analysis and Management, 15,* 252-270.

Harrison, B., & Weiss, M. (1998). *Workforce development networks: Community-based organizations and regional alliances.* Thousand Oaks, CA: Sage.

Hodson, R., & Sullivan, T. A. (1990). *The social organization of work.* Belmont, CA: Wadsworth.

Judy, R. W., & D'Amico, C. (1997). *Workforce 2020: Work and workers in the 21st century.* Indianapolis, IN: Hudson Institute.

Kain, J. (1968). Housing segregation, Negro employment, and metropolitan decentralization. *Quarterly Journal of Economics, 82*(2), 175-197.

Melendez, E. (1996). *Working on jobs: The Center for Employment Training.* Boston: Mauricio Gaston Institute.

Myers, D. (1992). *Analysis with local census data: Portraits of change.* Boston: Academic Press.

Osterman, P. (1988). *Employment futures: Reorganization, dislocation, and public policy.* New York: Oxford University Press.

Tigges, L. M., & Green, G. P. (1994). Small business success among men- and women-owned firms in rural areas. *Rural Sociology, 59,* 289-310.

Tilly, C., & Tilly, C. (1998). *Work under capitalism.* Boulder, CO: Westview.

ADDITIONAL SUGGESTED READINGS

Readings ■

Berry, D. E. (1998). The jobs and workforce initiative: Northeast Ohio employers' plan for workforce development. *Economic Development Quarterly, 12*(1), 41-53.

Fitzgerald, J. (1998). Is networking always the answer? Networking among community colleges to increase their capacity in business outreach. *Economic Development Quarterly, 12*(1), 30-40.

Gibbs, R. M., Swaim, P. L., & Teixeira, R. (Eds.). (1998). *Rural education and training in the new economy: The myth of the rural skills gap.* Ames: Iowa State University Press.

Holzer, H. J. (1996). *What employers want: Job prospects for less-educated workers.* New York: Russell Sage.

Melendez, E., & Harrison, B. (1998). Matching the disadvantaged to job opportunities: Structural explanations for the past successes of the Center for Employment Training. *Economic Development Quarterly, 12*(1), 3-11.

Molina, F. (1998). *Making connections: A study of employment linkage programs.* Washington, DC: Center for Community Change.

Streeck, W. (1989). Skills and the limits of neo-liberalism: The enterprise of the future as a place of learning. *Work, Employment and Society, 3*(1), 89-104.

Web Sites ■

U.S. Bureau of Labor Statistics (BLS). <www.bls.gov>. The BLS site is a major source for national labor market information, with data sets of state and metropolitan area data. This is a large and complex Web site containing hundreds of data sets, including local area unemployment statistics, industry employment estimates, and projections.

National Longitudinal Surveys. <www.bls.gov/nlshome.htm>. The Bureau of Labor Statistics sponsors the collection and production of data from the National Longitudinal Surveys (NLSs). Each survey gathers information at multiple points in time on the labor market experiences of five groups of American men and women. Each of the NLS groups consists of 5,000 or more members.

Employment Cost Trends. <www.bls.gov/ecthome.htm>. The employment cost trends program produces two ongoing surveys: the Employment Cost Index (ECI) and Employers' Costs for Employee Compensation (cost levels). The ECI measures the change over time in the cost of labor, including the cost of wages and salaries and employee benefits. Cost levels data provide average costs per hour worked for wages and salaries and specific benefits.

Employee Benefits Survey. <www.bls.gov/ebshome.htm>. This survey provides comprehensive data on the incidence and detailed provisions of selected employee benefit plans in small private establishments, medium and large private establishments, and state and local governments.

Occupational Compensation Survey. <www.bls.gov/ocshome.htm>. These annual or biennial surveys provide information on average weekly or hourly earnings for selected occupations in the nation and certain metropolitan areas, as well as related benefits data for white- and blue-collar workers.

Multifactor Productivity. <www.bls.gov/mprover.htm>. This program develops productivity measures for nonfarm business and manufacturing sectors of the economy as well as for nonfinancial institutions.

Employment Projections. <www.bls.gov/emphome.htm>. The Office of Employment Projections develops and publishes estimates on the economy and labor market 10 to 15 years into the future. Included are projections of the labor force, potential gross domestic product, industrial output, and employment by industry and occupation.

U.S. Census Bureau. <www.census.gov>. The Bureau of the Census Web site contains data from all the bureau's data collection efforts: the Decennial Census (1990), the Current Population Survey, the economic censuses, and the monthly economic surveys. It is a large and complex site of data, including population estimates and projections, migration, journey to work, income and poverty, educational attainment, and much more.

National Center for Education Statistics (NCES). <www.ed.gov/pubs/stats.html>. This Web site offers access to data sets, reports, guides, and research studies. Several NCES reports are available in their entirety: "The Condition of Education," "The Digest of Education Statistics," "Projections of Education Statistics," and "Youth Indicators."

U.S. Bureau of Economic Analysis (BEA). <www.bea.doc.gov>. BEA is a major producer and compiler of economic, business cycle, and labor market data. BEA has built a large on-line source for these data compiled from more than 50 federal agencies, called STAT-USA. This is a fee-based site.

University of Michigan. <www.lib.umich.edu/libhome/Documents.center/stats.html>. The University of Michigan Library provides a "catalog" of Web sites of statistical information from numerous agencies. The listing is organized by major topic: demographic, economic, income, labor market, and so on. It is a very useful site for locating sources.

America's Labor Market Information System (ALMIS). <www.doleta.gov/almis/index.htm>. The U.S. Department of Labor, Employment and Training Administration sponsors ALMIS. This Web site offers information about ALMIS projects; calendars of upcoming events; state-maintained bulletin boards, products and services, labor market information contacts, and news releases of interest to the labor market information community. In addition to Web links to various states' Web sites, there are links to national statistics sources.

CHAPTER 6

Social Capital
Building Trust, Norms, and Networks

C ommunity development practitioners have long recognized the importance of social relationships in mobilizing community residents and in affecting the success of projects. People frequently become involved in community-based organizations (CBOs) because their friends or neighbors are involved or because they want to meet new people. Who becomes involved often will shape the direction and the outcomes of the development effort. Similarly, community residents often depend on neighbors and families for assistance. CBOs can help build on these relationships and social ties in their efforts to promote development.

Social scientists consider these social relationships and ties as a form of capital (referred to as social capital) that facilitates collective action in communities. Social capital can be considered an asset that contributes to the development of other forms of community capital—human, financial, physical, and environmental. Social capital also may directly affect individual well-being through its effects on health and happiness, safe and productive neighborhoods, education, and children's welfare (Putnam, 2000). In this chapter, we examine the role of social relationships and networks in the community development process. We are especially interested in how communities can build the types of social relationships and networks that will serve as assets in the community development process in the future.

In Chapter 1, we distinguished between the concepts of "community of place" and "community of interest." *Community of place* refers to social relationships based on residence in a particular locality, whereas *community of interest* refers to social relationships based on a common set of interests. Community of interest is promoted through professional associations and national organizations associated with specific interests (e.g., environmental protection, abortion rights). Although *social capital* can refer to both types of communities, we focus again in this chapter on the nature of social capital in communities of place. Like other community assets, the match between the demand for and supply of social resources may be weak. In particular, individuals may be forming more social ties and networks around their community of interest than around place. Clearly, there are plenty of examples of neighborhoods and communities that rally around local issues, such as the siting of a hazardous waste site or the location

---

| BOX 6.1 | **Social Capital Facts** |

- The number of Americans attending public meetings dropped from 22% in 1973 to 13% in 1993.

- Union membership declined from 33% in 1953 to 16% in 1992.

- Membership in the League of Women Voters declined 42% from 1969 to 1997.

- Membership in the PTA declined from 12 million in 1964 to 7 million in 1997.

- Membership in the Jaycees declined 44% from 1979 to 1997.

- Membership in the Masons declined 39% from 1957 to 1997.

SOURCE: Putnam (2000).

---

of a "big box" store, such as Wal-Mart or Home Depot. But this mobilization does not institutionalize these localized relationships in most communities. Our discussion of social capital focuses on long-term social relationships that build expectations and reciprocity.

Social Capital Definition and Issues

Social relationships and networks serve as a form of capital because these social resources require investments in time and energy, with the anticipation that individuals can tap into these resources when necessary. The more individuals invest in these resources, the more they are likely to receive benefits in the future. These resources are frequently referred to as social capital. Social relationships are considered capital because they can be productive and improve the well-being of residents.

Social capital has been defined in a variety of ways (see Coleman, 1988; Putnam, 1993b; Temkin & Rohe, 1998). There is a common emphasis, however, on the aspects of social structure (trust, norms, and social networks) that facilitate collective action. The most frequent indicators of social capital are voter turnout, newspaper readership, participation in voluntary organizations, and attendance at meetings in local organizations. Others have looked, however, at the specific structures of social networks and ties of individuals and communities as indicators of the level of social capital (Green, Tigges, & Diaz, 1999).

As indicated in Box 6.1, there is growing evidence that Americans are becoming less involved in local associations and organizations. The assumption has been made that this trend has resulted in the loss of social capital in most neighborhoods and communities. Putnam (2000) argued that there are several plausible reasons for the decline in social capital. Among the more frequent reasons given are

- *Increased time pressures:* People don't have as much time for meetings and participation in local activities.

- *Residential mobility:* Because people move more frequently than they used to (today people move, on average, every 7 years), they are probably less involved and attached to their community.

- *Increased labor force participation of women:* Women are disproportionately involved in community organizations. Because women are much more likely to be employed than they have been in the past, they probably have less time for participation in these organizations and activities.

- *The growth of the welfare state:* In the past, communities relied heavily on voluntary organizations to provide social support. Many of these activities have been replaced by the welfare state over the past 50 years, thereby usurping a primary mechanism for civic involvement.

- *Erosion of civic culture in the 1960s:* Many social analysts have argued that the culture of the 1960s emphasized a more individualistic rather than a social orientation.

- *The growth of suburbs:* Similarly, recent critics of suburbs argue that suburban development has fostered alienation and individualistic behavior, thereby undermining civic culture.

- *Generational effects:* There is substantial evidence that there has been a decline in organizational participation over the last few generations that cannot be explained by individual aging processes.

- *Television:* Television is often blamed for the lack of community involvement because it takes time away from community activities.

After careful consideration of the possible explanations, Putnam (2000) eliminated all except television and generational effects. First, television requires large amounts of time. The average household watches television for several hours per day. This time may have been devoted to civic organizations and associations in the past. Second, television may affect the outlook of viewers, increasing their pessimism about human nature and inducing passivity. Individuals who are more pessimistic about their ability to change things will probably be less involved in local organizations and associations. Finally, there is some evidence that television may have especially negative effects on children. Television viewing may increase aggressiveness and reduce school achievement, which may be related to participation in local organizations. If Putnam is correct, the way to increase social capital is to lure people away from TV and back into social arenas.

Although there has been an erosion in most membership organizations in the United States over the past 30 to 40 years, there also has been a growth in the number of advocacy groups (such as the Sierra Club, National Organization for Women, and the American Association of Retired Persons). These organizations limit the role of member participation; the primary element of membership is the financial support necessary for the organization to pursue its goals. There also has been growth in nonprofit organizations and local support groups, which are really not associational organizations. These organizations may address community issues, but they do not directly involve their membership in shaping the activities of the organization. Thus, although there has been a proliferation of advocacy groups and national organizations that are issue oriented, these organizations do not enhance the social capital of communities or enhance the community's capacity to act collectively.

Several questions related to social capital should be considered in the community development field: Are social relationships and networks a form of capital or resources that can serve as assets in developing a community? Can social relationships and networks affect community development efforts? Do these social ties facilitate or impede development? What are some of the effects of strong and/or weak social ties on community development efforts? Can communities build social networks and ties to enhance their chances of development?

Key Concepts and Debates

The concept of social capital has been applied to a variety of issues: families and youth behavior problems; schooling and education; work and organizations; democracy and governance; and general collective action problems. In general, the literature has pointed to the importance of social capital in addressing common problems that are not easily resolved by individual actions. In this sense, social capital is central to building other forms of capital (human, financial, physical, and environmental) because of the limited efficacy of individual actions in solving these collective problems.

One of the problems in defining social capital may be that there are different types of social capital. An important distinction is between bonding capital and bridging capital. Bonding capital refers to bringing people together who already know each other. The goal is to strengthen the relationships that already exist. Mark Granovetter (1974), for example, also made a distinction between strong and weak ties. Strong ties involve large investments of time and energy, whereas weak ties are basically ties of acquaintanceship. Strong ties may be helpful for gaining access to emotional support and help in the case of emergencies, whereas weak ties may be especially helpful in finding jobs or housing. Bridging capital brings together people or groups who did not previously know each other. The goal is to establish new social ties so as to provide new information and access additional social networks and to fill the "structural holes" in the system of networks in the community (Burt, 1992). Woolcock (1998) also referred to linking capital, or the ties between people in communities and their local organizations.

There may be both advantages and disadvantages to promoting bonding capital. Increasing the level of interaction between those who already know each other may improve information flows, raise the level of reciprocity, and generate greater trust among individuals. At the same time, increasing the density of relationships (the frequency of interaction among people who already know each other) may make it less likely that this network will reach out to other individuals outside the network. In this sense, strong social ties may fragment the community and make it more difficult to achieve collective action.

The development of bridging capital addresses these concerns by encouraging the formation of new social ties and relationships. These issues are especially important when we consider community leadership. There are several advantages to having a broad set of leaders rather than the same set of individuals serving as leaders in a variety of organizations. These new leaders may bring new information and ideas, as well as additional contacts and resources that may not be available in the existing network.

What does social capital provide for individuals? Social relationships can provide both emotional and instrumental support. Emotional support includes advice, support, and friendship. Instrumental support includes material aid and services, information, and new social contacts. More specifically, instrumental support includes activities such as taking care of children, getting a ride from someone, or lending money to someone. The types of interpersonal contacts that provide the bulk of emotional and instrumental support are with kin (family), friends, and neighbors. Some institutions, such as churches, however, may play a strong role of providing emotional and instrumental support in some neighborhoods. Many times churches are able to combine this type of support with assistance in housing and job training as well.

Several factors may influence the extent to which individuals rely on informal sources of support. For example, individuals with few economic resources may need to rely more heavily on social ties to compensate for their lack of resources in the marketplace. The poor, therefore, may have to rely on informal arrangements for child care and other services instead of purchasing these services. The poor, however, tend to rely heavily on family and friends, who may have few resources themselves to support them. Thus, the poor are faced with greater need for instrumental support but fewer sources in their network that can help them.

Racial and ethnic differences frequently exist in the size of social networks and the frequency of social interaction (Taylor, 1986). Whites have the largest networks, followed by Hispanics and then African Americans. Most accounts of these racial and ethnic differences emphasize the importance of culture and values in explaining the differences, although some point to differences in family structure and social class as the real determinants (Hofferth, 1984). Networks of African Americans have a lower proportion of kin than do those of whites, whereas sex diversity is highest in the networks of whites, even when kin/nonkin composition is controlled (Marsden, 1987).

Research also suggests that although women generally have smaller social networks, they place greater emphasis on close relationships than do men (House, Umberson, & Landis, 1988). Women generally are more likely than men to seek or accept informal support, even when controlling for need.

Finally, Wilson (1987) argued that the structure of ghetto neighborhoods may explain the different forms of social capital between African Americans and whites. Neighborhoods with high concentrations of poverty isolate their residents from social contacts with mainstream society because inner-city African Americans seldom have ties with friends or relatives in more stable areas of the city or in the suburbs. The high concentration of poverty affects not only the nature of the social relationships but also attitudes toward work and information about job opportunities outside the neighborhood.

This discussion suggests that community development efforts may face serious obstacles in developing social capital in poor and minority communities. The poor may be more dependent on social relationships to meet their needs, but family and friends may have fewer resources to support them. Some groups, such as Hispanics, maintain very strong social ties and seldom have ties to individuals outside their local neighborhood or family. And in many urban neighborhoods, the loss of social institutions has made it more difficult to develop social capital. Ironically, this may suggest the need for residents to broaden social ties to individuals outside the neighborhood or family.

A concept that is related to the strength of the social tie is multiplexity. Lois Verbrugge (1979) defined multiplexity as the overlap of roles, exchanges, or affiliations in social relationships. A close friendship with someone who also is a coworker or neighbor is an example of a multiplex relationship. James Coleman (1988) sees multiplexity in social relationships as enriching social capital because it allows social organization to be appropriated from one situation to another. For example, if people are bound together by emotional ties, they also can exchange information about job openings or job expectations. This multiplexity may enhance the normative and informational functions of social capital. Individuals who are "strongly tied" to job searchers through multiple relationships, however, are likely to have experiences and characteristics similar to those of the job searchers and therefore will probably not gain much new information (Granovetter, 1974).

Recently, there have been two debates regarding the importance of social capital in the community development process. Putnam (1993a), whose early work on the role of social capital in regional development in Italy ignited much of the recent interest in the topic, argued that social capital has systematically declined in recent decades. He contended that social capital is highly correlated with economic development; regions in Italy that have high levels of social capital have more economic development (higher-quality jobs and income) than those with low levels of social capital. In his article "Bowling Alone," Putnam (1995) argued that membership and involvement in organizations has declined dramatically, especially since the 1960s.

Putnam has been criticized for his argument about the relationship between social capital and economic development. The link between strong and vibrant civic organizations, economic growth, and development is tenuous. Although aspects of social capital, such as voting and participation in civic organizations, may help establish democratic institutions, making a link between these activities and economic development at the regional and local level is problematic. There are so many other factors affecting a region's economy that it would be difficult to identify the relative influence of social capital.

Critics have argued that social capital cannot be built or destroyed quickly. They contend that although people may be less tied to their local neighborhood, they have become more involved in professional organizations and other organizations that represent their interests. This view suggests that the concept of community has become more liberated from place and based on relationships to people with very similar interests. A liberated community may contribute to an increased number of bridging ties for individuals.

But is this version of community the same as the ties that bring together people in a neighborhood? Though individuals may still be active in regional and national organizations, and developing social ties with people outside their local neighborhood or community, it is not the same. Interacting with others through the Internet or over the phone may not produce the same set of shared norms, expectations, and reciprocity that develops through face-to-face interaction with neighbors and other community residents. More important for community development, involvement in these "communities of interest" does not provide participants with as much experience in resolving conflicts and differences of opinion among community members. Communities of interest focus on fairly narrow interests that bind them. Communities of place are faced with a broad set of issues and sets of interests that are much more likely to be different. Although communities of interest may establish the social networks that prove to be useful, they do not provide some of the other benefits that are gained through the development of a community of place.

Another issue that has received an increasing amount of attention is the negative aspects of social capital (Portes & Landolt, 1996). In some cases, the strong bonds and social ties that exist among individuals may prove to be an obstacle to development. A couple of examples may help demonstrate this point. Many minority groups that rely heavily on family and friends to find jobs through their networks may be lacking different sources of job information that may be more valuable to them. Lack of ties to the larger, mainstream economy may produce obstacles to their mobility.

Another example of the limited benefit of strong social capital is the role that social networks play in helping small entrepreneurs in many cities (Waldinger, 1995). Ethnic entrepreneurs may benefit by serving an ethnic economy because it helps them establish a client base and market. Yet dependence on the ethnic economy alone may be limiting and may restrict the ability of the entrepreneur to enter new markets outside this niche.

These examples suggest that social capital may be least effective in the cases where there are primarily strong ties and an absence of weak ties. One could imagine cases, however, where neighborhood residents lacked the strong ties necessary to provide emotional and instrumental assistance.

Community-Based Organizations and Social Capital

First, community residents need space to permit social interaction. Social gatherings are a frequently used method for creating that space. This is why community buildings, recreational centers, and other public buildings (e.g., schools) are so critical to the development of communities. Community organizations can promote social gatherings as a way to develop informal and formal networks. Proponents of new urbanism have argued that the physical design of communities has a major influence on social relationships (Katz, 1994; Kunstler, 1993). They have been very critical of the sprawling pattern of metropolitan settlement that has developed over the past 40 years. New urbanist communities are designed with the intention of promoting social interaction in a variety of ways. Mixing of residential and commercial uses tends to decrease traveling time to work, which increases the opportunities for community participation. New urbanist design also tends to promote more social interaction through building of porches and patios in front of houses, where families will most likely interact with their neighbors.

Second, CBOs can use public debate to encourage participation. Visioning sessions (discussed in Chapter 3), for example, offer a venue for residents to identify shared purpose and common concerns. These opportunities to develop a vision of the community are most important in planning for development of the community. Some communities are experimenting with using new technology, especially the Internet, to create more dialogue among community residents.

Third, CBOs can promote social capital by ensuring that they have a diverse leadership rather than relying on the same individuals all the time. This practice can help promote community norms for public life: Everyone is expected to participate, and everyone has access to leadership roles.

Putnam (2000) also suggested that there is a role for CBOs in encouraging the arts and cultural programs as a means for promoting social capital. In particular, he emphasized the need to promote cultural activities, such as group dancing, community theater, and song festivals. These types of community recreation were once popular throughout the United States and played an especially important role in bringing together diverse sets of citizens.

Social Capital and Local Economic Development

How does social capital affect local economic development? To examine this relationship, we need to consider both micro and macro forces. Micro factors are those specific social ties and networks among residents. It is useful to distinguish between intracommunity ties (integration) and extracommunity networks (autonomy). Both types of social capital may improve the prospects for local economic development. Intracommunity ties are beneficial because they allow individuals to draw on the social resources in their community and increase the likelihood that the community will be able to adequately address its collective concerns. Extracommunity networks are an equally important source of social capital (Flora, Green, Gale, Schmidt, & Flora, 1992). These social ties provide access to external resources that may facilitate the development process. For example, many communities may need to access external sources of information or financial capital that is not available locally. Extracommunity networks also provide new ideas that can stimulate development activities locally.

In addition to these intra- and intercommunity networks, there are two macro aspects of social capital that can affect local development. First, the level of social ties that connect citizens and public officials, referred to as synergy, can affect local development. There may be several ways to create synergy, such as through public hearings and listening sessions, public-private development partnerships, and citizen-appointed boards. Social capital theorists argue that in communities that have more interaction between citizens and public officials, there is a greater likelihood of public trust in local government officials and accountability of public officials.

Another macro element of social capital is the organizational integrity of the local government. Organizational integrity is the institutional coherence, competence, and capacity of the local government. It is a form of social capital because it affects how citizens interact with their local government and the amount of trust they have in it. If the local government is arbitrary and has a limited capacity to deal with local issues, citizens are less likely to support government programs.

Thus, social capital is highest when the organizational integrity of the local government is high and there is a high level of synergy between citizens and public officials. This situation is referred to as a development state. Other possible combinations of organizational capacity and synergy are less desirable.

Assessing Social Capital

As we have indicated earlier, a variety of indicators have been used to measure social capital. Among the most common indicators are voter turnout, newspaper readership, participation in voluntary organizations, and attendance at meetings of local organizations. These definitions are largely based on the approach toward social capital taken by Putnam (1993b, 2000). But these indicators of social capital are narrow and in many cases are not very useful for community-based development organizations. More useful indicators of social capital might be those advanced by Temkin and Rohe (1998). They distinguished between two aspects of social capital: sociocultural milieu and institutional infrastructure.

Sociocultural milieu can be defined as having four elements: (a) the feeling that the community is spatially distinct; (b) the level of social interaction among residents; (c) the degree to which residents work and socialize in the community; and (d) the degree to which residents use neighborhood facilities. Most of these data are not available from existing sources and must be obtained through surveys of residents or records from local organizations.

Institutional infrastructure includes (a) the presence and quality of neighborhood organizations, (b) voting by residents, (c) volunteer efforts, and (d) visibility of neighborhood to citywide officials. Again, these data may be obtained through surveys and records of organizations.

Summary and Conclusions

Although there continues to be debate about the definition and importance of social capital in national development, there is much more consensus about the importance of these resources in community development. One of the obstacles to community development has been the greater reliance on social ties and networks outside one's community. The loss of local organizations and institutions in communities has facilitated this change. The establishment of local organizations that encourage local exchanges and interaction is crucial to the development of social capital in communities. At the same time, we have argued that the greater reliance on social ties and networks outside the locality may not undermine but rather actually enhance social capital. Because residents now have access to more information and resources, these bridging ties may be more useful for the development of the community. The challenge is to create a common vision that will harness these resources.

The other obstacle that communities face with regard to social capital is how to overcome the negative effects of social capital. Many communities have a core set of residents who are strongly connected to one another and have a disproportionate influence over local policies and activities. In particular, local developers and realtors may work together to promote their narrow interests against the general welfare of the community. They clearly have developed a strong basis for social capital, but it may undermine attempts to promote community development. These negative effects of social capital need to be addressed by encouraging more widespread involvement in community activities and policies.

KEY CONCEPTS

Autonomy	Integration	Sociocultural milieu
Bonding capital	Linking capital	Strong ties
Bridging capital	Multiplexity	Synergy
Emotional support	New urbanism	Weak ties
Institutional infrastructure	Organizational integrity	
Instrumental support	Social capital	

QUESTIONS

1. What is the definition of social capital? What are some key indicators of social capital? What are some of the trends in terms of the level of social capital in the United States?

2. What can CBOs do to promote social capital?

3. How does social capital affect local development? What are the micro and macro forces that affect the relationship between social capital and local development?

EXERCISES

1. Identify a local voluntary organization in your community that has been active for several years. Go back through the records of the organization and examine the membership trends, participation in local meetings, and the social backgrounds of the leadership of the organization over the years.

2. Among the major voluntary organizations in your community, identify the leaders (such as the board of directors) in each organization. How much overlap is there in the leadership between these organizations? Try to identify any common organizational ties among these individuals to assess how diverse the leadership is in your community.

REFERENCES

Burt, R. (1992). *Structural holes: The social structure of competition.* Cambridge, MA: Harvard University Press.

Coleman, J. S. (1988). Social capital in the creation of human capital. *American Journal of Sociology, 94*(Suppl.), S95-S120.

Flora, J. L., Green, G. P., Gale, E. A., Schmidt, F. E., & Flora, C. B. (1992). Self-development: A viable rural development option? *Policy Studies Journal, 20,* 276-288.

Granovetter, M. (1974). *Getting a job: A study of contacts and careers.* Cambridge, MA: Harvard University Press.

Green, G. P., Tigges, L. M., & Diaz, D. (1999). Racial and ethnic differences in job search strategies in Atlanta, Boston and Los Angeles. *Social Science Quarterly, 80,* 263-278.

Hofferth, S. (1984). Kin networks, race, and family structure. *Journal of Marriage and the Family, 46,* 791-806.

House, J. S. (1981). *Work, stress, and social support.* Reading, MA: Addison-Wesley.

House, J. S., Umberson, D., & Landis, K. (1988). Structures and processes of social support. *Annual Review of Sociology, 14,* 293-318.

Katz, P. (1994). *The new urbanism: Toward an architecture of community.* New York: McGraw Hill.

Kunstler, J. H. (1993). *The geography of nowhere: The rise and decline of America's man-made landscape.* New York: Simon & Schuster.

Marsden, P. V. (1987). Core discussion networks of Americans. *American Sociological Review, 52*(1), 122-131.

Portes, A., & Landolt, P. (1996, May-June). The downside of social capital. *American Prospect, 26,* 18-23, 94.

Putnam, R. D. (1993a). *Making democracy work: Civic traditions in modern Italy.* Princeton, NJ: Princeton University Press.

Putnam, R. D. (1993b, Spring). The prosperous community: Social capital and public life. *American Prospect, 13,* 35-42.

Putnam, R. D. (1995). Bowling alone: America's declining social capital. *Journal of Democracy, 6*(1), 65-78.

Putnam, R. D. (1996, Winter). The strange disappearance of civic America. *American Prospect, 24,* 34-48.

Putnam, R. D. (2000). *Bowling alone: The collapse and revival of American community.* New York: Simon & Schuster.

Taylor, R. J. (1986). Receipt of support from family among black Americans: Demographic and familial differences. *Journal of Marriage and the Family, 48,* 67-77.

Temkin, K., & Rohe, W. (1998). Social capital and neighborhood stability: An empirical investigation. *Housing Policy Debate, 9*(1), 61-88.

Verbrugge, L. M. (1979). Multiplexity in adult friendships. *Social Forces, 57,* 1286-1309.

Waldinger, R. (1995). The "other side" of embeddedness: A case-study of the interplay of economy and ethnicity. *Ethnic and Racial Studies, 18,* 555-580.

Wilson, W. J. (1987). *The truly disadvantaged.* Chicago: University of Chicago Press.

Wilson, W. J. (1996). *When work disappears: The world of the new urban poor.* New York: Knopf.

Woolcock, M. (1998). Social capital and economic development: Toward a theoretical synthesis and policy framework. *Theory and Society, 27,* 151-208.

ADDITIONAL SUGGESTED READINGS

Readings ■

Cohen, J., & Rogers, J. (1992). Secondary associations and democratic governance. *Politics and Society, 20,* 393-472.

Fernandez, R., & Harris, D. (1992). Social isolation and the underclass. In A. Harrell & G. Peterson (Eds.), *Drugs, crime, and social isolation: Barriers to urban opportunity* (pp. 257-293). Washington, DC: Urban Institute Press.

Fukuyama, F. (1995). *Trust: The social virtues and the creation of prosperity.* New York: Free Press.

Gittell, R., & Vidal, A. (1998). *Community organizing: Building social capital as a development strategy.* Thousand Oaks, CA: Sage.

Portes, A. (1998). Social capital: Its origins and applications in modern sociology. *Annual Review of Sociology, 24,* 1-24.

Verba, S., Schoolman, K., & Brady, H. (1995). *Voice and equality: Civic voluntarism in American politics.* Cambridge, MA: Harvard University Press.

Web Sites ■

World Bank. <www.worldbank.org/poverty/scapital/index.htm>. This site is an excellent resource for social capital research. It includes references, data, published and unpublished papers, questionnaires, Web guides, and more.

Civic Practices Network. <www.cpn.org/sections/tools/models/social_capital.html>. The Civic Practices Network (CPN) is a nonpartisan project focusing on the new citizenship movement. The site provides case studies and essays on civic innovation.

Robert D. Putnam. <www.BowlingAlone.com>. This Web site provides important resources for analyzing social capital and includes the data used by the author in his book *Bowling Alone.*

Videos ■

Social Capital and Sustainability: The Community and Managing Change in Agriculture, produced and directed by Dan Mundt, Publication EDC-88. This excellent video links social capital with sustainability in agriculture. Available from Iowa State University Extension Publication Distribution, 119 Kooser Drive, Ames, IA, 50011.

CHAPTER 7

Physical Capital
The Role of Housing in Community Development

People's view of a place is dominated by that place's physical capital: its roads, buildings (houses, businesses, warehouses), and other physical features (railroad tracks, bridges, vacant land). In the context of community development, physical capital refers to buildings (houses, retail stores, factories) and infrastructure (roads, water, sewer). When physical capital (a house) is constructed, an individual or a household is making an investment and expects a return on that investment, whether it is going to be sold at a later date for profit or whether heirs will inherit it. This investment, however, has a return to other community residents as well. One unique aspect of physical capital is its immobility. Although on occasion houses are moved, water and sewer lines are replaced, and factories are razed, these are costly endeavors, so, to a great degree, physical capital endures over a long period of time and is rooted in place. Thus, the quality of local physical capital is important in a community development context and in relation to other forms of community capital.

In this chapter, we focus on affordable housing and the role of community-based organizations (CBOs). Affordable housing has been one of the chief concerns among community development organizations in the United State for decades now. We examine several questions related to affordable housing. Why is affordable housing important in a community development context? How do communities create affordable housing? What role do CBOs play in the provision of affordable housing? In this chapter, we review the key concepts and issues surrounding affordable housing, the major actors and institutions, and the primary strategies and tactics for making housing more affordable, accessible, and available in a community. CBOs, because of their unique relationship with communities, can help establish networks that are part of a broader affordable housing strategy while addressing local housing concerns and providing information on affordable housing to a broad array of actors and institutions. There is a consensus that the way housing markets operate makes it difficult to provide affordable housing and that the federal government is relying increasingly on CBOs to meet these needs.

| BOX 7.1 | **Housing Facts** |

- Housing is the single largest form of fixed capital investment in the United States.

- As of 1998, for the first time, the majority (50%) of central-city households were home owners.

- As of 1998, a total of 69.9 million families owned their homes.

- From 1994 to 1998, the number of owner households grew by 5.4 million, with minority households contributing over 40% of this growth.

- However, poor urban residents continue to face an affordable housing crisis and related problems of poverty.

- Between 1991 and 1995, 337,000 unsubsidized units affordable to extremely low-income renters were lost.

- Almost 3.9 million unsubsidized renters with extremely low incomes spent more than 50% of their incomes on rent in 1995. But in 1994 for the total population, personal consumption expenditures on housing accounted for 14.9% of household budgets.

- In 1998, the nation lost 17,000 subsidized units as owners opted out of federal programs. During the next 5 years, contracts on two thirds of all Section 8 units, involving 14,000 properties and 1 million apartments, are set to expire.

SOURCES: HUD (1999), Joint Center for Housing Studies of Harvard University (1999), Green and Malpezzi (2000).

Housing Issues

Housing is an important feature of any community and in many ways defines it. Housing is where people live; it is the private spaces for our families and friends to share common concerns. Housing quality, its physical appearance, matters. It can provide a community with a positive image, suggesting that the community cares about place, and it can have the reverse effect as well.

Housing is a major component in the bundle of goods that define social and economic well-being for American families. It is an indicator of the social status of families and individuals. It is the largest investment most people make and makes up the majority of most families' net worth. It is also the largest part of most households' budgets, generally around 20%, but often a third or more for families of limited means (Clay, 1992, p. 93).

Efforts to produce and renovate affordable housing are place-based strategies in community development. Although the construction of affordable housing benefits individuals who may reside in those units, housing is tied to a particular community, a neighborhood. A house cannot be easily moved, although it can be rehabilitated. If vacant land is available, new housing can be constructed.

The Problem

In most communities, there are a range of housing types from apartments and manufactured homes to town homes and duplexes to single-family homes that can span from the very small and modest to the very large and luxurious. A variety of housing options are available for the diverse range of incomes, tastes, and values that exist in most communities. Many people, however, experience a number of problems related to housing.

- Excessive cost burdens can approach 40% to 50% (often as high as 70%) of an individual's or family's income.

- Housing may be overcrowded or physically inadequate, lacking indoor plumbing and heating, for example.

- First-time buyers may have difficulty in making the transition to home ownership.

- Homelessness is a widespread and increasing problem.

- Special needs groups (such as people with AIDS) and migrant farmworkers have difficulty obtaining housing.

- Few housing options may be available as people make the transition from one life phase to another.

- Rural areas often have an older housing stock in conjunction with the nonadoption and enforcement of codes, a lack of plumbing, a lack of lending institutions, lower family incomes combined with uncertain futures, and few qualified builders and craftspeople.

- Subtle and pervasive forms of housing discrimination have kept communities segregated along racial lines. Racial segregation has affected the neighborhoods where people live and their choice of available housing in terms of types, tenure, and cost.

- Sprawl adds to the cost of providing services and often the price of a home.

Housing problems can be divided into four general issues:

1. Housing affordability refers to the median housing costs within a community in relation to household income. Housing is considered affordable when households do not pay rents that exceed 30% of household income.[1]

2. Housing adequacy refers to a community's housing inventory, specifically the physical condition of the housing stock and its age.

3. Housing availability refers to a community's housing inventory, specifically the quantity of the housing stock and its distribution by type (e.g., single family, multifamily).

4. Housing accessibility refers to institutional barriers or other issues, such as racial segregation, financing, and local regulations, that make access to particular types of housing difficult (Bogdon, Silver, & Turner, 1994).

In the following, we focus on the concepts behind these issues. We must understand how the housing market operates in order to address the above issues.

Key Concepts and Debates

To understand housing in any community, one needs to understand the local housing market. Local housing markets are complicated and complex systems. A housing market occurs within a region and is shaped by an interaction of demand and supply forces. These forces include the number and characteristics of households and their purchasing power, the composition and condition of the existing housing stock, type of tenure, degree of household formation, ability to pay for housing of decent quality, extent of poverty, and degree of government subsidies and the regulatory environment (Huttman, 1988, pp. 6-7). Other factors shaping the housing market include the abundance of or restraints on economic resources, the general money market situation, land availability, construction technology, costs of building and maintaining housing units, and the cost of land (Huttman, 1988, pp. 8-9). Because local housing markets are influenced by many factors, CBOs, to be effective, need to understand the housing market: that is, the supply and demand of housing as well as the institutional mechanisms that regulate it.

In Table 7.1, we outline each phase of housing production in the left-hand column. In the middle column are the influences on each phase. It should be noted that virtually all the influences listed are institutional (i.e., formal and informal rules, laws, and regulations). Although regulations and laws are critical in keeping the housing market functioning fairly and efficiently, it should be noted that regulations can create perverse incentives. For example, home ownership rates can decline under stringent regulatory environments, and more regulations can increase house prices (Green & Malpezzi, 2000). The right-hand column outlines the players involved in each phase of the process.

The institutions (informal and formal laws and regulations) that affect the housing market are key factors in understanding how housing markets work in particular communities. Regulations such as zoning, subdivision regulations, and building codes are important sources of information that also affect house construction. Most local jurisdictions have some regulations that are necessary to ensure the welfare and safety of the public. Do these regulations allow for alternative development models, such as cluster housing? Regulations can lead to patterns of segregation or exclusion (large-lot zoning, zoning of insufficient land for multifamily dwellings) by race or income. Another primary stumbling block for many individuals and families in owning a home is access to capital, or the issue of housing finance (Chapter 8 focuses on financial capital).

Economists argue that the market, when operating correctly (i.e., uninhibited by regulation), will produce the right mix of housing types and prices (availability and affordability). However, the market cannot simply rectify the situation. If the market were producing the right mix of housing, we would not see issues of affordability, availability, adequacy, and accessibility continue to plague local housing markets. There are

TABLE 7.1

Major Influences and Participants in the Housing Market

Market Phase	Influences	Participants
Preparation: land acquisition, planning and zoning amendments	Real estate law Recording regulations and fees Landowner Banking laws Zoning Subdivision regulations Private deed restrictions Public master plans	Developer Lawyers Real estate brokers Title companies Architects and engineers Surveyor Planners and consultants Zoning and planning officials
Production: site preparation, construction, and financing	Banking laws Building and mechanical codes Subdivision regulations Utility regulations Union rules Rules of trade and professional associations Insurance laws Laws controlling transportation of materials	Developer Lending institutions Federal Housing Administration (FHA), Veterans Administration (VA), or private mortgage insurance company Contractors Subcontractors Craftspeople and their unions Material manufacturers and distributors Building code officials Insurance companies Architects and engineers
Distribution: sale (and subsequent resale or refinancing)	Recording regulations and fees Real estate brokers Real estate law Transfer taxes Banking laws Rules of professional associations	Developer Lawyers Lending institutions Title companies FHA, VA, or private mortgage companies
Service: maintenance and management, repairs, and improvements and additions	Property taxes Income taxes Housing and health codes Insurance laws Utility regulations Banking laws Union rules Rules of trade and professional associations Zoning Building and mechanical codes Laws controlling transportation of materials	Owner Maintenance firms and employees Property management Insurance companies Utility companies Tax assessors Repair people, craftspeople, and their unions Lending institutions Architects and engineers Contractors Subcontractors Material manufacturers and distributors Local zoning officials Local building officials

SOURCE: From *Shelter and Subsidies: Who Benefits From Federal Housing Policies,* by H. Aaron, 1972, Washington, DC: Brookings Institution Press. Copyright 1972 by the Brookings Institution Press. Reprinted with permission.

several reasons why the market cannot rectify the situation. First, private housing developers often are unwilling to rehabilitate or construct new housing in low-income neighborhoods or communities. Second, developers cannot make a reasonable profit when construction costs are high because of labor and materials and when the available buyers are unwilling or cannot afford to buy in a particular neighborhood at a particular price. Third, private housing developers can create higher profit margins by producing middle- and high-income housing units in new subdivisions (previously farms or green space) than by rehabilitating or constructing affordable housing. Fourth, regulations can produce perverse incentives, or at least not the right incentives for creating affordable housing. Some economists would argue that getting rid of regulations would allow developers and therefore the housing market to operate more efficiently and effectively.

One important process that occurs within local housing markets is filtering. Filtering is a key concept for understanding changes in the housing market. It is the process by which high-income households buy and move into new homes, leaving behind a house that is bought by someone of slightly lesser means, who in turn leaves behind a house that is bought by someone of lesser means. This process "filters" houses downward from richer to poorer families (Adams, 1984).

Myers (1990) noted that there are three interacting components in the definition of filtering: change in occupancy (turnover), declining price, and declining income (p. 276). Baer and Williamson (1988) noted several criticisms of the filtering model: (a) Absorption rates of new units to filter down are inadequate; (b) the correlation between decreasing quality/cost of units and age is not inevitable; (c) discrimination makes minorities, particularly blacks, more dependent than others on the filtering process; (d) owners and renters may exhibit different behaviors in the filtering process; and (e) overproduction of new units at the top may mean that new units compete with older units at the same value and represent an income loss to owners (p. 131).

The concept of filtering is useful and explains some of the dynamics in the housing market. The criticisms noted above, however, are important, especially for racially segregated neighborhoods. CBOs, especially if they are in neighborhoods that are experiencing a "filtering down" process, may be able to slow it through their efforts.

Another key concept is that of a dual housing market. Some analysts argue that the supply of subsidized housing has created a dual housing market: that is, the creation of two markets operating side by side, one for private market units and the other for public housing units. In reality, both private and public sector housing is supported by subsidies (Huttman, 1988, p. 4). Forms of public housing are direct governmental allocations, whereas private housing gets governmental support from guarantees on housing mortgages and insurance and, most important, through favorable tax deductions for home owners.

The Debate Over Affordable Housing

In discussions of housing policy, analysts turn to whether affordable housing is a supply or demand problem and whether a supply-side or demand-side solution is called for. The federal government originally saw the problem as a supply problem and called for public housing as a solution. From the 1960s to the present, the federal government shifted its position to the demand side. The shift from a supply-side to a demand-side model means that the nature of the problem and the range of possible solutions are viewed differently. Under a demand-side model, it is assumed that there is an adequate supply of housing but that low-income households do not have adequate incomes to afford available units. The solution is to help households by supplying them with vouchers, for example, so that they can meet the costs of housing.

The key question is whether supply-side or demand-side housing assistance is more efficient and cost-effective and achieves the goals of housing policies. One argument is critical of demand-side housing assistance, such as federal Section 8 certificates or vouchers. This argument suggests that the Section 8 program may benefit property owners more than renters. Rents are at their highest level in more than 20 years, we have lost 1.4 million low-rent housing units (that have not been replaced), and many renters reside in structurally inadequate units (Nenno, 1996, p. 137). There is counterevidence to suggest, however, that rents in real terms are no higher than 30 years ago (Green & Malpezzi, 2000). One of the problems is that in the 1960s and 1970s many cities through redevelopment efforts began to eliminate single-room occupancy housing (SROs) through demolition and conversion of those buildings to other uses. SROs were an important source of low-cost housing in many downtown areas of major cities. A number of cities now have programs to create and/or preserve SROs. There is a Section 8 SRO program that provides rent subsidies to tenants in newly rehabilitated SROs (Goetz, 1993).

In contrast, critics of supply-side housing assistance find evidence that housing conditions are improving and that some areas have high vacancy rates. This leads to the conclusion that the problem is rent burden; thus, the need is for certificates or vouchers, not provision of housing per se.

Because housing markets are dynamic—that is, the supply of housing fluctuates—at any given time supply-side or demand-side programs may provide a more appropriate solution. CBOs have an important role in neighborhoods in keeping pace with federal, state, and local programs but also in keeping tabs on national, regional, and local economies to gauge what is happening to housing markets in their area.

Another important debate in the community development and housing literature is the level and scope of government and community involvement in housing markets. The federal government, as we see from the previous discussion, has both direct and indirect effects on housing. Indirect effects come from the use of taxation (tax credits and deductions) and regulations that actually dwarf the effects of public production. Since Nixon's "New Federalism" and Reagan's more accelerated efforts at devolution, the federal government has used block grants (in which the federal government gives general guidelines over the use of funds, allowing local governments some discretion over how funds are used) rather than categorical assistance (in which the federal government allocates funds for specific programs, allowing little or no discretion over how funds are used) to help fund what were federal government functions for 50 years, including welfare assistance, housing, and urban development. Public housing has been one important source of affordable housing.

The United States now produces fewer than 30,000 new public housing or federally subsidized units each year compared to an average of more than 150,000 units per year during the late 1970s. Subsidized units formerly not only served to fill the critical gaps of low-income housing supply but also represented a major resource for minority households (Clay, 1992, p. 99).

The federal government has moved away from producing public housing to making funds available to lower levels of government and to organizations. One argument for this policy change is that lower levels of government are more aware of their citizens' needs and can be more responsive and innovative in delivering services. Although devolving responsibility to lower levels of government may make sense theoretically, in practice state and local governments do not have the resources to assume the same level of activity as the federal government undertook in the past. State and local governments vary in the types of housing policies they use and in their level of financial and technical support. Even so, the trend is to retreat from direct housing provision, in the hopes that the private sector and CBOs will respond, given the "right" incentives.

In the next section, we review a chronological history of housing policy in the United States to bring a contextual dimension to the previous discussion and prepare for the following section on the efforts of CBOs.

The Federal Government's Role in Housing

The federal government first became involved directly in the housing market at the turn of the century. It played two critical roles. One role was to help ensure that home ownership was widespread by creating subsidies for middle- and upper-income households.[2] The other role was to directly provide housing to low-income households.

During the Depression, almost all home mortgages were in default, and 1,000 foreclosures a day were occurring (Goetz, 1993, p. 20). The federal government acted on a variety of fronts to help the country through the crisis. Organizations were created from 1932 to 1934 to refinance troubled mortgages (the Home Owner's Loan Corporation); to address a lack of mortgage insurance (the Federal Housing Administration [FHA]); and to address inadequate funds for home lending (the Federal National Mortgage Association) (O'Connor, 1999, p. 91). The creation of these organizations subsidized middle- and upper-income households. In later years, the policy of subsidizing home owners has continued. The tax code provides a major subsidy to middle- and upper-income home owners. Home owner deductions dwarf all other housing expenditures, and the overall pattern of benefits from government housing aid is inequitable (Dolbeare, 1986, pp. 264-268). In general, the income tax system benefits owners over renters and benefits higher-income home owners over lower-income home owners.

The U.S. Congress affirmed the goal of a decent home and suitable living environment for every American family in the Housing Act of 1949 and reaffirmed it in subsequent housing acts in 1968 and 1990. Over time, a myriad of programs addressed affordable housing and urban development under the U.S. Department of Housing and Urban Development, by one estimate about 200 programs (Van Vliet, 1997). As we already have suggested, the trend in these programs is away from providing public housing and toward funding CBOs.

The purpose of urban renewal (1949-1974) was slum clearance and reuse of land, part of which would be designated for public housing. Despite thousands of projects and over 400,000 dwelling units on committed land, its critics claimed that it eliminated more affordable housing than it ever produced, that it was used as an economic development tool to revitalize downtown land, and that it primarily benefited urban real estate interests (Nenno, 1996, p. 30). It was criticized for destroying working-class neighborhoods, displacing poor people and people of color from their neighborhoods without giving them adequate assistance to relocate (Goetz, 1993, p. 23; Marcuse, 1986, p. 254; O'Connor, 1999, p. 97). The Model Cities Program (1966-1974) carried out demonstrations including housing projects in selected blighted areas to revitalize them in their entirety. It was believed that a comprehensive approach was needed to eradicate blight. Because of the high number of eligible communities and a lack of funding, however, the program largely failed in its demonstration effort.

The Community Development Block Grants (CDBG) program was established under President Nixon when several programs were consolidated into a single program (urban renewal, Model Cities, neighborhood facilities, open space, water and sewer, and public works assistance). These grants were allocated to cities and urban counties by a formula based on need. Smaller places and rural areas had to compete within their state under a state CDBG program. Over time, CDBG funds have been increasingly used for gap financing in private or nonprofit affordable housing developments.

> It is clear that cities could not pursue housing activities at anywhere near current levels without CDBG support. Three-quarters of officials in cities reported that CDBG was their primary housing resource. CDBG remains critical to city housing rehabilitation efforts. (Nenno, 1996, p. 40)

Although urban renewal, Model Cities, and CDBG are important programs for provision of affordable housing, HUD has had many specific programs directly related to housing provision. Housing assistance through HUD ranges from public housing (a supply-side program) to Section 8 and HOME (demand-side programs). Public housing assistance was directed at very low income families by the late 1960s. In 1974, Congress created the Section 8 private leasing programs. These programs provided a cash-based housing allowance for qualifying families, based on a percentage of median income. The Section 8 program supported both new construction and existing, rehabilitated housing. By 1983, the new construction portion of the program was canceled and was replaced with the Housing Development Action Grant (HODAG). HODAG lasted for 6 years until 1989, when it too was canceled. Section 8 has played and continues to play an important role by giving a housing allowance to eligible and certified low-income tenants who can search for rental units that meet certain physical standards. Landlords receive the difference between 30% of the tenant's adjusted income and the fair market rent (Green & Malpezzi, 2000, p. 88). In theory, a low-income family, for example, has a much wider choice of housing; the rental housing market is opened up to a much greater degree than is possible without the allowance.

The Low-Income Housing Tax Credit (LIHTC) is an important element in affordable housing provision. Through its use, an average of 1,300 projects and 56,000 units are placed in service annually (Abt Associates, 1996, p. 3.1). The LIHTC was created by the Tax Reform Act of 1986 and was renewed in Congress in 1992.

> The LIHTC provides a federal income tax credit . . . for ten years to private investors who provide equity capital for new construction or the cost of substantially rehabilitated affordable housing units. The credit applies to the proportion of units occupied by eligible low-income households. (Rosen & Dienstfrey, 1999, p. 450)

LIHTC has become the primary subsidy tool for low-income housing production. The program provides the equivalent of more than $3 billion in annual budget authority to state housing agencies. This program is another important funding source for CBOs, and these organizations are responsible for about 25% of LIHTC production overall. CBOs produce about 30% of LIHTC units in metropolitan areas and about 29% in suburbs but only about 8% in nonmetro areas (Abt Associates, 1996, p. 4.6).

In 1990, the National Affordable Housing Act was passed. Under this act, the HOME program was established.

> It is a formula allocation program (based on comparative local housing needs rather than an application grant program) intended to support a wide variety of state and local affordable housing programs. . . . HOME funds can be used for acquisition, construction, reconstruction, and moderate or substantial rehabilitation, and also for tenant-based rental assistance. (Nenno, 1996, p. 133)

An important piece of this legislation was housing vouchers that go directly to the tenant rather than to the landlord, as in Section 8. This program allows tenants to shop for rental housing that costs more than their voucher, in which case they need to pay the difference, or to choose to shop for units that are less than the voucher, in which case they can keep the savings.

Another important part of this program is that 15% of its funds are set aside for CBOs that develop housing. Another part of the 1990 Act was the Homeownership and Opportunity for People Everywhere (HOPE) program. Under Secretary Kemp of HUD, the idea was to empower low-income persons by assisting them in owning a home. HOPE concentrated on selling public housing to residents, assisting ownership for families in FHA-distressed multifamily properties, and promoting home ownership of publicly held, single-family properties through nonprofit organizations, among other elements (Nenno, 1996, pp. 86-87).

The above history focused on programs that aimed to create housing units through either supply- or demand-side policies. However, another important piece of legislation has influenced housing in this country. The Fair Housing Act was enacted in 1968 because of widespread racial segregation that has been and continues to be a problem in this country.

> The Act was, in theory, the pinnacle of civil rights reform in this country, because it offered equal access to a home, a mortgage, and neighborhoods that accompanied equal access to the voting booth, education, jobs, hotels, and other major arenas of life. (Goering & Squires, 1999, p. 1)

In assessing what the act has accomplished, even with amendments in 1988 that gave stronger enforcement powers to the Secretary of HUD and the Attorney General, national and local housing audits have found widespread discrimination (Kushner, 1995). It is estimated that from 2 to 10 million cases of housing discrimination occur each year in the United States (Feagin, 1999, p. 82).

BOX 7.2   **Information Sources**

- Local libraries

- Local building inspector/commissions

- County building inspector/department

- County planning department

- Regional planning department

- State planning agencies

- State data center

- U.S. Bureau of the Census

- U.S. Department of Commerce, construction statistics

- Private data providers

The Role of Community-Based Organizations in Housing Provision

So far, we have shown that there have been two primary approaches to address the problems of affordable housing: federal government programs and the housing market. A third approach that has gained momentum and popularity is the use of CBOs to address housing issues. Many actors and institutions are involved in the private housing market, as shown in Table 7.1. Note that no CBOs are mentioned. Nevertheless, CBOs involved in housing need to understand how the private sector housing market works if they are to participate in the development or rehabilitation of affordable housing. Like the private housing market, CBOs act as the developer in the first three stages and often take on various roles in the fourth phase, service, particularly maintenance and property management.

Models of Community-Based Housing Provision

Because private sector housing developers are reluctant to construct affordable housing, especially in neighborhoods that have high rates of unemployment, poverty, minorities, crime, and other social problems, CBOs have stepped in as developers to provide affordable housing in many neighborhoods where the private sector either has assumed that the process of filtering is taking care of the low-cost portion of the market or is simply ignoring that part of the market. CBOs are well situated to respond to housing needs in a community or neighborhood. They are physically located within the community or neighborhood and can listen and respond to neighborhood needs. They are connected to local voluntary organizations as well as governmental bodies, financial institutions, and philanthropic organizations. Without financial support from

---

BOX 7.3   **Types of Data**

- Age of the housing stock
- Age of the housing as a percent of the total housing stock
- Type of dwelling unit (multifamily, duplex, single-family)
- Median household income
- Monthly cost of owner-occupied housing
- Value of owner-occupied housing
- Monthly gross rent
- Tenure of owners and renters
- Vacancy rates
- Housing occupancy by status and unit type
- Actual cost of housing construction
- Utility costs

---

government and other sources, however, CBOs could not act as suppliers of affordable housing. Part of the strength of CBOs is the active membership of people in the community who are involved in deciding on the CBOs' roles and activities.

There are many organizational models for community-based housing provision. They are not mutually exclusive; all can exist and produce affordable housing within a community. Community development corporations (CDCs) are the most common organizational model outlined. Other CBOs are important in providing both affordable and alternative forms of housing such as community land trusts (CLTs) and cooperative housing (cohousing).

CDCs are vital players in community development, especially in the housing sector. As Table 7.2 shows, CDCs are involved in many kinds of activities, with housing development and rehabilitation dominating their work. Even though CDCs contribute only a small proportion of the total number of housing units constructed per year, they meet the needs that the private sector does not (Squires, 1994, p. 61). By the early 1990s, CDCs had produced about 320,000 units of affordable housing (Sullivan, 1993, p. 1). (See Case Studies 7.1 and 7.2.)

Some of the reasons for this de facto specialization are that housing establishes a foundation for other community activities, such as economic development and social services; housing is a visible product, so CDCs can establish a viable track record; and financial tools are more readily available for housing than for other community activities (Rosen & Dienstfrey, 1999, p. 439; Stoutland, 1999, p. 202). In Table 7.3, we show the various organizations from which CDCs obtain funding in their efforts at transforming communities. To get a housing project off the ground, many CDCs rely on from five to seven sources of funds (Rosen & Dienstfrey, 1999, p. 445).

TABLE 7.2
Percentage of Neighborhood-Based Urban CDCs Participating in Activities by Category, 1994

Category	% of All CDCs
Housing development and rehabilitation	
New housing construction	51
Housing rehabilitation	85
Home repair, weatherization	32
Construction management	44
Housing-related services	76
Own/control and manage housing	62
Own/control but no managing	10
Commercial and industrial	
New construction	15
Building rehabilitation	24
Business development	
Business owner and operator	8
Any business development role for nonowner/operator CDCs	11
Planning, advocacy, and organizing	
Advocacy and community organizing	75
Education and youth development	
Youth services and programming	32
Child care	12
Security and public safety	
Anticrime activities	23
Workforce development	
Job training or placement	26
Other sectors	
Emergency food assistance	12
Health services	6
Arts and culture activities	15
Senior citizen services	15
Mean number of active categories (of the 20 listed above)	6.35
Number of CDCs in urban neighborhood sample	538

SOURCE: From "Introduction," by R. F. Ferguson and W. T. Dickens, in *Urban Problems and Community Development,* edited by R. F. Ferguson and W. T. Dickens, 1999 (pp. 1-32). Washington, DC: Brookings Institution Press. Copyright 1999 by the Brookings Institution Press. Reprinted with permission.

There are two types of community land trusts (CLTs): (a) conservation trusts that focus on land conservation and do not promote any development and (b) CLTs that focus on housing and community development (White & Matthei, 1987). CLTs separate ownership of the house from the property it is on, thereby retaining ownership of the land in trust and according the benefits of home ownership to families. Keeping the land in trust removes it from the speculative market. Residents do not own the land; the title to the land is held in trust for the community by the CLT. Residents lease the land

CASE STUDY 7.1

CDCs: A Rural Example—South East Alabama Self-Help Association

Formed in 1967 to help small farmers in a 12-county area of southeast Alabama, the South East Alabama Self-Help Association (SEASHA) realized that housing development funds were more readily available than funds for cooperative farming and that a major problem in the area was the lack of decent, affordable housing. The organization's first initiative was part of a HUD-financed national experiment to design and build a prototype home for low-income people. HUD discontinued the program, but SEASHA learned enough to continue on its own. Within 12 years, SEASHA had constructed 269 single-family garden-style homes for low- and moderate-income families. Another successful experiment was a 100-unit rental complex for elderly and handicapped residents. SEASHA linked a range of auxiliary services to the apartment complex. It created a subsidiary, SEASHA Homes, that has constructed over 300 new single family homes, rehabilitated 75 existing homes, and constructed 192 multifamily apartments for elderly and handicapped citizens. The organization makes use of subsidies offered through HUD and Farmers Home Administration programs to make the homes affordable to low-income families.

SOURCE: From "Community Development Corporation Oral History Project," <www.picced.org/advocacy/bldghope.htm>, February 1997. Pratt Institute Center for Community and Environmental Development, Brooklyn, NY. Copyright 1997 by the Pratt Institute Center for Community and Environmental Development. Reprinted with permission.

from the CLT, which acts as the legal instrument to allow the CLT to control the resale price of the home. CLTs figure the maximum resale price of the land each year by considering the initial investment, the increase in local wages, and any improvements made. The buyer can expect a fair return on his or her investment, and the resale price restriction guarantees that the home remains affordable for future buyers (Goetz, 1993; Peterson, 1996) (see Case Study 7.3).

A major issue for many CLTs is financing. Without financing, CLTs rely on property owners to voluntarily conserve land, for example. Many CLTs would like to do more, especially when a piece of property is for sale, but without financing, they cannot take the initiative. The Institute for Community Economics (ICE) is a nationally based organization that helps CLTs with seed money provided from its revolving loan fund. Like CDCs, CLTs cobble together various financing resources from as many as five to seven sources, including CDBG funds and other HUD program funds, state land trust/land bank programs (as in Connecticut, Vermont, Maine, and Minnesota), commercial mortgages and construction loans, and tax credit dollars to finance their projects (Baker, 1992; Peterson, 1996). CLTs can act as land bankers by acquiring property and

CASE STUDY 7.2

CDCs: An Inner-City Example—
New Community Corporation

In 1969, about a year after its creation, New Community Corporation (NCC) began to plan its first housing project, New Community Homes. NCC, located in Newark's black inner city, successfully reached out to neighboring white suburban communities and created the New Community Foundation, raising funds for its project. To plan for the project, 60 families living in public housing were asked to participate in a process to develop the housing project. Their design was unlike any the state had seen and went against specific state rules for costs of low-rise housing. However, the state agreed to build the 120-unit New Community Homes project as planned, and the project was opened in 1975. With this success, NCC completed five major building projects over a 5-year period, creating an additional 829 units of affordable housing. In 1989, NCC built a transitional housing facility for previously homeless families. By 1992, NCC was employing 1,200 people and owning and managing over 2,500 housing units.

SOURCE: From "Community Development Corporation Oral History Project," <www.picced.org/advocacy/bldghope.htm>, February 1997. Pratt Institute Center for Community and Environmental Development, Brooklyn, NY. Copyright 1997 by the Pratt Institute Center for Community and Environmental Development. Reprinted with permission.

TABLE 7.3
Sources of CDC
Funding, 1991-1993

Source	% of CDCs	Source	% of CDCs
Federal		Private sector	
LIHTC	28.0	Foundation	52.1
CDBG	60.4	Bank	52.8
HOME	37.2	Local or national intermediary	37.1
McKinney Act	10.2		
State government	46.4	Corporation	31.7
Local government	42.6	Religious	14.4

SOURCE: From "The Economics of Housing Services in Low-Income Neighborhoods," by K. T. Rosen and T. Dienstfrey, in *Urban Problems and Community Development*, edited by R. F. Ferguson and W. T. Dickens, 1999 (p. 445). Washington, DC: Brookings Institution Press. Copyright 1999 by the Brookings Institution Press. Reprinted with permission.

holding it until a CDC or some other community developer can build affordable housing.

Shared housing is an important way for low-income households and families to afford housing in many communities. "Shared housing combines common facilities for joint use and shared responsibility for governing this use" (Hemmens, Hoch, &

**Land Trust: H.O.M.E., Inc. and the
Covenant Community Land Trust**

H.O.M.E. formed in 1970, originally focused on job training and education. The organization's focus expanded to include a store, a market stand, a learning center, a prison program for women and children, a health center, various studios and workshops for artisans, a food bank, and housing. H.O.M.E.'s initiation into housing occurred when it built four shelters for use by the homeless or battered women and children. In 1974, they created a community land trust and helped build 14 family farm houses. Because CLT land is kept in trust and out of the market, H.O.M.E. is able to build affordable housing in a growing community.

SOURCE: Flora et al. (1991).

Carp, 1996, p. 1). Many types of shared housing are found in communities. Many are informal arrangements, and some can be illegal: That is, they do not conform to zoning regulations or building codes. Shared housing occurs when neighborhood or community demographics and economic needs do not mesh with the available housing stock and its price. Shared housing ranges from co-ops to accessory apartments to group homes and condominiums. Several variations are possible, as evidenced by the list of kinds of shared housing, but these various forms need varying kinds of institutional/legal and financial support. Many types of shared housing are supported and created by CBOs, who can act as developers, advocates, or financiers.

Collaborative housing (cohousing) is a form of shared housing. A group of people buy, design, and construct a group of housing units and share community buildings and open space. This movement started in Denmark and only moved to the United States during the 1990s. The first cohousing community was built in 1991 in Davis, California. Over 170 cohousing communities have been built, are under construction, or are currently planned (Bader, 1998). Cohousing communities have several characteristics: participatory process, intentional neighborhood design, extensive common facilities, and complete resident management (Levinson, 1991). Like other alternative organizational forms, cohousing faces financial hurdles, specifically construction financing, and sometimes zoning problems depending on state and local laws as well as attitudes of planning boards and local councils (Levinson, 1991). A number of cohousing communities are concerned with affordability issues. They have used government subsidies to make some units in the community affordable to low- and middle-income households. Other ways to make cohousing communities affordable to low- and middle-income households are to build in rural areas or on urban in-fill land, build on a large scale to achieve economies of scale, develop densely, use sweat equity, and use prefabricated parts (Bader, 1998).

BOX 7.4	**Kinds of Shared Housing**

- Shared
  - Collective
  - Co-op
  - Condo
- Private
  - Boarding
  - Rooming
  - SRO
  - Accessory
  - Echo (temporary housing built as an accessory unit onto a single-family home)
- Institutional
  - Congregate
  - Transitional
  - Women's shelter
  - Group homes

SOURCE: Hemmens et al. (1996).

Employer-assisted housing reminds people of the idea of company towns, but today employer-assisted housing "means the offering of one or more housing benefits to non-management workers" (Schwartz, Hoffman, & Ferlauto, 1992, p. 4). Although relocation packages for management have been standard fare in corporations for a long time, helping nonmanagement employees with buying a house or renting is a fairly new idea. Part of the reason for this new benefit is the realization that many communities offer housing only at prices unaffordable to workers. Companies find it difficult to retain loyal and qualified employees, so they have turned to benefit packages to address the affordable housing problem that these employees face. In these programs, employers help pay the interest charged to home buyers or the down payment required on the new home. In general, there are two categories of employee-assisted housing: demand-side programs that enable employees to buy housing available on the market and supply-side programs that produce housing units for employees. Case Studies 7.4 and 7.5 give examples of each category. The problem with these programs, particularly demand-side programs, is that many people like their benefits portable: In other words, they like the option of getting another job in another city or town and taking their pension with them. Nevertheless, these programs give employers in difficult labor market situations with tight housing markets an option to explore. Several states now have employer-assisted programs that help subsidize employers for these programs.

CASE STUDY 7.4

Employer-Assisted Housing, With Employer Constructing Employee Housing

Winnebago, a town of 1,600 in Faribault County, Minnesota, is experiencing household and job growth but is lacking an adequate supply of affordable housing. Employers are unable to attract and retain employees because they are unable to find housing in the community. One employer, Weerts Company, decided to do something about the housing shortage by taking the initiative to develop new affordable housing. Weerts Company, a construction and landscaping company, invested $233,585 in the production of eight two- and three-bedroom rental units for its employees and will own and operate the project. The city also contributed to this project by waiving hookup and permit fees for these units. The Greater Minnesota Housing Fund contributed a $120,000, 0% deferred loan to the project.

SOURCE: From "Employer Assisted Housing: Minnesota Examples," <www.gmhf.com/Pages/eahmnexamples.htm>, November 2000. Greater Minnesota Housing Fund. Copyright 2000 by the Greater Minnesota Housing Fund. Reprinted with permission.

CASE STUDY 7.5

Employer-Assisted Housing, With Employer Providing Down-Payment Assistance

Coming up with a down payment and closing costs is often the most difficult barrier to home ownership for low- and moderate-income families to overcome. In Edgerton, Minnesota, Fey Industries is helping its employees overcome that barrier by providing up to $5,000 per employee in down-payment assistance. Fey Industries, a manufacturing company, is expanding and wants to attract a stable workforce to its community. This program is one method of obtaining this goal. The down-payment assistance is in the form of a 0% interest loan that is forgivable over 5 years as long as the employee remains employed with the company. Fey Industries is partnering with the Southwest Minnesota Housing Partnership, an experienced nonprofit housing organization, to administer the program. The Greater Minnesota Housing Fund is contributing a grant of $2,000 per employee to the program.

SOURCE: From "Employer Assisted Housing: Minnesota Examples," <www.gmhf.com/Pages/eahmnexamples.htm>, November 2000. Greater Minnesota Housing Fund. Copyright 2000 by the Greater Minnesota Housing Fund. Reprinted with permission.

Research has shown, however, that the programs tend to pay for themselves by reducing the employee turnover rate because workers are required to pay back the subsidy if they leave their employer within a set period, such as 3 to 5 years.

Mutual housing associations are more widely used in western Europe but are becoming more prevalent in the United States. These organizations are structured as nonprofits, with tenants controlling their rental housing. Like CLTs, mutual housing associations aim to take affordable housing units out of the market to prevent speculation and keep those units affordable to low-income residents over a long period of time (Hovde & Krinsky, 1997; White & Matthei, 1987).

Limited-equity cooperatives aim to control price through cooperation with other home owners. They are based on the idea of a housing cooperative, which is a nonprofit association of members who jointly own the building in which they live. Members purchase "shares" that convey the right to occupy a particular unit. Limited-equity co-ops are attempts to control escalating housing costs by controlling equity appreciation (Goetz, 1993, p. 89).

Housing trust funds use the idea of dedicating specific revenue sources to a particular function. Since the 1980s, with the housing crisis fueled by federal devolution, states, cities, and counties have turned to dedicating funds for housing purposes. Real estate transfer taxes and linkage fees (fees paid by commercial and industrial development to offset the impact of additional employees on the local housing supply) are examples of such revenue sources (Brooks, 1997, p. 230). Housing trust funds exist across the United States, with well over 100 in operation. They have several common characteristics: They have a dedicated source of revenue that acts to remove the need for funding from an annual budgetary process; they are local programs; there is a large amount of variation in program requirements; there is an assumption that other financial institutions are involved in affordable housing projects and that the housing trust fund is not the sole financier; and they are dedicated to housing and allocated to low-income and very low-income households (Goetz, 1993, pp. 101-104).

The Impact of CBOs

The preceding discussion has identified a variety of CBOs involved in housing issues, especially related to supply. The remaining question is, How effective are CBOs in the delivery of housing? In Table 7.4, we report the estimated number of affordable housing units produced by CDCs in the late 1980s. Interestingly, it about equals the federal government's production or output during the same period. This means that CDCs have developed a production capacity about equal to HUD's (Goetz, 1993, p. 118). Another source of affordable housing is manufactured homes. These are produced by the private sector. Private housing starts represent the largest output of units, representing almost 2% of the housing stock in any given year. All other housing output is far less than 1% of the total housing stock.

If CBOs are producing far less than 1% of the current housing stock, does this mean they are ineffective or inefficient? These data can lead one to believe that CBOs have little impact on communities, but we would be ignoring the context in which CBOs operate. Most CDCs and CBOs operate in communities with difficult conditions: poverty,

	No. of Units	% Relative to Housing Stock
Goetz survey, CDC produced	23,000[a]	>1%
NCCED survey, CDC produced	23,120[b]	>1%
New School survey, CDC produced	45,000[c]	>1%
HUD-subsidized housing completions	38,682[d]	>1%

SOURCE: Green and Malpezzi (2000).
NOTES: a. In 1989, 17,000 units were estimated from the survey. Goetz (1993) then extrapolated to 177 U.S. cities over 100,000 to arrive at 23,000 (pp. 117-118).
b. For the years 1986-87 (Goetz, 1993).
c. Production for 1989 (Goetz, 1993).
d. Per year 1986-87 (excluding vouchers and Section 8 rental certificates).

unemployment, building abandonment, disinvestment, crime, and pollution. Also, we would be ignoring the comprehensive approach that many CBOs bring to community development. That CBOs are having an impact in neighborhoods and communities with these conditions should be seen as an accomplishment. For the lives that CBOs touch, for the people who live in the homes that CBOs are building, in neighborhoods where a variety of projects are taking place along with housing, such as job training, open space improvements like community gardens, recreational programs, social services, health care services, and day care provision, CBOs make an impact and a difference.

Summary and Conclusions

Housing has become the "meat and potatoes" of community development work. It has been an area where CBOs could have an impact and show success and where the federal government was willing to lend a hand in promoting these activities. Some critics have charged that CBOs have focused too much on housing issues and should diversify their activities and pay more attention to community organizing issues (see Chapter 4). Other critics claim that housing is one of the few things that CBOs can do effectively and that they should stay focused on these issues and stay out of the economic development realm.

CBOs will most likely continue to be the lead actors in housing markets in most low-income neighborhoods. They now have the experience, funding, and skills to carry out these activities in these difficult settings. There probably is a need for CBOs to focus on the production of rental units rather than almost exclusively on home ownership. This shift could be facilitated by consideration of some of the alternative housing models that have been discussed here.

Of course, one of the major limitations of housing projects developed by CBOs is that they do not address the racial segregation of neighborhoods that limits the opportunities of low-income residents. These issues can best be addressed through regional strategies and policies.

KEY CONCEPTS

Block grants	Fair Housing Act	Housing availability
Categorical assistance	Filtering	Physical capital
Community Development	HOME	Public housing
Block Grants (CDBGs)	Housing accessibility	Section 8
Demand-side model	Housing adequacy	Single-room occupancy
Dual housing market	Housing affordability	Supply-side model

QUESTIONS

1. Why is housing and its quality important in and to communities?

2. What is a housing market?

3. What are the forces that affect a housing market?

4. What is the difference between supply- and demand-side policies?

5. What is filtering, and why is it important?

6. Why are CDCs important actors in the affordable housing market?

7. Discuss another type of CBO and its role in community housing.

EXERCISES

1. Examine the range of organizations in your community that are interested in housing issues. What aspects of housing does each organization focus on? Do organizations compete or are they involved in a network—that is, do they work cooperatively or competitively? Why?

2. Sample term paper question: Choose a community in your state. Examine the housing market, particularly for affordable housing, and the organizations involved in delivering affordable housing. Use the following questions to guide you:

   ■ What is the current demand for housing in the community and region, and how is it likely to change in the future?

   ■ What is the current supply of housing, and how is it likely to change in the future?

   ■ How are the private and public sectors meeting the supply and demand for housing? Is there unmet demand?

NOTES

1. If we agree that housing or shelter is a necessity, some would say a right, then the question is, How can low-income households in particular afford shelter? And what per-

centage of income devoted to housing is excessive? When you look at the income distribution in the United States, you find that the lower the income, the higher the percentage of income devoted to housing. A common rule of thumb is that spending more than 30% of household income on housing implies that it is not affordable. HUD uses this rule of thumb in its official calculations. This is a normative policy decision. For an argument about what is affordable, see Green and Malpezzi (2000).

2. Green and Malpezzi (2000) noted that not all home owners benefit from the mortgage interest deduction. A married couple's itemized deductions need to be more than the standard deduction of $7,500.

REFERENCES

Abt Associates Inc. (1996). *Development and analysis of the national low-income housing tax credit database.* Washington, DC: U.S. Department of Housing and Urban Development.

Adams, J. S. (1984). The meaning of housing in America. *Annals of the Association of American Geographers, 74,* 515-526.

Bader, E. J. (1998, January/February). Cohousing: Collective living for the 90s. *Dollars and Sense,* pp. 22-25, 41.

Baer, W. C., & Williamson, C. B. (1988). The filtering of households and housing units. *Journal of Planning Literature, 3*(2), 127-152.

Baker, A. (1992). This land is not for sale. *Social Policy, 22*(4), 25-35.

Bogdon, A., Silver, J., & Turner, M. A. (1994). *National analysis of housing affordability, adequacy, and availability: A framework for local housing strategies.* Washington, DC: U.S. Department of Housing and Urban Development.

Brooks, M. E. (1997). Housing trust funds: A new approach to funding affordable housing. In W. Van Vliet (Ed.), *Affordable housing and urban redevelopment in the United States* (pp. 229-245). Thousand Oaks, CA: Sage.

Clay, P. L. (1992). The (un)housed city: Racial patterns of segregation, housing quality and affordability. In G. C. Galster & E. W. Hill (Eds.), *The metropolis in black and white: Place, power and polarization* (pp. 93-107). New Brunswick, NJ: Rutgers University, Center for Urban Policy Research.

Dolbeare, C. (1986). How the income tax system subsidizes housing for the affluent. In R. G. Bratt, C. Hartman, & A. Meyerson (Eds.), *Critical perspectives on housing* (pp. 264-271). Philadelphia: Temple University Press.

Feagin, J. R. (1999). Excluding blacks and others from housing: The foundation of white racism. *Cityscape, 4*(3), 79-91.

Flora, J. L., Chriss, J. J., Gale, E., Green, G. P., Schmidt, F. E., & Flora, C. (1991). *From the grassroots: Profiles of 103 rural self-development projects* (Staff Rep. No. 9123). Washington, DC: U.S. Department of Agriculture, Rural Economy Division, Economic Research Service.

Goering, J., & Squires, G. (1999). Guest editors' introduction: Commemorating the 30th anniversary of the Fair Housing Act. *Cityscape, 4*(3), 1-17.

Goetz, E. G. (1993). *Shelter burden: Local politics and progressive housing policy.* Philadelphia: Temple University Press.

Green, R. K., & Malpezzi, S. (2000). *A primer on U.S. housing markets and housing policy.* Bloomington, IN: American Real Estate and Urban Economics Association.

Hemmens, G. C., Hoch, C. J., & Carp, J. (1996). Introduction. In G. C. Hemmens, C. J. Hoch, & J. Carp (Eds.), *Under one roof: Issues and innovations in shared housing* (pp. 1-16). Albany: State University of New York Press.

Hovde, S., & Krinsky, J. (1997, March/April). Watchful stewards: Mutual housing associations and community land trusts preserve affordable housing. Shelterforce. <www.nhi.org/online/issues/92/mha.html>

Huttman, E. (1988). Introduction. In E. Huttman & W. Van Vliet (Eds.), *Handbook of housing and the built environment in the United States* (pp. 1-20). Westport, CT: Greenwood.

Joint Center for Housing Studies of Harvard University. (1999). *The state of the nation's housing 1999.* Cambridge, MA: Author.

Kushner, J. A. (1995). *Fair housing: Discrimination in real estate, community development, and revitalization* (2nd ed.). Colorado Springs, CO: Shepard's/McGraw-Hill.

Levinson, N. (1991). Share and share alike. *Planning, 57*(7), 24-26.

Marcuse, P. (1986). Housing policy and the myth of the benevolent state. In R. G. Bratt, C. Hartman, & A. Meyerson (Eds.), *Critical perspectives on housing* (pp. 248-263). Philadelphia: Temple University Press.

Myers, D. (1990). Filtering in time: Rethinking the longitudinal behavior of neighborhood housing markets. In D. Myers (Ed.), *Housing demography: Linking demographic structure and housing markets* (pp. 274-296). Madison: University of Wisconsin Press.

Nenno, M. K. (1996). *Ending the stalemate: Moving housing and urban development into the mainstream of America's future.* Lanham, MD: University Press of America.

Nenno, M. K. (1997). Changes and challenges in affordable housing and urban development. In W. Van Vliet (Ed.), *Affordable housing and urban redevelopment in the United States* (pp. 1-21). Thousand Oaks, CA: Sage.

O'Connor, A. (1999). Swimming against the tide: A brief history of federal policy in poor communities. In R. F. Ferguson & W. T. Dickens (Eds.), *Urban problems and community development* (pp. 77-137). Washington, DC: Brookings Institution Press.

Peterson, T. (1996). Community land trusts: An introduction. *Planning Commissioners Journal, 23,* 10.

Rosen, K. T., & Dienstfrey, T. (1999). The economics of housing services in low-income neighborhoods. In R. F. Ferguson & W. T. Dickens (Eds.), *Urban problems and community development* (pp. 437-472). Washington, DC: Brookings Institution Press.

Schwartz, D. C., Hoffman, D. N., & Ferlauto, R. C. (1992). *Employer-assisted housing: A benefit for the 1990s.* Washington, DC: Bureau of National Affairs.

Squires, G. D. (1994). *Capital and communities in black and white: The intersections of race, class, and uneven development.* Albany: State University of New York Press.

Stoutland, S. E. (1999). Community development corporations: Mission, strategy, and accomplishments. In R. F. Ferguson & W. T. Dickens (Eds.), *Urban problems and community development* (pp. 193-240). Washington, DC: Brookings Institution Press.

Sullivan, M. L. (1993). *More than housing: How community development corporations go about changing lives and neighborhoods.* New York: New School for Social Research, Community Development Research Center, Graduate School of Management and Urban Policy.

U.S. Department of Housing and Urban Development. (1999). *The state of the cities 1999: Third annual report.* Washington, DC: Author.

Van Vliet, W. (1997). Learning from experience: The ingredients and transferability of success. In W. Van Vliet (Ed.), *Affordable housing and urban redevelopment in the United States* (pp. 246-276). Thousand Oaks, CA: Sage.

White, K., & Matthei, C. (1987). Community land trusts. In S. T. Bruyn & J. Meehan (Eds.), *Beyond the market and the state: New directions in community development* (pp. 41-64). Philadelphia: Temple University Press.

ADDITIONAL SUGGESTED READINGS

Readings ■

Aaron, H. J. (1972). *Shelter and subsidies: Who benefits from federal housing policies.* Washington, DC: Brookings Institution.

Belden, J., & Weiner, R. (1995). *A home in the country: The housing challenges facing rural America.* Washington, DC: Fannie Mae Office of Housing Research.

Bratt, R., Hartman, C., & Meyerson, A. (Eds.). (1986). *Critical perspectives on housing.* Philadelphia: Temple University Press.

Dolbeare, C. (1990). *Out of reach: Why everyday people can't find affordable housing.* Washington, DC: Low Income Housing Information Service.

Ferguson, R. F., & Dickens, W. T. (1999). Introduction. In R. F. Ferguson & W. T. Dickens (Eds.), *Urban problems and community development* (pp. 1-31). Washington, DC: Brookings Institution.

Ferguson, R. F., & Stoutland, S. E. (1999). Reconceiving the community development field. In R. F. Ferguson & W. T. Dickens (Eds.), *Urban problems and community development* (pp. 33-75). Washington, DC: Brookings Institution.

Gramlich, E. (1991). *Comprehensive housing affordability strategies: A citizen's action guide.* Washington, DC: Center for Community Change.

Moore, B. (1992, April). Not in my backyard: Removing the barriers to affordable housing—A review and critique. *Planning and Zoning,* pp. 12-17.

Vidal, A. (1992). *Rebuilding communities: A national study of urban community development corporations.* New York: New School for Social Research, Community Development Research Center, Graduate School of Management and Urban Policy.

Web Sites ■

American Planning Association. <www.planning.org/>. This site offers a variety of information about the association. It has a large publications list that is very useful for all kinds of planning-related issues. Another useful site is that of the association's Planning Advisory Service. PAS reports can be accessed at <www.planning.org/pas/passtuff3.htm>.

Co-Housing Network. <www.cohousing.org>. This coalition works to promote cohousing and help people start cohousing communities.

Enterprise Foundation. <www.enterprisefoundation.org>. The Enterprise Foundation was started in 1982 by James Rouse, a real estate developer known, among other projects, for the development of Inner Harbor in Baltimore. The organization's purpose is to bring lasting improvements to distressed communities. It is a national, nonprofit housing and community development organization.

Fannie Mae Foundation. <www.fanniemaefoundation.org>. The mission of this foundation is to transform communities through innovative partnerships and initiatives that revitalize neighborhoods and create affordable home ownership and housing opportunities across America.

Housing Assistance Council. <www.ruralhome.org>. The Housing Assistance Council is a national nonprofit corporation created in 1971 to increase the availability of decent housing for rural low-income people.

Internet Resources for the Built Environment. <www.cyburbia.org>. This site has a list of over 7,500 links in its resource directory. There is a planning resource directory that has a list of housing-related sites. Also, an architectural resource directory focuses on buildings, construction, historic preservation, and green architecture.

Local Initiatives Support Corporation. <www.liscnet.org>. This national intermediary was started with a $10 million grant from the Ford Foundation and six Fortune 500 companies for the renovation of 100 neighborhoods. The purpose of LISC is to assist CDCs that are committed to comprehensive residential and commercial development. LISC helps CDCs redevelop neighborhoods and communities in urban and rural settings.

Farmworkers and Colonia Communities. <www.hud.gov/migrant.html>. This section of the HUD home page contains listings and links to a wide variety of resources for individuals and organizations interested in farmworker housing.

National Housing Institute (NHI). <www.nhi.org>. This nonprofit organization focuses on affordable housing in a community context. It publishes Shelterforce, which is available by subscription either on-line or in hard copy. NHI searches for innovative strategies, unique partnerships, and effective ways to organize low-income communities.

National Low Income Housing Coalition. <www.nlihc.org>. This organization was established in 1974 and is dedicated to ending America's affordable housing crisis. The NLIHC is committed to educating, organizing, and advocating to ensure decent, affordable housing within healthy neighborhoods for everyone. The Web site provides information on housing affordability across most areas of the United States.

Neighborhood Reinvestment Training Institute. <www.nw.org/training/institute.htm>. This organization provides training to CDCs and other CBOs that are committed to community development—in particular, affordable housing, neighborhood economic development, and the quality of community life.

Neighborhood Reinvestment Corporation. <www.nw.org/nrc/index.html>. The Neighborhood Reinvestment Corporation, a national nonprofit, was created in 1978 by the Neighborhood Reinvestment Act (Public Law 95-557) to revitalize communities. It is a national intermediary and supports local CBOs.

National Housing Conference. <www.nhc.org>. This organization is a diverse coalition of housing leaders from the public and private sectors. Since 1931, NHC has worked to forge consensus and develop innovative approaches to meet our nation's housing needs.

U.S. Department of Housing and Urban Development. <www.hud.gov>. This site lists all the available programs from HUD. It also has information on mortgages, best practices, and so on. Also visit HUD User at <www.huduser.org>. It is the primary source for federal government reports and information on housing policy and programs, building technology, economic development, and urban planning.

Videos ▪

Homes and Hands: Community Land Trusts in Action (1998), produced by Women's Educational Media, directed by Helen S. Cohen and Debra Chasnoff. This video features the stories of CLTs in Durham, North Carolina; Albuquerque, New Mexico; and Burlington, Vermont. Available from the Institute for Community Economics, 57 School Street, Springfield, MA 01105-1331; phone (413) 746-8660.

CHAPTER 8

Financial Capital
Community Development Loan Funds

Poor and minority communities generally lack access to financial capital. Why are they disadvantaged in credit markets? Is it a problem of collateral or of the credit history of the residents in the community? Or is it a result of the discriminatory practices of lending institutions in the area? What can community-based organizations (CBOs) do to address these problems?

In this chapter, we examine why credit markets tend not to respond the needs of poor and minority communities. Many poor and minority communities are developing alternative credit institutions (e.g., community development credit unions, community development banks, revolving loan funds, and microenterprise loan funds) to address their credit needs. We evaluate whether these community development credit institutions are able to overcome the obstacles that businesses and individuals face in these communities. We also assess how these local institutions can be strengthened.

One of the basic assumptions of the asset approach outlined in this book is that there are existing resources in most communities that are underused. This is especially the case when we look at the availability of financial capital. In even some of the poorest communities, family savings are deposited in institutions that invest the capital outside the area. These assets need to be mobilized to serve local needs. One of the problems is that the returns on these investments are often higher when invested outside rather than inside the community. The alternative community credit institutions examined here seek to reinvest these resources in the community to promote development. They are still driven by profits, but with the constraint that the capital should be invested at the source. In other words, they attempt to create a balance between economic and social objectives of investing.

Like the other assets discussed in this book, there is a strong relationship between financial capital and the other forms of capital. Much of the focus on physical capital has been on developing financial mechanisms to provide affordable housing. Human capital strategies focusing on self-employment often emphasize the importance of debt and equity capital to help new businesses start and grow. Strategies for building environmental capital also rely heavily on developing pools of capital to purchase land. Finally, we will discuss how social capital is often intimately tied to access to financial

---

BOX 8.1 **Financial Capital Facts**

- Studies by the Federal Reserve indicate that in 1989, black and Hispanic applicants were denied mortgage loans two or three times more often than whites.

- The greatest gaps in the availability of capital exist for equity financing of small and new business, loans for nontraditional organizations, businesses in low-income neighborhoods, and home mortgage loans to minorities.

- In 1988, black businesses in minority communities with the same characteristics of black businesses in a nonminority area received $40,000 less in loan funds.

SOURCE: Parzen and Kieschnick (1992).

---

capital in many communities. In many ways, financial capital is the lifeblood of communities.

Financial Capital Issues

Communities face a variety of issues related to credit. Most of these issues are concerned with the demand for and supply of capital and with the institutions involved in the credit market. Among the most important issues are the following:

1. Do consumers and firms face an adequate supply of credit in the community? Is the cost of credit an obstacle for consumers and firms? If there is a problem, is long-term or short-term credit the problem?

2. What types of credit are being demanded by consumers and firms? What have been the experiences of consumers and firms in trying to obtain credit in the community?

3. What is the structure of credit institutions in the community? How much competition is there among lenders? What is the history of branch openings and closings in the community?

4. How well are local credit institutions meeting the needs of local residents? What proportion of the assets of credit institutions is invested locally?

5. How well do credit institutions that serve a community market their services and products? How aware are residents concerning the types of credit services and products available?

6. Are minorities, women, or small businesses discriminated against in the local credit market?

Key Concepts and Debates

Economic theory suggests that markets should be the most efficient means of allocating credit. Yet there are several reasons why capital markets may not operate in the most efficient manner and may deny credit to low-income and minority individuals, to small businesses, and to residents in poor neighborhoods that are deserving of credit. Among the most important reasons are

1. *Incomplete information.* Probably the most important reason why capital markets may not operate the way they are supposed to is that lenders have imperfect or incomplete information about loan applicants. Lenders have a difficult time evaluating the risk involved in making loans. If they rely on willingness to pay interest charges as an indicator of risk, however, they may make loans that are too risky. If they use collateral as their primary indicator, they may not be taking enough risk. Instead, lenders may use factors such as the neighborhood one lives in or the location of the business as a means of assessing the risk of the loan. This strategy typically works against minorities, low-income individuals, and people who live in poor neighborhoods.

2. *Transaction costs.* One reason why small borrowers may be disadvantaged in credit markets is the transaction costs involved. Transaction costs are the costs associated with reviewing and structuring an investment. The administrative costs of making large loans are about the same as the costs of making small ones. Banks also make more profit off large residential and commercial loans than they do off smaller ones. The result is that banks may prefer to make loans to wealthier applicants than to small businesses or poor applicants.

3. *Regulation.* Banking regulations may affect the ability of lending institutions to take risk. Regulators may encourage lenders to rely more heavily on collateral as a determinant in the loan process, which may work against low-income and minority loan applicants. Conversely, regulators may attempt to create more competition in local capital markets, which may improve access to credit in poor and minority neighborhoods.

4. *Bias/discrimination.* Studies continue to show that some lenders discriminate against minorities and minority communities. Two types of studies demonstrate this finding. First, some studies have used audits that are based on having white and black loan applicants with similar credit histories apply for loans at a bank. Whites are more likely to receive loans than are blacks. Second, statistical studies based on data from the Federal Reserve show that whites are more likely to receive loans than are blacks. Critics of these statistical studies, however, point out that they do not consider the credit history of applicants or the success rates of applicants.

5. *Competition.* Finally, credit markets may not work properly in some communities because of the lack of competition. Communities with only a few lenders may not face enough competitive pressure to efficiently allocate credit. This issue may be especially important for rural communities that are relatively isolated and may only have one or two banks.

When we discuss community credit needs for poor and minority communities, it is important to distinguish between equity capital and debt capital. Equity capital is a direct and permanent investment, such as cash or other assets (e.g., land, buildings), in a project. As a result of the investment, the investor can claim a portion of the earnings after the project pays its debts. Equity capital is usually the long-term operating funds for a business. Debt capital is usually short-term credit, and the borrower must repay the principal amount, usually with interest. Normally, credit institutions tend to specialize in providing either equity or debt capital, not both. Another type of capital that is somewhat related to equity capital is venture capital. Venture capital is usually an investment in a high-risk enterprise in the form of equity. The investment is often associated with a new product or service, and the investor is taking a risk on receiving a high return on this new market.

There are several approaches to dealing with market imperfections in credit markets, most involving some mix of government regulations and market-driven programs. The first approach, a pure market approach to solving the credit problems of poor and minority neighborhoods, focuses on removing the obstacles to the flow of capital into and out of these communities, such as the lack of competition among financial institutions or regulatory constraints that make it difficult to take risk on the investments in these communities. The assumption is that the market will correct the uneven investment of capital when poor neighborhoods become attractive for capital investment. One of the major factors affecting the flow of capital across neighborhoods might be the cost and availability of land. As land becomes more costly in other areas of cities, poor neighborhoods become more attractive for investment. However, the gentrification process may not benefit the local residents who wish to remain in the neighborhood. Gentrification can lead to higher tax rates because of the increasing demand for services and may ultimately push out residents who live on a fixed income.

The second approach is to use regulations to influence the allocation and pricing of credit. One example of this approach is the Community Reinvestment Act of 1978 (CRA). During the 1970s, banks and thrift institutions were charged with "redlining" in allocating credit. Redlining is arbitrary geographic discrimination in the granting of credit. Redlining was seen as contributing to the economic decline that affected many minority neighborhoods. In response to such charges, Congress passed the CRA to encourage financial institutions to meet the credit needs of local communities.

Another example of a regulatory approach is to provide private institutions with incentives for investing in minority and low-income communities. Some states have developed linked deposit programs that provide banks with deposits from state government if the banks are meeting certain criteria for lending in desirable areas. Another example is to provide loan guarantees to businesses and individuals in communities that have been identified as underserved with respect to credit.

A third approach to improving the access to credit in minority and poor communities is to assist in the development of community credit institutions that focus on development in a geographic area. Examples of these types of institutions are community development credit unions (CDCUs), revolving loan funds (RLFs), community development loan funds, and microenterprise loan funds. These types of institutions may allocate credit differently from private lenders for several reasons. First, because they are more actively tied to CBOs, they may be able to provide more complete information on the risk of loan applicants, which may increase the level of lending in these areas. Second, although these institutions are interested in profit making, they also have a set of social objectives they are trying to achieve. So most of these institutions make loans only to applicants in a certain geographic area or to individuals who may have less access to credit, such as low-income women in the case of some microenterprise loans or small businesses in the case of RLFs. Although market and regulatory approaches to addressing the credit needs of poor and minority communities may have some impact on the flow of capital, community-based credit institutions offer the most promise because they consider "community" at the heart of the investment decision.

Community Credit Institutions

There are several examples of community development loan funds. In this section, we focus on the most popular ones that are used today: CDCUs, community development loan funds, microenterprise loan funds, and RLFs. We discuss the distinguishing characteristics of these institutions, provide some examples, and evaluate their performance in poor and minority communities.

CDCUs are credit unions that have a geographic or associational bond where a majority of the members are low income. There are approximately 400 CDCUs in the United States, ranging in size from $25,000 to $30 million in assets. Many CDCUs are organized by neighborhood residents to address credit needs, such as personal loans or home rehabilitation loans, that are not being met by commercial lending institutions. A CDCU is essentially organized like any other credit union—it is a nonprofit cooperative governed by its member-elected board of directors. A cooperative form of organization is owned and controlled by the people who use the services (see Case Study 8.1).

One of the persistent criticisms of credit unions has been that they have begun to operate like commercial banks and have less interest in social objectives than they had in the past. CDCUs are more immune from this criticism than other types of credit unions because they limit their investments to the community or neighborhood they are serving. Probably the main limitation of these organizations is that there are so few of them.

Community development loan funds are privately owned, nonprofit organizations that make loans to assist low- and moderate-income people, women, and minorities in obtaining housing and jobs. These institutions serve as financial intermediaries that accept loans from socially motivated investors and reinvest in CBOs and projects. These funds often support nontraditional investments, such as land trusts, cooperative housing developments, and others. As a result, many of their loans carry a higher risk than is acceptable to most commercial banks (see Case Studies 8.2 and 8.3).

Community development loan funds are proliferating across the country. Some of these loan funds are limited to cities or neighborhoods, such as the Boston Community Loan Fund, and a few make loans available at the state level, such as the New Hampshire Community Loan Fund. Probably the most visible community development loan fund in the United States is the South Shore Bank in Chicago (see Taub, 1988). This bank has served as a model for many of the loan funds that have been developed over the past decade.

CASE STUDY 8.1

Community Development Credit Unions: The Lower East Side People's Federal Credit Union

This credit union was established in response to a branch bank's closing on the Lower East Side of New York City. The neighborhood used the CRA to challenge the Manufacturers Hanover Trust Company's decision to close the branch and received the vacated building for 3 years, rent free, plus a $100,000 deposit in the credit union.

CASE STUDY 8.2

Community Development Banks: The New Hampshire Community Loan Fund (NHCLF)

This fund has been operating since 1983. NHCLF takes investments from socially oriented investors and church groups and makes loans to CBOs, such as tenant groups, community land trusts, housing cooperatives, and community development corporations. The average-size loan ranges from $40,000 to $100,000.

CASE STUDY 8.3

Community Development Banks: The Boston Community Loan Fund (BCLF)

This fund was established in 1985 by a coalition of religious institutions and community leaders. BCLF focuses on developing and preserving housing for low-income people in Boston. It also provides technical assistance to groups so they can become qualified developers and borrowers.

The Clinton administration had plans to fund several hundred community development loan funds, but there was never much political support for the project. Although there are some very successful cases of community development loan funds, they are scattered around the United States, and only a few communities have them.

Microenterprise loan funds are nonprofit corporations that make very small, short-term loans for debt capital to microenterprises. The primary purpose of microenterprise

Microenterprise Development Programs: The Good Faith Fund

The Good Faith Fund was one of the first programs in the United States to build a lending program similar to the Grameen Bank's (Bangladesh) group-lending model. Created in 1988, the Good Faith Fund offers group and individual loans to entrepreneurs in rural, sparsely populated counties within the state of Arkansas. The objective of the program is to increase access to credit for women, minorities, and dislocated workers. The project was started by the Winthrop Rockefeller Foundation. It allocates an average of about $500 per loan to approximately 200 members.

loan funds is to provide opportunities to the poor and underemployed by developing business skills and establishing small businesses that require small amounts of capital to operate.

Several funds that are now operating in the United States were adapted from the Bangladeshi Grameen Bank, which creates small groups to provide loans. The Grameen Bank has made loans to approximately 700,000 of the poorest women in Bangladesh. The average size loan is $67. The repayment rate is 98% and the average interest rate is 16%. The bank uses a personal sense of obligation as a tool to encourage loan repayment, relying explicitly on peer pressure. Potential borrowers join small groups, which make credit available to any member of the group, contingent upon repayment of loans by every member. The peer group concept appears to work best when the groups range from five to eight members. The Grameen Bank has had a 2% loan loss rate, which is much lower than the 3% to 4% loss rate for most commercial banks. Most of the programs that have used this model in the United States can have loan losses as high as 10% in the early years, but most get down to 2% to 5% within 5 to 10 years.

Some of the U.S. microenterprise loan funds rely on the Grameen principles and some do not. Some examples of microenterprise funds in the United States are the Good Faith Fund (Case Study 8.4), the Women's Self-Employment Project (Case Study 8.5), and the Lakota Fund (Case Study 8.6). Most of these programs limit the size of loan to $25,000 and serve a fairly limited population.

Microenterprise loan funds face several obstacles. First, because the businesses participating in these programs are so small, most start out in their homes. Many municipalities prohibit home work. Adding expenditures for rent and other associated costs may be too much of an obstacle for microenterprises.

Second, licensing requirements may be prohibitive for many microenterprises. In some urban areas, the costs of licenses are equivalent to the maximum size of loans permitted under the loan fund.

Third, because many of the microenterprise loan funds are oriented toward helping individuals make the transition from welfare to work, borrowers often face bureau-

---

CASE STUDY 8.5

Microenterprise Development Programs: The Women's Self-Employment Project

This project provides credit, technical assistance, and training to low- and moderate-income women in the Chicago area. Its goal is to assist these women to achieve self-sufficiency. The loan program was established in 1983 and provides a maximum loan of $2,500. It has provided loans to a few hundred women. It requires a business plan, and the organization provides consulting and training to businesses in support of the loan. The project is largely funded through the Small Business Administration (SBA).

CASE STUDY 8.6

Microenterprise Development Programs: The Lakota Fund

This fund is located on the Pine Ridge Indian Reservation in South Dakota. It helps support the development of Lakota-owned and operated businesses. Its circle banking project uses the group-lending model of the Grameen Bank. The project began in 1987 and has made nearly $400,000 in loans to 200 tribal members. The project has a capital fund of $600,000 and accepts investments of more than $1,000. The fund does place several requirements on borrowers: Business owners must obtain business training, have collateral, and develop a business plan.

---

cratic obstacles. In some cases, individuals may run the risk of losing their public aid if their business begins to show a profit. There needs to be a transition period where profits from the business are not counted against any support that borrowers may be receiving from public aid.

Finally, most microenterprise loan funds are simply not large enough to become self-sustaining. Because of the administrative costs and the turnover in credit, a loan fund must be fairly large to support itself. Assuming that the loan fund charges an average interest rate of 16% and sets aside reserves for a 7% loss rate, the break-even point would be an $8 million loan fund, which is much higher than most microenterprise loan funds. In an area where population and employment are not very high, a microenterprise loan fund will usually face some serious obstacles. In most cases, the loan funds are actually subsidized by foundations or government sources.

Revolving Loan Funds: Thief River Falls, Minnesota

In the late 1980s, when Land O'Lakes announced the closing of its turkey-processing plant, which affected not only workers at the plant but also 32 area turkey growers who faced loss of their market, the community began seeking other options. The city established a revolving loan fund to help start Northern Pride, Inc., a grower-owned cooperative that purchased the processing facility outright and ran it as a for-profit corporation. Much of the grant came from the Economic Development Administration as well as other sources.

Most of the early microenterprise loan funds were first started in developing countries. These experiences have produced several important lessons about what makes these loan funds work properly. The evidence suggests that they should be demand driven, which means that providing loan funds to a business for which there is no market is not going to work. Most of these businesses will never graduate to commercial banks, so the loan programs need to be flexible enough to meet the needs of these businesses as they change and grow.

RLFs are designed to provide financing of housing and business development, frequently using terms that are not available through conventional lenders. As the loans are repaid, the money returns to the fund to be loaned out again. Many RLFs are funded by government programs. For example, the Community Development Block Grants (CDBGs) are a major source of funding for RLFs throughout the United States. Generally, RLFs do not make as many small and high-risk loans as other types of programs, such as microenterprise loan funds. A recent study by the Corporation for Enterprise Development (CFED) found that among the RLFs studied, a median of 276 jobs per fund had been created (Levere, Clones, & Marcoux, 1997).

There are numerous examples across the United States of successful RLFs. Two interesting examples are the fund established by Thief River Falls, Minnesota (Case Study 8.7), which has focused on new industry to replace jobs that have been lost, and Glacier Garden Rainforest Adventures in Juneau, Alaska (Case Study 8.8). Among the various community development credit institutions examined here, RLFs have probably proven to be the most successful and widely adapted throughout the United States. Part of their success has been due to the funding base for these loan funds and the ease with which they can be replicated.

Context for Community Credit Institutions

One of the major reasons for the growing interest in local credit markets has been the deregulation of the banking industry over the past 20 years. The merits of banking deregulation have been widely debated. Proponents contend that deregulation has

Revolving Loan Funds: Glacier Garden Rainforest Adventures

The Juneau Economic Development Council made a $300,000 loan to construct a greenhouse and site preparation for landscaping and construction of cart pathways. The facility gives tourists and local residents an opportunity to observe the rainforest environment with a tour guide/naturalist familiar with the flora and fauna of the area. Private financing matched the RLF dollars 2 to 1. The new businesses created four full-time and 23 part-time jobs.

improved efficiency and competition in banking markets and placed banks on a level playing field with nonfinancial institutions that have entered banking markets. As a result, banks are able to provide a wider variety of services and charge less for those services and for credit.

Critics of deregulation charge that banking deregulation has increased concentration of financial resources, ultimately leading to higher costs for banking services and credit. In addition, banking deregulation is alleged to have an especially deleterious effect on poor and minority communities because lending institutions can more easily shift credit to growing areas. As local banks have merged with larger banks, critics have charged that there has been a net flow of capital out of poor communities because the banks now can get a higher return on their capital by investing outside these communities.

Banking deregulation has focused on three issues: interest charges, geographic restrictions, and the types of services offered by financial institutions. Before 1980, Regulation Q placed a ceiling on the interest rates that commercial banks could pay on deposits. Regulation Q was removed because of increased competition for capital from funds from newly developed alternative investment instruments (e.g., money market funds). With the elimination of Regulation Q, commercial banks are allowed to compete for deposits, allowing savers to earn more but increasing interest rates for borrowers. One of the unintended consequences of this act, however, was that lending institutions began competing more through prices, and some took more risk in their investments to cover the additional costs (Glasberg & Skidmore, 1997).

The second element of banking deregulation has concerned geographic limitations on the activities of lending institutions. Before the mid-1980s, banks were not permitted to cross state lines. The spark to merger mania was the Supreme Court's decision in 1985 that interstate banking was constitutional. Today, we have effectively created interstate banking across the country.

Finally, before the 1980s, nonfinancial institutions were immune from banking regulations because they were not considered "banks" by the regulators. Commercial banks are defined as institutions that take deposits and make loans; if a firm only does one of these activities, it is not considered to be a commercial bank. In the 1980s, firms such as Sears and Merrill Lynch began entering the financial arena by making loans. Financial institutions asked regulators for permission to become more involved in activities not related to finance, such as real estate, insurance, and securities. The wall that had divided nonfinancial and financial institutions since the Depression was eliminated. This wall had reduced the risk in the financial sector, which had been a major factor in the Depression of the 1930s.

Ironically, the deregulation of the 1980s that was perceived to be so threatening to low-income and minority neighborhoods has actually turned out to be an important resource for CBOs to pressure banks to lend more in their area. The federal agencies that must approve the bank mergers require that the lending institutions demonstrate that they are meeting the credit needs of the communities they serve. CBOs have used this provision to challenge the practices of lending institutions, and as a result the lending institutions have made available relatively large amounts of credit for community development purposes.

Another piece of legislation that influenced the field of community development banking in the 1990s was the Community Development Banking and Financial Institutions Act of 1994 (the CDFI Act). The purpose of the act was to create a fund for community development financial institutions (CDFIs). The fund assists CDFIs through equity investments, capital grants, loans, and technical assistance. The support can be used for a wide variety of community development activities, including housing for low-income people, businesses owned by low-income people, financial services, commercial facilities promoting job creation or retention, and technical assistance.

The CDFI fund was originally set up as an independent agency but was eventually placed in the U.S. Treasury Department. In its first three rounds, the CDFI has awarded more than $119 million to 122 awardees; $58 million to 172 banks, thrifts, and CDFIs for lending in low-income communities under the Bank Enterprise Award program; and $3 million to 70 organizations in the Technical Assistance Component funding.

To be eligible for a CDFI Fund award, an organization must meet six criteria:

1. Its primary mission must be community development.

2. It must serve an investment area or targeted population.

3. It must provide development services and equity investments or loans.

4. It must maintain accountability to residents of its investment area or targeted population.

5. It must not be a public agency or institution.

6. It must be primarily a financing entity.

Key Actors and Institutions

Several federal agencies are responsible for regulating lending institutions in the United States: Comptroller of the Currency, Board of Governors of the Federal Reserve System, Federal Deposit Insurance Corporation, and the Office of Thrift Supervision. The reason why there are so many agencies involved in the regulation of lending institutions is that they all have some impact on capital markets in the United States. The primary way that these agencies affect CBOs is through the Community Reinvestment Act (CRA). Several states have become much more active in this arena and have developed policies beyond the federal CRA.

Some states are becoming involved in efforts to improve the social responsibility of commercial banks. A few states have enacted reinvestment laws that establish a quid pro quo policy. For example, in New York, banking powers are linked to CRA activity; with a better rating, banks are allowed to invest a larger proportion of their assets in real estate. In Massachusetts, CRA ratings are tied to eligibility to receive deposits of state funds. In Maine, financial institutions acquiring in-state banks are required to demonstrate that the transaction will lead to a net increase in funds to the state and will benefit the communities being affected.

Other states have developed new institutions to provide credit to underdeveloped sectors and regions and to small businesses and minority groups. State programs range from seed capital and venture capital programs to small business and home mortgage loan programs. A central concept behind many of these financial institutions is the pooling of risk. Capital access programs and business industrial development corporations are two examples of innovative institutions designed to fill the credit gap of poor communities.

One mechanism for directing capital to borrowers who have difficulty obtaining loans from commercial banks and venture capitalists is a Business Industrial Development Corporation (BIDCO). BIDCOs use an approach referred to as a risk return initiative. Developed in the early 1970s, BIDCOs are structured to meet the financial needs of small businesses that fall into this credit gap. They use two different means of channeling credit to businesses. First, BIDCOs can make Small Business Administration (SBA) loans and sell the guaranteed portion on the secondary markets. By selling these loans, it is possible to leverage capital up to 10 to 1. Second, BIDCOs can borrow from private sources and make non-SBA loans.

Another example of a state credit institution is a capital access program (CAP). CAPs are based on a different principle than the traditional type of insurance or guarantee program. These programs are based on a portfolio or pooling concept. An example of this program is the Loan Loss Reserve Program developed by the Michigan Strategic Fund. Under this program, a special reserve is established for banks participating in the program to cover loan losses. The reserve is established through matched payments made by the borrower and the bank.

In addition to these state and federal agencies, a plethora of intermediary organizations have emerged to help neighborhoods and communities with their credit problems. One of the premier organizations in the country is the Woodstock Institute in Chicago. This organization has worked for years with Home Mortgage Disclosure data and in designing CRA programs and initiatives.

Other national organizations are more specialized. For example, the National Association of Development Organizations (NADO) provides a training program for revolving loan managers. The Association of Community Organizations for Reform Now (ACORN) is a coalition of low- and moderate-income people with members in 26 states. The organization has worked to eliminate redlining practices in many cities. The National Association of Community Development Loan Funds serves as a resource center and an advocate for issues related to community development loan funds.

Assessing Local Credit Markets

There are two basic components to any assessment of credit markets: the supply of and the demand for credit in the community. In addition, any analysis must begin by identifying the market area for credit institutions. One way of identifying the market is to use Community Reinvestment Act (CRA) statements to identify the service area of local lending institutions. This area should be about the same for most services.

There are many types of information available on capital markets. One of the most widely used is the information provided through the Home Mortgage Disclosure Act of 1975 (HMDA). Financial institutions are not required to disclose much about their lending practices. But HMDA requires that banks and thrifts with more than $10 million in deposits in Metropolitan Statistical Areas (MSAs) report (a) the annual number and volume of residential loans, (b) the volume and amount of mortgage loans by census tract and zip code in MSAs, and (c) the aggregate number and volume of mortgage loans outside the MSA. The HMDA was recently amended by the Financial Institutions Reform, Recovery, and Enforcement Act of 1989 (FIRREA) to expand disclosure requirements. FIRREA requires lenders to disclose the race, sex, and income of loan applicants and recipients. HMDA data are of little value to rural communities because information on capital flows outside MSAs is not provided by lending institutions.

The CRA also requires lenders to provide information on their activities. Four agencies regulate lending institutions: the Comptroller of the Currency, the Board of Governors of the Federal Reserve, the Federal Deposit Insurance Corporation, and the Office of Thrift Supervision. These regulators require the following in a CRA statement:

1. A delineation on a map of each community served by the institution. The overriding concern is that the banks are not arbitrarily excluding certain neighborhoods from their area.

2. A list of the specific types of credit that the institution is prepared to offer within each community.

3. A copy of the CRA notice indicating where to get copies of the statement, written comments, and the institution's lending performance.

4. Information on efforts to assess and to help meet credit needs of the community.

The regulators consider a number of additional pieces of information in their evaluation of lending institutions. Examiners consider the institution's attempts to assess credit needs, marketing of credit services, geographic distribution and record of opening and closing offices, discrimination and other illegal credit practices, and participation in community development and redevelopment projects/programs.

The CRA, along with HMDA, was designed to address the problems of redlining neighborhoods on the basis of race or economic class. National organizations concerned with redlining, such as the National Center for Policy Alternatives, the Center for Community Change, and the Woodstock Institute have recognized that CRA taps only a small segment of the financial industry and have argued that nonregulated institutions should also be monitored. These organizations contend that a broader approach to monitoring is needed.

Several other data sources on lending institutions may be useful. Several guides provide basic information on the practices of lending institutions. But one of the problems with using secondary data sources to analyze the performance and behavior of lending institutions is that the data are reported by bank and not by branch. This means that if there are only branch banks in a neighborhood or community, it will be impossible to examine the lending patterns of those institutions. HMDA does require banks to report lending by census tract, but it does not require this of all banks, and this information is not available from other types of lenders. Obviously, an alternative is to collect your own information on lending patterns, but this can be very costly and time consuming for community organizations.

Strategies for Building Local Credit Markets

Communities may adopt several strategies for building their local credit market. Below, we have identified some of the most common strategies.

Build Community Development Financial Institutions

CBOs can play an important role in helping to build community credit institutions. Most of the institutions that have been discussed in this chapter could be operated by CBOs, but they may need help with technical assistance or funding. A variety of financial intermediaries exist for this purpose. Many community development corporations have established revolving loan funds to help revitalize their neighborhoods. In some cases, the loan funds have eventually spun off into separate organizations. But there are advantages, at least initially, for a community development financial institution to be affiliated with a CBO that has an established reputation and can help build the financial base and links to borrowers.

Pressure Local Credit Institutions to Serve Community

Experience with the CRA suggests that communities can achieve important results by challenging the lending practices of local credit institutions. CRA challenges require a rigorous analysis of the lending practices of these institutions and evidence that the community is being underserved. Community organizations also have found that it frequently takes a well-organized effort to make lenders respond to local credit needs. Some financial institutions, however, are looking for ways to demonstrate that they are serving their local community, and CBOs should take advantage of these resources. Many lenders find the CRA regulations rather ambiguous, and community organizations can educate them on areas where they can invest in the community at relatively low risk.

Use Informal Credit Markets

Some communities have been successful in promoting informal credit markets to address local needs. CBOs can play an integral role in matching borrowers with available capital. These organizations can help identify available sources of financial capital and make them go to work in the local community.

Identify External Sources of Credit

Most borrowers find credit in their local community. But borrowers who have a specialized need may find intermediaries outside the community that can serve them. One example would be a worker-owned firm. There are several credit sources for these types of institutions. CBOs, again, can play a special role in helping match these intermediaries with local firms.

Summary and Conclusions

There continues to be concern among policy makers and community activists that poor and minority communities suffer from a lack of capital. Some people contend that the credit gap is due to discriminatory lending practices of financial institutions. Others argue that the credit gap is due to the risk of investing in these neighborhoods. In response to these problems, a variety of community credit institutions have been created. Our brief review suggests that government programs and market-based solutions have not adequately addressed the credit problems in these communities. Over the past few decades, community credit institutions have emerged to fill this need.

Although some of these models are very promising, most of the evaluations of these institutions suggest that they have only had limited impact on the credit markets in poor and minority communities. Although they have been able to funnel more dollars into poor neighborhoods, they have not come close to meeting the demand for credit in these areas. In many cases, the community credit institutions have received a substantial amount of support from foundations and the federal government, but they have not proven to be sustainable yet. The evidence also suggests that these institutions are supplemented with technical support and other types of assistance to communities.

KEY CONCEPTS

Business industrial development corporation (BIDCO)

Capital access programs (CAPs)

Community development credit union (CDCU)

Community development loan fund

Community Reinvestment Act of 1978 (CRA)

Debt capital

Deregulation

Equity capital

Home Mortgage Disclosure Act of 1975 (HMDA)

Linked deposit programs

Microenterprise loan fund

Redlining

Revolving loan fund (RLF)

Transaction costs

QUESTIONS

1. What are some of the explanations for why minorities and residents in low-income neighborhoods are disadvantaged in capital markets? What are some strategies that communities can use to address these problems?

2. What are some features that distinguish a traditional commercial lender from a community development loan fund?

3. What have been the major elements of financial deregulation over the past two decades? What have been the implications of deregulation for poor and minority communities in the United States? How can deregulation be used to the advantage of these communities?

EXERCISES

1. Go to your local bank and obtain a copy of its Community Reinvestment Act Performance Evaluation. Discuss with a loan officer the most recent evaluation, and assess how well the lending institution is meeting local needs. With what types of activities is the bank involved in your community? How does the bank assess the community's credit needs?

2. Analyze the local credit market in your community. What are the various types of institutions supplying credit into the community? How well do these institutions serve the community? How well does the supply of credit match the demand? Are there any credit gaps that you can find in the community?

3. Meet with some local businesses and discuss their experiences with obtaining credit from local banks and other lenders. Do they believe that there are any major obstacles to obtaining credit in the local community? Has the lack of credit ever prevented them from expanding into new markets and growing their business? If so, how have they responded to these problems?

REFERENCES

Glasberg, D. S., & Skidmore, D. (1997). *Corporate welfare policy and the welfare state: Bank deregulation and the savings and loan bailout.* New York: Aldine de Gruyter.

Levere, A., Clones, D., & Marcoux, K. (1997). *Counting on local capital: A research project on revolving loan funds.* Washington, DC: Corporation for Enterprise Development.

Parzen, J. A., & Kieschnick, M. H. (1992). *Credit where it's due: Development banking for communities.* Philadelphia: Temple University Press.

Taub, R. P. (1988). *Community capitalism.* Boston: Harvard Business School Press.

ADDITIONAL SUGGESTED READINGS

Readings ■

Bates, T. (1993). *Banking on black enterprise: The potential of emerging firms for revitalizing urban economies.* Washington, DC: Joint Center for Political and Economic Studies.

Caftel, B. J. (1978). *Community development credit unions: A self-help manual.* Berkeley, CA: National Economic Development and Law Project.

Dominguez, J. (1976). *Capital flows in minority areas.* Lexington, MA: Lexington.

Dunham, C. R. (1986, March/April). Interstate banking and the outflow of local funds. *New England Economic Review, 2,* 7-19.

Hogwood, A. W., Jr., & Shabecoff, A. (1992). *Lending for community economic development: A guide for small town and rural lenders.* Washington, DC: Community Information Exchange.

Parzen, J., Shabecoff, A., Vandenberg, L., & Berman, G. (1990). *Capital and communities: A community guide to financial institutions.* Washington, DC: Community Information Exchange.

Rosen, D. P. (1988). *Public capital: Revitalizing America's communities.* Washington, DC: National Center for Policy Alternatives.

Squires, G. D. (Ed.). (1992). *From redlining to reinvestment: Community responses to urban disinvestment.* Philadelphia: Temple University Press.

White, K. (1987). *The community loan fund manual.* Springfield, MA: Institute for Community Economics.

Web Sites ■

Coalition of Community Development Financial Institutions. <www.cdfi.org>. This Web site provides information for those interested in community development financial institutions. The coalition was developed in 1992 as an ad hoc policy development and advocacy initiative and represents more than 350 community development financial institutions (CDFIs) in 50 states. The coalition is a primary source of information for the general public, the media, public officials, and the private sector about CDFIs.

Woodstock Institute. <www.woodstockinst.org>. The Woodstock Institute is a Chicago nonprofit organization that works to promote community reinvestment and economic development in lower-income and minority communities. The institute engages in applied research, policy analysis, technical assistance, public education, and program design and evaluation. Their primary activities are CRA and fair lending policies, financial and insurance services, community development financial institutions, and economic development strategies.

Enterprise Development Website. <www.enterweb.org/communty.htm>. This Web site is an excellent resource for finding information on a wide variety of programs related to community economic development, including several sites on financing.

Community Reinvestment Fund. <www.crfusa.com>. The Community Reinvestment Fund (CRF) is a nonprofit organization that provides a secondary market for economic development loans. This Web site also provides information and resources for lenders, such as information on fair lending, lender liability, and housing-related sites.

National Federation of Community Development Credit Unions (NFCDCU). <www.natfed.org>. The NFCDCU's Web site provides basic information on and resources for community development credit unions.

National Community Capital Association. <www.Communitycapital.org>. The National Community Capital Association is a membership organization of nonprofit groups that invest in poor communities.

Videos ■

Faith, Hope, and Capital: Banking on the "Unbankable" (2000), produced by Tenth Street Media, Inc., directed by Lynn Adler and Jim Mayer (Item No. BLV10148). This video examines the workings of community development financial institutions. It provides case studies of several institutions that provide capital and technical assistance to businesses in poor and neglected communities. Available from Films for the Humanities and Science, P.O. Box 2053, Princeton, NJ 08543-2053.

CHAPTER 9

Environmental Capital
Controlling Land Development

What is environmental capital? To review, capital in the context in which we have defined it is a type of community asset that can be employed to produce more assets; capital should not be equated just with wealth generation by individuals or businesses. Others use the term *assets* as a way to examine, analyze, and create community. John Kretzmann and John McKnight (1993) are now well known for their asset-based approach to community development. Ronald Ferguson and William Dickens (1999) also have spoken of community development assets as different forms of capital: physical, human, social, financial, and political. They have captured Kretzmann and McKnight's definition within these different forms of capital. Ferguson and Dickens, however, have ignored an important form of capital: environmental capital. Increasingly, community-based organizations (CBOs) are faced with issues related to their natural environment. In this chapter, we discuss some of the dilemmas, strategies, and tactics involved in the community-based efforts to build a community's environmental capital.

Environmental capital includes several aspects of a community's base of natural resources: air, water, land, flora, and fauna. Why do communities need to be concerned about environmental capital? There are several possible reasons. First, we need to be concerned about the ecological functions that natural resources play, such as flood control, water catchment, and waste assimilation. Second, natural resources have direct use value, primarily as marketed outputs (e.g., timber, crops, renewable energy) and unpriced benefits (e.g., recreation and landscape). Finally, natural resources may have nonuse values, such as the ability to pass on a natural area for future generations or simply the satisfaction that is derived from knowing that the natural resources are being preserved. Because natural resources may produce a variety of values, it is important to consider what is the best use of the resources for the long-term viability of the community.

We need to make a few comments at the outset about the relationship between natural resources and economic development. In the past, natural resources have been viewed primarily in terms of their productive value, but increasingly communities are considering the consumer value of their natural resources and viewing their natural resources as amenities. Amenities are natural and manmade features of a community that cannot be re-created or transferred to other communities. Examples of an amenity would be a wildlife ecosystem, a recreational area, a historical site, or even the social and cultural traditions of a community. Amenities are usually restricted in an absolute sense, and once their consumer value has been destroyed, it is impossible to restore their initial value.

What is the relationship between an amenity and economic development? Most people immediately think of the first scenario in which development leads to the destruction of an amenity. An example might be a development project that is proposed for a wetland site. There are, however, other possible relationships between amenities and economic development. In some cases, nondevelopment can lead to the destruction of amenities. For example, the loss of people in some rural areas may lead to the loss of farms and the landscape that so many people appreciate. Another possibility is that preservation or promotion of amenities can lead to nondevelopment. Residents may limit economic activities or take land out of the market to preserve natural resources. Finally, preservation or promotion of amenities can promote higher levels of development, as in the case of a recreation area.

For many of us, the natural environment is in the background of our communities. We accept its existence without thinking about it. In a city, a suburb, or village it is more obvious to observe what is going on in the downtown area or with new housing developments. We generally do not notice when a wetland is filled in or a few trees are felled for a new industrial or residential development. But many communities are beginning to recognize that wisely managed natural resources, a community's environmental capital, play a major role in community satisfaction and economic development.

Few communities have considered the complicated needs of natural systems included within their political boundaries. Numerous laws, strategies, and programs address parts of our ecological support system (e.g., sewage treatment districts, shoreland preservation regulation, priority watershed plans, lake management districts, farmland preservation zoning, and wellhead protection zones). In contrast to these regulatory and management approaches, CBOs can offer an alternative approach to protecting a community's environmental capital, especially in places that do not have the broad support necessary for protecting key environmental resources.

Many minority and poor communities face a disproportionate number of environmental problems; this situation is referred to as environmental racism. Many of these communities have become the sites for hazardous waste or illegal dumps (Bullard, 1994). Residents in these communities often suffer from high rates of cancer and other diseases. These communities are mobilizing around the environmental problems in their communities.

In this chapter, we examine why CBOs are sometimes better able to address a community's environmental capital than either government or market-based strategies. We also examine the kinds of obstacles and issues that CBOs need to address to become more effective and successful in considering environmental capital issues. We focus on community land trusts to illustrate how CBOs can address environmental capital issues, particularly the issue of sprawl and open space. In particular, we are interested in how CBOs can promote development that benefits the economy, the community, and the environment.

Forms of Environmental Capital

Depending on where your community is located, the natural environment may play a role in local image and quality of life. Many communities rely on their local environmental capital for beauty, as an economic resource, and/or for recreational opportunities. Your community probably has some connection with its environmental capital, whether for tourism, industry, or recreation.

Local environmental capital provides important functions to communities. Undeveloped lands, especially wetlands, act as flood control and part of a system of water storage. Trees and plants hold soils in place and act as air purifiers. Natural areas also provide aesthetically pleasing environments and, if large enough, provide plant and animal diversity. Finally, natural areas provide opportunities for economic development and recreation, education, and spiritual enrichment.

Communities have changing relationships with their local natural resources. During their early history, economic development was probably based on the extraction of natural resources. Change is a part of natural ecosystem dynamics, but air, water, land, or an ecosystem can become degraded through human activities. Surface water (lakes, rivers, or streams) may degrade over time: Algae blooms can occur regularly, or water can become murky or overly acidic—clear and lifeless. Closely allied with degradation is the depletion of natural resources. There are fewer trees, prairies, and wetlands and fewer of the birds and other animals and plants that are associated with those kinds of ecosystems.

Pollution is often the source that degrades natural resources. Pollution comes from point and nonpoint sources. Nonpoint source pollution is the most difficult to address; it cannot be traced to a specific source. Urban streets and agricultural fields are common sources of nonpoint pollution. Point source pollution, in contrast, is specific output from a production process and can be traced to its source. Some examples of point source pollution are pollution from manufacturing firms, such as paper plants, or utilities, such as coal-fired power plants. Clean water and air are used as part of the production process, but the output of water or air is "dirtier" than it was when it was used as an input. Reduction, degradation, or loss of natural resources also translates to loss of beauty and loss of ecosystem functions, such as air and water purification, sediment filtration, and water flow control.

The following is a list and description of environmental resources or capital that are important to communities.

Aesthetic Qualities/Scenic Resources

The aesthetic qualities of natural resources and the built environment are important aspects of a community. Aesthetic qualities of the built environment can be enhanced by selective emphasis on certain natural features, such as preservation of a scenic waterway or the use of prairie plants, native trees, and native shrubs in community plantings. The built community can enhance the natural beauty of surrounding resources by emphasizing building materials and colors that blend with local scenery. Variety and unique features are important components of aesthetic quality. Examples of unique features might include forests, farmland, wetlands, and prairies; small communities; urban communities; utilities; highways; water-related areas such as streams, rivers, and lakes; landforms such as hills, cliffs, plains, valleys, and glacial features; and view potential, such as vistas and panoramic views.

Agricultural Land Resources

Productivity and size are two important aspects of a community's agricultural resource. Potential productivity for traditional agricultural activities can be determined through a review of agricultural land: slope, available water, soil particle size, amount of organic matter, depth of root zone, permeability of soils, depth to groundwater table, and length of growing season. Productivity can be judged by comparison to an indicator crop or use of an agricultural lands rating system. Size of the land also may be important for agricultural purposes. Some crops and farming practices require the use of large equipment or other management practices that can govern optimal size for a farm unit.

Cultural Features

Cultural features include historical, architectural, and archaeological structures and sites. They may also include sites that have no historical importance but have local interest. Cultural features and sites may include a building, a group of buildings, natural features (such as an Indian mound), trails, gardens, cemeteries, old farms, and stagecoach routes. Review of cultural features and sites can lead to a decision about preservation but may also be useful in decisions about whether to adapt a significant site to recreation, education, or economic objectives. Determining the relative significance of cultural features should partly depend on the community's vision of itself.

Geographic Setting and Soils

The topography, drainage patterns, soil characteristics, mineral deposits, and other geological features of a community can influence and be influenced by a whole variety of activities within the community. Geological and geographical considerations affect community aesthetics, wildlife habitat, economic resources, location of roads, soil erosion, surface water runoff, and many other land use factors. Geology also affects the community water supply.

Understanding the geographic setting involves mapping watersheds and subsurface geology and their drainage patterns, and geological phenomena such as outcrops, bluffs, cliffs, glacial features, sand dunes, and caves for their significance from both aesthetic and wildlife habitat perspectives and identifying local rock types and deposits.

Human Health/Environmental Hazards

Air quality, water quality, climate, and noise issues are now considered when assessing natural resources. Air quality concerns are part of the landscape no matter where you live in the United States. Urban areas are at greatest risk of noncompliance with air standard regulations. Pesticide use and other agricultural activities in rural areas, construction, nonmetallic mining, and vehicle exhaust, however, all contribute to air pollution.

Careful monitoring of community human health categories is needed to ensure fair distribution of community businesses or services that have an impact on local air, water, or noise quality. Although a site may be ideal for location of a business, factory, or highway in economic terms, it may not be ideal in ecological terms: A change in local air, water, or noise may have an impact on the health of surrounding human, plant, or animal communities.

Plant Communities

Natural vegetation provides local scenery and contributes to the quality of life in the community. Vegetation is also significant for the role it plays in the ecology of the area and maintaining adequate water supply. Ecological interactions include soil quality, wildlife habitat, nutrient cycling, and climate impacts. Presence or absence of vegetation and the type of vegetation affect the ability of the land to absorb water and to conserve soil and nutrients. Identifying current plant communities and evaluating their aesthetic, recreational, ecological, and conservation impacts assists communities in discovering where change should be encouraged and where it should be avoided. The character of plant communities can be summarized by reviewing such qualities as size, frequency of occurrence, diversity, fragility, significance, plant community/species types, age of plants, canopy cover and openings, density of plant stands, signs of physical or insect damage, and location in relation to other features.

Wildlife and Wildlife Habitat

Wildlife includes turtles, snakes, salamanders, frogs, toads, fish, birds of prey, songbirds, waterfowl, and insects. All need a natural resources habitat appropriate to their food, resting, mating, and shelter needs. The amount and characteristics of the habitat space varies from animal to animal. Birds and animals travel along "corridors" of habitat that also include flight paths. For some species, these "corridor" habitats are also vital to their survival. Undisturbed areas have many benefits for the community as well as the wildlife, such as education, nature study, outdoor enjoyment, and comparative information.

Surface Water Resources/Water Supply

Surface water resources are integral to numerous natural systems. They replenish atmospheric water lost in precipitation and accept surface runoff. Plant and animal ecosystems are dependent on a certain quality, temperature, rate of flow, and volume of water. Lakes, rivers, and streams are a source of drinking water for humans; a source of water supply for agriculture, industry, and tourism; an avenue for transportation and waste disposal (industrial, agricultural, utility, sewer, and urban runoff); and a source of recreation and passive enjoyment.

Evaluation of surface water features considers alteration of lakes, rivers, or streams as a result of human activity; scarcity of quality surface water; water resource hazards, such as flooding; and resource sensitivity, such as areas where increased shoreland development would be incompatible or would degrade the water resource and its accompanying role in the natural system.

Groundwater/Water Supply

Agriculture and many other industries depend heavily on large supplies of high-quality groundwater. For small communities and rural homes, groundwater is the only economical source of high-quality water for domestic use. For example, in rural areas nitrogen and phosphorus can affect water quality. Quality and availability of groundwater can vary locally, on a site-to-site basis, depending on the specific geologic and hydrologic conditions of the area. Groundwater is sensitive to local contamination, depending on pollutant characteristics and soil permeability. Once present in groundwater, pollutants travel with or through the groundwater, depending on their chemical characteristics.

The supply of groundwater is not infinite. It must be recharged through the hydrologic cycle: Precipitation percolates into the ground or enters the ground from surface water bodies. Poorly constructed wells, improper well spacing, and excessive pumping can lead to pronounced decreases in water storage, interference between wells, interchange of water between aquifers or basins, and interference with surface water levels. Evaluation of groundwater supplies should consider supply and uses, sensitivity and threats, and hazards.

Although we continue to improve our understanding of the components of natural systems and their potential benefits, we must still proceed with caution in local management decisions. We now know, for example, that wetlands serve important functions. Wetlands help to maintain water quality, reduce the chances of flooding, offer habitat for numerous species, and provide a source of water in dry years. In the past, soils present in wetland areas were valued primarily for their agricultural potential. Wetlands were often drained for the perceived economic benefit of crop sales. The loss of potential long-term economic and environmental benefits from water quality/quantity protection, aesthetic appeal, and recreation uses was ignored. Thus, decisions about a community's environmental capital can have both short- and long-term effects.

Land Use and Environmental Capital

Many human-related activities affect local environmental capital. Below, we examine two distinct problems that can affect a community's environmental capital. One problem, which exists on the fringes of urban America, is called sprawl. The other problem, which exists in central cities and other locations of the United States, is vacant land resulting from deindustrialization and depopulation of central cities. Two important issues involving vacant land are abandoned buildings and brownfields. In the next few sections, we will define and discuss these terms and examine how CBOs are addressing these issues.

| BOX 9.1 | **Sprawl Facts** |

- As of 1998, approximately 4.7 million acres of land—wetlands, wildlife habitat, ranches and farms, shorelines, forests, recreation land, and other property of ecological significance—had been protected by local and regional land trusts (Land Trust Alliance, 2001).

- From 1970 to 1990, Detroit's population shrank by 7%, but its urbanized area increased by 28%. Pittsburgh's population shrank 9% in the same period while its area increased by 30%. Chicago's population did increase between 1970 and 1990 by 1%, but meanwhile its urbanized area grew by 24%. Phoenix sprawl provides a similar picture: While its population grew 132% from 1970 to 1990, its urbanized area grew by a significant 91% (Sierra Club, 2001a).

- Sprawl-like development can use many more resources—five times more pipe and wire, five times as much heating and cooling energy—than urban living. Sprawl also costs us 35 times as much land, and it requires 15 times as much pavement as compact urban living (Sierra Club, 2001b).

- Between 1970 and 1990, more than 19 million acres of rural land were developed (Sierra Club, 1998).

Sprawl

Many people and organizations today argue that sprawl is one of the biggest threats to a community's environmental capital. Sprawl can be defined as low-density, often residential development on the fringe of or beyond the border of suburban development (Office of Technology Assessment, 1995). Existing laws and regulations, such as local land use planning efforts, have inadequately protected the natural environment (Daniels & Bowers, 1997).

Several factors contribute to sprawl. Zoning policies frequently discourage higher-density development and mixed-use development projects. Highway building provides an incentive for families to move to the suburbs and commute to their jobs. Housing policies such as federal programs that encourage middle-class home ownership have provided a powerful incentive for the growth of the suburbs. Competition for tax revenue among municipalities encourages businesses to move out to the suburbs, where the costs of doing business may be lower. Finally, social and economic conditions in the inner city, such as property values and concentrated poverty, may encourage less dense development.

What are the impacts of sprawl? There are several problems associated with sprawl. Many people point to the tendency for sprawl to contribute to a loss of a "sense of place" because the development looks the same across most communities. Sprawl means a loss of land, especially of prime farmland adjacent to cities. There continues to be concern

---

Characteristics of Sprawl

- Unlimited outward extension

- Low-density residential and commercial settlements

- Leapfrog development

- Fragmentation of powers over land use among many small localities

- Dominance of transportation by private automotive vehicles

- No centralized planning or control of land uses

- Widespread strip commercial development

- Great fiscal disparities among localities

- Segregation of types of land uses in different zones

- Reliance mainly on the trickle-down or filtering process to provide housing to low-income households

SOURCE: PlannersWeb (2000).

---

that sprawl increases costs to local government because services must be provided over a larger area rather than to more dense settlement. Sprawl increases auto dependence and associated fuel consumption, which contributes to air pollution and other environmental problems. Outward expansion of cities tends to lead to abandonment of the inner city, which tends to create greater racial segregation. Finally, sprawl has been found to contribute to the loss of wildlife habitat and wetlands (PlannersWeb, 1999).

There are several strategies to deal with sprawl, including creating a sense of place, preserving open space and farmland, concentrating growth and investment, changing transportation strategies and priorities from automobile dependence, and establishing regional cooperation. Case Study 9.1 describes a growing practice of encouraging higher-density development.

Vacant Land

Due to deindustrialization and depopulation of central cities, thousands of structures and acres of land have been abandoned over the past 30 years. With this abandonment have come a number of problems for residents in these abandoned areas. The problems include visual blight, increased crime and safety issues for those left behind, lost tax revenue, public expenditures related to demolition of buildings, and contaminated sites or brownfields.

Brownfields are especially a problem because of the cost and legal liability issues associated with cleanup. The Environmental Protection Agency (EPA) defined brownfields as sites with "actual or perceived contamination and an active potential for redevelopment or reuse" (National Congress for Community Economic Development [NCCED], 2000, p. 1). "The General Accounting Office estimates that there are any-

Cluster Development

When the Lowcountry Open Land Trust received a conservation easement on the 314-acre former cotton plantation located on Wadmalaw Island and known as Oakhart, the family agreed to cluster a development of no more than seven houses on a 30-acre area, leaving more than 85% of the farm permanently undeveloped and available for forestry, agriculture, and recreational uses. Existing zoning regulations would have allowed construction of approximately 70 houses. The conservation easement is the 15th received by the Lowcountry Open Land Trust on Wadmalaw Island, bringing the land conserved there to more than 2,500 acres. Lowcountry Open Land Trust has conserved more than 18,800 acres of open space on the coast of South Carolina.

SOURCE: Land Trust Alliance (1999b).

where from 130,000 to 425,000 vacant industrial properties across the country" (NCCED, 2000, p. 1). To make these brownfield sites more attractive to developers, the federal and state governments have created programs that limit liability and mitigate risk and costs of cleanup.

At the federal level, a number of programs create incentives for redeveloping brownfields. These include the General Service Administration's Brownfield Redevelopment Initiative; the Treasury Department's Brownfields Tax Incentive; the EPA's grant monies and pilot projects, national annual conferences, and guidelines for state voluntary cleanups; the U.S. Department of Housing and Urban Development's Community Development Block Grant program and Brownfields Economic Development Initiative; and the Economic Development Administration's Technical Assistance, Economic Adjustment, and Public Works Programs. Incentives also are provided through the Community Reinvestment Act. In addition, 32 state governments have voluntary cleanup programs.

For local governments, the goal is to physically redevelop these areas to similar densities to what they had before. Community development corporations (CDCs) that operate in such neighborhoods or areas often are focused on physical development too, producing safe and affordable housing, retail projects, and industrial parks. CDCs throughout the country are addressing brownfields sites in a number of ways (see Case Studies 9.2 and 9.3).

The Roles of Government and the Market

Environmental capital has been addressed primarily through debates about who should have control over natural resources—the government, individuals, or corpora-

Vacant Land and Brownfields: The Facts

- Philadelphia—15,800 parcels of vacant land and 27,000 vacant structures

- New Orleans—14,000 vacant lots

- Chicago—70,000 vacant lots

- Milwaukee—2,500 acres of vacant land, 4 square miles, or 4% of total land area

- St. Louis—13,000 tax-delinquent parcels, 1,200 acres, or 3% of total land area

- Trenton, New Jersey—900 acres or 18% of total land area

- Detroit—46,000 city-owed vacant parcels, 24,000 empty buildings

- Twenty-eight states now have brownfields redevelopment programs to clean up abandoned and often polluted industrial sites.

- Every dollar of public money spent for a brownfields development effort leveraged an average $2.48 in private sector funds.

SOURCE: Sierra Club (1999).

Brownfields Projects in Trenton, New Jersey

Isles, Inc., a Trenton, New Jersey, CDC focuses on four areas: urban greening and land recovery, environmental education, affordable housing, and job training. Isles is cooperating with the city of Trenton and the New Jersey Department of Environmental Protection to reclaim abandoned industrial facilities, beginning with the seven-acre former Magic Marker site and redevelopment of an abandoned battery-manufacturing site. Isles is bringing together area residents, government, and technical assistants to help clean up the site, plan its reuse, and participate in its redevelopment while educating young people about this important New Jersey issue. Isles' Brownfields Restoration Program collaborates in three communities with Rutgers University, the New Jersey Institute of Technology, and the Department of Environmental Protection. Isles has linked the problems of brownfields with job training by establishing a nationally recognized program by training residents through an accredited curriculum in Geographic Information Systems.

SOURCE: U.S. Environmental Protection Agency (1995).

CASE STUDY 9.3

Brownfields Projects in Chicago

In Chicago, three CDCs have undertaken brownfields projects. Bethel New Life has cleaned up two sites in preparation for development and is identifying the most reusable properties in its neighborhood. Bethel has linked its work in brownfields to job training and placement and economic development. The Greater Southwest Development Corporation (GSDC) has redeveloped the former site of a dry cleaners and movie theater. A fast-food restaurant is now on the site. GSDC is examining a second site for possible use as an industrial park. Finally, the Chicago Association of Neighborhood Development Organizations is a citywide network that operates a Brownfield Initiative that focuses on organizational capacity of CDCs located in empowerment zones.

SOURCE: National Congress for Community Economic Development (2000).

tions operating in the free market—and what are the best ways to maintain, conserve, and protect those resources—manage, regulate, or buy and sell.

The Government

Daniel Mazmanian and Michael Kraft (1999) identified three environmental epochs. The first epoch, from the early 1970s to the early 1980s, was characterized by command-and-control regulation. The aim during this period was to clean up the nation's polluted waterways, air, and land, at the same time protecting this nation's natural resources. Critics of this approach charged that it was costly, inefficient, inflexible, reliant on remedial measures rather than preventive actions, complex in its rule-making process, cumbersome, and adversarial and that it used a piecemeal approach (Mazmanian & Kraft, 1999, p. 4). There seems to be a consensus, however, that this approach did make large strides toward cleaning up environmental problems in the United States.

In the second epoch, business interests and others were very critical of this stringent regulatory approach and the overreliance on command-and-control regulation. This epoch, which began in the 1980s and extended into the 1990s, shifted to a more market-based approach that was flexible and used incentive-based techniques, was cost-efficient, and shifted responsibilities for compliance and enforcement to the state and local levels.

The third epoch, beginning in the 1990s, emphasizes sustainability. The ultimate responsibility for regulating and managing the natural resources lies with the local government; the federal government acts as a guiding force and as oversight. In this epoch, public/private partnerships and local/regional collaborations are the predominant organizational means of implementing community sustainability objectives (Mazmanian & Kraft, 1999, pp. 10-12). (See Box 9.4 on goals of the EPA.)

BOX 9.4 **EPA's National Goals**

- Clean air

- Clean and safe water

- Safe food

- Preventing pollution and reducing risk in communities, homes, workplaces, and ecosystems

- Better waste management, restoration of contaminated waste sites, and emergency response

- Reduction of global and cross-border environmental risks

- Expansion of Americans' right to know about their environment

- Sound science, improved understanding of environmental risk, and greater innovation to address environmental problems

- A credible deterrent to pollution and greater innovation to address environmental problems

- Effective management

SOURCE: U.S. Environmental Protection Agency (2000).

As this third epoch evolves, the federal government continues to approach natural resources in two fundamental ways: management and regulation. The agencies that take a management approach fall under the Departments of the Interior and Agriculture and include the Forest Service, the Bureau of Land Management, and the National Park Service. Under these agencies and a few others, the federal government owns about 630 million acres or about one third of the land area of the United States. These agencies manage environmental resources for timber, grazing, minerals, and recreation. Generally, they manage large tracts of land that are generally located in the western United States and are beyond community boundaries. Thus, communities concerned with their local environmental resources do not turn to these agencies except in specific circumstances. For example, the Urban and Community Forestry program of the Forest Service is involved with education and creating partnerships to assist communities in planting and/or managing urban forests.

The regulatory approach is exemplified in the work of the EPA. The EPA was established in 1970 as a regulatory and enforcement agency. Some of the more well-known environmental laws under its jurisdiction are the Clean Air Act, the Clean Water Act, the Endangered Species Act, the National Environmental Policy Act, and the Occupational Safety and Health Act. The agency has shifted to acting as an environmental watchdog, making sure that specific industrial plants are not polluting and that local governments in large metropolitan area, such as Los Angeles, are implementing plans to clean up their air. When it comes to assisting communities that are interested in preserving their local natural resources, the EPA also acts as an educator, a facilitator, and a technical resource. Thus, the EPA encourages local governments and CBOs to create ways to protect their environmental resources.

The Market

In contrast to the federal or state governments attempting to preserve the environment, the market could be left to operate unregulated (Gordon & Richardson, 1997). Some argue that all environmental resources should be bought and sold like other commodities. The Cato Institute, for example, proposes that all federally owned lands should be auctioned off and that these lands would be better managed both financially and ecologically through the free market (Anderson, Smith, & Simmons, 1999). The free market, however, tends to favor short-term decisions and those that bring a profit to the individual. Because land is a commodity, under a free market system it is understood that it should be developed to its highest and best use (Ewing, 1997).

Under this scenario, the most expensive land markets are in downtown central business districts, and land prices decrease as one moves away from the center. It is relatively easy to value land in terms of its development potential, but valuing lands such as wetlands, prairie, and forests in terms of their unique environmental or aesthetic attributes is far more difficult. Economists are trying to understand the value of natural resources through a variety of techniques. Environmental groups, however, generally object to the notion that natural resources can have values (prices) established for them.

In this section, we have argued that neither the government nor the market is adequate to the task of addressing environmental capital in communities. Generally, the government, particularly both federal and state governments, operates at a level that does not take into account community-level natural resources. They are too small to manage, and sometimes are too small to regulate, even though a particular natural resource may be an important asset to a community. The market also has difficulty with accounting for natural resources for their environmental value rather than their monetary value, so the market cannot be trusted to manage a community's environmental assets.

Within the present institutional setting, sprawl will continue if not actually be promoted, and with less financial support from federal and state governments, other organizations need to fill the gap to conserve and preserve natural resources. Land trusts and CDCs are two types of organizations that are concerned with their community's environmental capital. In the next section, we examine how CBOs represent an alternative to government and to the market in managing, conserving, and preserving environmental assets.

Community-Based Organizations

Among the organizations that are interested in protecting a community's environmental capital and dealing with sprawl are CBOs, such as CDCs and community land trusts. For the most part, environmental organizations in the United States have taken the lead in addressing concerns over the conservation, preservation, or degradation of natural resources. Many national environmental organizations, such as the Sierra Club, the

Audubon Society, and the Nature Conservancy, have local chapters that address local concerns or issues. But local chapters of national organizations may not always have place as their chief concern; the larger organization and its interests may matter more. We are interested in CBOs that are rooted in a place, are supported by residents, and have as their missions a focus on the community as a geographic entity.

Specific issues become important to communities for a variety of reasons. In this next section, we address debates on two problems, sprawl and abandonment of land (e.g., brownfields) and buildings, that are taking place simultaneously; but sprawl is occurring primarily at the intersection between urban and rural places, and abandonment of land and buildings is occurring primarily within cities. Although we can find sprawl occurring on the outskirts of small rural communities in counties that are experiencing rapid growth and we can find brownfields in rural areas, these two phenomena occur mostly in suburbs and inner cities.

CBOs in such places as Detroit, Michigan; Atlanta, Georgia; Ventura, California; Houston, Texas; Racine, Wisconsin; Jefferson Parish, Louisiana; Oakland, California; and St. Louis, Missouri, are coming up with ways to deal with sprawl, vacant land, and brownfields while preserving the natural environment. One particularly popular organization is the community land trust.

What Is a Community Land Trust?

A land trust is a nonprofit, voluntary organization that works with landowners to protect land, usually open space and green space. Land trusts use a variety of techniques to protect land, such as conservation easements. The first land trust was created in Massachusetts in 1891. According to the Land Trust Alliance (1999a), as of 1999 there were more than 1,200 land trusts in the United States. In 1985, there were only 743.

Some of the diverse purposes of these organizations are to protect open space and green places threatened by sprawl and development, save individual landowners money, protect local quality of life, create affordable housing, and ensure a safe, reliable, and affordable food supply. Local land trusts have protected over 4.7 million acres, and national land trusts have protected an additional 13 million acres of forests, wetlands, farmland, and greenways (Fisher & MacDowell, 1999). Increasingly, land trusts are used to purchase and develop brownfields. Because individual developers are not likely to take the risk in investing in these projects, land trusts can overcome some of the obstacles to developing the community.

Land trusts vary in their size, scope, mission, staff (volunteers or experts), boards of directors, and membership. They receive funds from members, land donors, other nonprofits, government agencies, foundations, and corporate partners (Fisher & MacDowell, 1999).

What Do Land Trusts Do?

A land trust "works to conserve land by undertaking or assisting land transactions with landowners in order to permanently protect the natural, scenic, agricultural, historic or cultural attributes of their land" (Fisher & MacDowell, 1999, p. 1). Land trusts accomplish this objective by obtaining some degree of legal control over the land. Com-

---

| BOX 9.5 | **Examples of Kinds of Land Protected by Land Trusts** |

- Wetlands
- Wildlife habitats
- Ranches
- Shorelines
- Forests
- Scenic views
- Farms
- Watersheds
- Historic estates
- Recreational areas

SOURCE: Land Trust Alliance (1999a).

---

munity land trusts typically acquire and hold land but sell off any residential or commercial buildings that are on the land. In this way, the cost of land in the housing equation is minimized or eliminated, thus making the housing more affordable (Peterson, 1996, p. 11).

Land trusts face four challenges in their operations: raising funds; educating landowners about the financial benefits of land preservation; assisting communities in creating land protection strategies; and selecting the "right" projects (Daniels & Bowers, 1997). Several regional and national organizations have been established to help land trusts address these challenges.

The primary tool used by land trusts is the conservation easement. This tool coincides with the general organizational philosophy of a voluntary approach to land management (Daniels & Bowers, 1997). Other tools advocated by land trusts to landowners to preserve their land include an outright donation to the land trust; bequest or donation of conservation easements; or sale of land at below-market value.

A conservation easement is a legal agreement by a landowner to permanently protect open space. The first conservation easement was prepared by Frederick Law Olmstead, Sr., in the 1880s to protect parkways in and around Boston (Land Trust Alliance, 1999a). The Tax Reform Act of 1976 explicitly recognized conservation easements as tax-deductible donations. As of 1999, all states have enabling legislation in place for conservation easements. Conservation easements can be legally complex and if not done well can be challenged in court successfully. Land trusts that accept land through a conservation easement should be prepared to enforce it. There are also agricultural conservation easements that are designed to protect farmland. These types of conservation easements are important in that they keep farmland in agricultural use and productivity (American Farmland Trust, 1999). (See Case Studies 9.4 to 9.8.)

CASE STUDY 9.4

Buying a Conservation Easement or Saving Farmland Forever

The Wisconsin Farmland Conservancy, dedicated to keeping farming alive in northwestern Wisconsin, helped to raise $30,000 in 1997 to buy a conservation easement on the 40-acre, community-supported Common Harvest Farm near Osceola, near the growing Minneapolis-St. Paul, Minnesota, corridor. The money ensured that Dan Guenthner and Margaret Pennings, who had been tenant farmers on five farms consumed by sprawl over the past decade, would be able to farm as long as they wished. The conservation easement guarantees that the land will be protected as a farm forever.

SOURCE: Land Trust Alliance (1999a).

CASE STUDY 9.5

Bequeathing Land

Lamenting that neighboring farms with views of the Smoky Mountains are quickly being transformed into cookie-cutter subdivisions, Jim and Gail Harris instead wrote their wills to bequeath their 400-acre farm near Knoxville to the Foothills Land Conservancy. The conservancy accepted a revocable trust on the farm, which land trust officials estimate will be worth several million dollars by the time it passes on to the conservancy. Then the Foothills Land Conservancy will either maintain or lease the farm or permanently protect it with a conservation easement before selling it.

SOURCE: Land Trust Alliance (1999a).

Why do people choose to use land trusts? For some people, saving specific pieces of land is important for what that land and the uses on it contribute to the community. For example, in New York City, Mayor Rudolph Giuliani planned to auction 115 lots throughout the city where community gardens had been functioning. The Trust for Public Land and the New York Restoration Project purchased the land to preserve the community gardens (Enzer, 1999). Other people donate a conservation easement or bequeath land to a land trust because they have a special connection to their piece of property and want it to remain undeveloped.

Do land trusts work? If someone donates a conservation easement, will it be enforced? First, if the amount of land is any indication of success, the Land Trust Alliance (1999a) has estimated that 4.7 million acres of land are being protected through

---

CASE STUDY 9.6

Donating a Conservation Easement

Having spent 25 years assembling parcels that became an 1,100-acre ranch of native mixed conifers just an hour's drive from Spokane, Washington, Steve Wilson, a retired firefighter, was unwilling to see it lost as open space. His solution was to donate a conservation easement to Pacific Forest Trust. The easement will permanently protect the land while permitting the landowner to manage it to restore native forest species. Today, the forest is home to waterfowl and moose and serves as a forage area for the threatened northern goshawk as well as the great blue heron.

SOURCE: Land Trust Alliance (1999a).

CASE STUDY 9.7

Use of Sales Tax to Buy a Conservation Easement

Using funds from a 1% sales tax that Gunnison County, Colorado, voters passed in 1997, as well as donations from area businesses and other sources, the Gunnison Ranchland Conservation Legacy by last December had helped place conservation easements on six ranches, permanently protecting 3,500 acres. Within the next 6 months, the land trust expects to complete 11 more projects, protecting an additional 6,000 acres. Ultimately, the fledgling land trust hopes to complete conservation easement agreements, to be held by organizations such as the Colorado Cattlemen's Agricultural Land Trust, on much of the 65,000 acres of prime ranch land in the county. Already, the land trust's Ranchland Protection Program, which purchases development rights from willing landowners, has protected a 12-mile ribbon along Tomichi Creek.

SOURCE: Land Trust Alliance (1999a).

---

land trusts. This figure is relatively small and covers only some of the most threatened land. Second, many of these organizations and the key tool they use, conservation easements, are relatively new. Recently, easement violations have sent land trusts to court in an effort to protect conservation easements. Biondo (1997) predicted that as protected land changes hands, land trusts will find themselves with legal expenses and possibly in court. According to her, enforcement of easements will be the true test of whether land trusts will be considered successful in their mission. Thus, for many land trusts it is too

---

Bargain Sale

Determined to ensure that their 222-acre Hamilton Cove property on the Bold Coast remained open space forever, the Bohlen family of Lubec offered the property as a "bargain sale," below fair market value, to Maine Coast Heritage Trust, a statewide land trust, which already owned the adjacent 154-acre property. Together, the properties formed the Hamilton Cove Preserve, the land trust's third preserve on Maine's renowned Bold Coast. The cove, open to the public for low-impact recreation, provides diverse habitats for moose, bobcats, coyote, migratory hawks, and breeding merlins and harriers; and the rare purple crowberry grows along its windswept ledges.

SOURCE: Land Trust Alliance (1999a).

---

early to tell whether they can be considered successful because the original owner who made the conservation easement continues to enjoy the land.

Given the amount and types of land that are protected through these tools, at this early stage land trusts can be considered successful in their limited, yet important purpose. Land trusts have had only a marginal impact on development processes because they control such a small amount of land. Yet there is a growing interest in using land trusts to preserve open space (as a result of development pressures) and to deal with abandoned property and structures in inner cities.

A growing number of land trusts are involved in brownfield redevelopment. Land trusts face several obstacles in these projects. The most difficult problem is the fear of legal liability. Federal legal liability is a result of the Comprehensive Environmental Response, Compensation and Liability Act (CERCLA)—usually referred to as the Superfund. Usually, landowners who did not know about the contamination are not legally responsible, but there can be cases where they will be held liable. Second, most land trusts lack funds for remediation costs. Finally, land trusts still face difficulty in finding end users for the land.

One of the most successful efforts by a land trust to acquire and own land that was a brownfield is the Dudley Street Initiative (see Case Study 1.1). The organization was able to receive the power of eminent domain from the city of Boston to acquire vacant land and buildings in their neighborhood. The land was eventually used for affordable housing projects. Several intermediary organizations are emerging to deal with the financing needs of redevelopment of brownfields. The Louisville Land Bank Authority uses profits from the sale of remediated brownfields to fund new projects (Leigh, 2000). The state of Wisconsin also is establishing a fund to help local governments and nonprofits deal with some of the financial needs of redevelopment.

Summary and Conclusions

A community's environmental capital is diverse because it comprises the entire range of natural resources in a community, from water to air to land and more. Environmental capital is complex, both in how it operates within a community and in how to preserve, conserve, and use that capital appropriately and with care. Because of this diversity and complexity, this chapter has focused only on land and has touched on only a couple of issues, sprawl and brownfields, that can affect environmental capital in its entirety. Further, it has focused only on ways that one kind of CBO can address some of the concerns associated with sprawl and brownfields.

The federal government has refocused its approach to managing and regulating natural resources and is acting as a technical resource and as enforcement oversight rather than a top-down command-and-control regulator. The market, or private sector approaches, especially related to community environmental capital, are not acting to preserve or conserve specific natural resources, instead tending to use and possibly abuse them. Thus, as in other areas of communities, CBOs are becoming an alternative organizational means of accomplishing community environmental goals.

KEY CONCEPTS

Aesthetic qualities	Environmental capital	Point and nonpoint source
Amenities	Environmental racism	pollution
Brownfields	Geographic setting	Regulatory approach
Command-and-control	Groundwater	Sprawl
regulation	Land trust	Surface water
Conservation easement	Management approach	Wetlands
Cultural features	Natural resources	Wildlife

QUESTIONS

1. Name three problems that can threaten a community's environmental capital.

2. Why are natural resources or the environment used in conjunction with the term capital? Is this a contradiction?

3. Why are CBOs an appropriate organizational level for dealing with a community's environmental capital?

4. What is sprawl? What causes sprawl? What are some strategies to deal with sprawl?

5. What is a brownfield? What are three causes of brownfields?

EXERCISES

1. Find out if there is a land trust organization in your community. What does it do? What kind of land has it preserved? How did the land trust do it? What kinds of tools did it use?

2. Are there any brownfields or abandoned buildings in your community? If there are, what is being done to redevelop them? Have any brownfields been redeveloped in your community in the past? How was it done? Which organizations were involved? Did any CBOs get involved?

3. What are the forms of environmental capital in your community? Is any organization taking care of parts of it? What is that organization doing? How successful is it in conserving or preserving environmental capital?

REFERENCES

American Farmland Trust. (1999). Good deals: Colorado farm hedges out sprawl. *LandWorks Connection, 11*(2), 5-6.

Anderson, T. L., Smith, V. L., & Simmons, E. (1999). *How and why to privatize federal lands* (Report No. 363). Washington, DC: Cato Institute.

Biondo, B. (1997, Winter). Dealing with conservation easement violations. *Exchange: The Journal of the Land Trust Alliance, 16,* 206-209.

Bullard, R. D. (1994). *Dumping in Dixie: Race, class and environmental quality* (2nd ed.). Boulder, CO: Westview.

Daniels, T. L., & Bowers, D. (1997). *Holding our ground: Protecting America's farms and farmland.* Washington, DC: Island.

Enzer, M. (1999). Land trust, actress save NYC community gardens. *American Forests, 105*(2), 11.

Ewing, R. (1997). Is Los Angeles-style sprawl desirable? *Journal of the American Planning Association, 63*(1), 107-126.

Ferguson, R. F., & Dickens, W. T. (Eds.). (1999). *Urban problems and community development.* Washington, DC: Brookings Institution.

Fisher, J., & MacDowell, M. (1999). *Land trusts: A new strategy for private lands conservation in Latin America.* Arlington, VA: Nature Conservancy.

Gordon, P., & Richardson, H. W. (1997). Are compact cities a desirable planning goal? *Journal of the American Planning Association, 63*(1), 95-106.

Kretzmann, J. P., & McKnight, J. L. (1993). *Building communities from the inside out: A path toward finding and mobilizing a community's assets.* Evanston, IL: Northwestern University, Center for Urban Affairs and Policy Research.

Land Trust Alliance. (1999a). *Land trusts: The front guards of land protection.* Washington, DC: Author. <www.lta.org/whatlt.html>

Land Trust Alliance. (1999b). Land trusts succeed every day. <www.lta.org/feature.html>

Land Trust Alliance. (2001). About land trusts: National Land Trust Census. 1990s bring surge in land conservation. <www.lta.org/aboutlt/census.shtml>

Leigh, N. G. (2000, September). Promoting more equitable brownfield redevelopment. *Land Lines,* pp. 1-3.

Mazmanian, D. A., & Kraft, M. E. (1999). The three epochs of the environmental movement. In D. A. Mazmanian & M. E. Kraft (Eds.), *Toward sustainable communities: Transition and transformations in environmental policy* (pp. 3-41). Cambridge, MA: MIT Press.

National Congress for Community Economic Development. (2000). *Brownfield resources.* Washington, DC: Author. <www.ncced.org/breakingnews/geninfo/brownfield.html>

Office of Technology Assessment. (1995). *The technological reshaping of metropolitan America* (OTA-ETI-643). Washington, DC: Government Printing Office.

Peterson, T. (1996, Summer). Community land trusts: An introduction. *Planning Commissioner's Journal, 23,* 10.

PlannersWeb. (1999). *Problems associated with sprawl.* Burlington, VT: Author. <www.plannersweb.com/sprawl/problems.html>

PlannersWeb. (2000). How do you define sprawl? <www.plannersweb.com/sprawl/define.html>

Sierra Club. (1998). Sprawl: The dark side of the American dream. <www.sierraclub.org/sprawl/report98/introtext.html>

Sierra Club. (1999). *The costs and consequences of urban sprawl.* San Francisco: Author. <www.sierraclub.org/transportation/sprawl/report99>

Sierra Club. (2001a). A complex relationship: Population growth and suburban sprawl. <www.sierraclub.org/sprawl/population.asp>

Sierra Club. (2001b). Costs of sprawl. <www.sierraclub.org/sprawl/community/costs.asp>

U.S. Environmental Protection Agency, Urban and Economic Policy Division; CONCERN, Inc.; Community Sustainability Resource Institute; Jobs and Environment Campaign. (1995, September). Sustainability in action: Profiles of community initiatives across the United States. <www.sustainable.org/casestudies/newjersey/NJ_epa_isles.html>

U.S. Environmental Protection Agency. (2000). EPA's national goals for protecting public health and the environment. <www.epa.gov/history/org/origins/goals.htm>

ADDITIONAL SUGGESTED READINGS

Readings ■

Daniels, T. L., Keller, J. W., & Lapping, M. B. (1995). *The small town planning handbook* (2nd ed.). Chicago: American Planning Association.

McHarg, I. L. (1971). *Design with nature.* New York: Doubleday.

Sargent, F. O., Lusk, P., Rivera, J., & Varela, M. (1991). *Rural environmental planning for sustainable communities.* Washington, DC: Island.

U.S. Environmental Protection Agency. (1997). *Community-based environmental protection: A resource book for protecting ecosystems and communities* (EPA 230-B-96-003). Washington, DC: Author.

White, K., & Matthei, C. (1987). Community land trusts. In S. T. Bruyn & J. Meehan (Eds.), *Beyond the market and the state: New directions in community development* (pp. 41-64). Philadelphia: Temple University Press.

Web Sites ■

American Community Gardening Association (ACGA). <www.communitygarden.org>. ACGA has a guidebook on starting community gardens, holds an annual conference, and has an annual newletter, *Community Gardening Review.*

American Farmland Trust. <www.farmland.org>. This organization's mission is to work to stop the loss of productive farmland and to promote farming practices that lead to a healthy environment. The site includes a current legislative agenda, conferences, tools and resources, and an on-line store with a publications section.

Council for Urban Economic Development. <www.cued.org>. This site provides information on brownfields and many other issues pertinent to economic development.

EPA-U.S. Environmental Protection Agency-Green Communities. <www.epa.gov/greenkit/>. This site provides a step-by-step guide for planning and implementing sustainable actions. It provides a multitude of information on tools, resources (financial, data, and other), and case studies.

EPA Software. Planning for Small Communities. <www.epa.gov/seahome/trilogy.html>. This program offers a complete one-stop introduction to a wide range of environment issues and decisions that affect small and medium-sized communities. It offers communities the chance to judge their own needs and preferences and to make informed decisions on their own.

Humane Society of the U.S. Wildlife Land Trust. <www.wlt.org/>. This land trust works with landowners to protect wild animals in their natural habitats.

Land Trust Alliance. <www.lta.org/>. The Land Trust Alliance promotes voluntary land conservation and strengthens the land trust movement by providing the leadership, information, skills, and resources that land trusts need to conserve land for the benefit of communities and natural systems.

Smart Growth Network. <www.smartgrowth.org/index2.html>. This Web site provides comprehensive information on smart growth activities and databases.

Sprawl Watch Clearinghouse. <www.sprawlwatch.org>. The Sprawl Watch Clearinghouse mission is to make the tools, techniques, and strategies developed to manage growth accessible to citizens, grassroots organizations, environmentalists, public officials, planners, architects, the media, and business leaders.

Trust for Public Land. <www.tpl.org>. This is a national land trust organization working to preserve land, open space, gardens, greenways, and riverways.

Urban Land Institute. <www.uli.org/indexJS.htm>. This organization's primary interest is in land use policy and real estate development. It publishes many useful publications, such as *Urban Land and Smart Growth.* It conducts many useful workshops and conferences on a variety of land use and real estate issues.

U.S. Department of Agriculture Natural Resources Conservation Service. <www.wi.nrcs.usda.gov/>. On this site, you can find "how-to" information on backyard conservation and conservation buffers.

Videos ■

Homes and Hands: Community Land Trusts in Action (1998), produced by Women's Educational Media, directed by Helen S. Cohen and Debra Chasnoff. Available from the Institute for Community Economics, 57 School Street, Springfield, MA 01105-1331; phone (413) 746-8660.

Ours to Decide (1999), produced and directed by Dorrie Brooks. Available from Shebang Media, 710 Woodward Drive, Madison, WI 53704 or e-mail shebang@execpc.com or see www.execpc.com/7Eshebang.

Laid to Waste (1997), produced and directed by Robert Bahar and George McCollough. Provides an excellent case study of a community fighting against a hazardous waste site. Available from University of California Extension, Center for Media and Independent Learning, 2000 Center Street, CA 94704.

PART III

Contributions of Community Development to Sustainability and International Development

CHAPTER 10

Community Sustainability

Originally a concept from ecology, sustainability has several definitions. In this chapter, we define key concepts and debates that pertain to community sustainability, examine where the idea originated and how it is used, and assess the role of community-based organizations (CBOs) in pursuing community sustainability. We evaluate how communities are attempting to build sustainability into their development strategies and the types of indicators that communities are using to address their progress.

Sustainability can be viewed as a concept, a method, and even a way of life. It allows communities to sort through development options and arrive at a strategy that takes into consideration the full range of economic, environmental, and social characteristics of a community (Beatley & Manning, 1997; Maser, 1997; Roelofs, 1996; Roseland, 1994; Sargent, Lusk, Rivera, & Varela, 1991; Van der Ryn & Calthorpe, 1986). The drive toward sustainable communities results from a host of problems such as rapid global population growth, global warming, species extinction, ozone depletion, widespread hunger and starvation, and deforestation. At a local level in the United States, the loss of farmland and open space, solid waste crises, crime, and widening income disparities are another set of problems driving the community sustainability movement.

What Is Community Sustainability?

To discuss sustainability, a vague term, it is useful to make the term relative to something else. Table 10.1 provides a series of indicators of unsustainability at the global, national (U.S.), and local levels. At the global level, the indicators address issues such as species extinction, soil degradation, and depletion of fisheries. At a local level, unsustainability is marked by sprawl, racial and economic segregation, and depletion and degradation of natural resources, to name a few features. Sustainability should be unsustainability's opposite. The section will provide some of the concepts with which to elaborate the idea of sustainability.

Three important dimensions of community, referred to as the three E's in the literature, underlie sustainability: economics, environment, and equity, or social justice. Each of these dimensions needs to be in balance for sustainability to be achieved. For example, if the economic dimension is too strong, it can create disparities in income or overuse of a particular animal or plant (e.g., overfishing the cod in New England). From a systems perspective, these three dimensions operate in complex ways and call

---

BOX 10.1 **Global Problems**

THE NATURAL WORLD

The Earth's natural ecosystems have declined by about 33% since 1970, with humans as the main cause of this depletion (World Wildlife Fund, 2000).

RAIN FORESTS

"The world's rainforests represent 3.4 million square miles of tropical forest. Almost two acres of tropical rainforest disappear every second" (Rainforest Site, 2000).

ENDANGERED SPECIES

"At present rates of extinction, as much as a third of the world's species could be gone in the next 20 years" (World Wildlife Fund, 2001).

TABLE 10.1
Indicators of
Unsustainability

Global	Local
Global warming	Suburban sprawl
Soil degradation	Segregation/unequal opportunity
Deforestation	Loss of agricultural land and open space
Species extinction	Depletion and degradation of groundwater resources
Declining fisheries	Traffic congestion and smog
Economic inequity	Disproportionate exposure to environmental hazards

SOURCE: James, Power, and Forrest (2000).

for cooperative functioning among individuals, communities, and institutions. As with any system that involves humans and a political process, there are compromises to be made. Advocates of sustainability believe that choices should be made to ensure that these three dimensions remain balanced (Berke & Kartez, 1995).

To understand community sustainability and these three dimensions more thoroughly, several other concepts are necessary. First, scale is an important part of sustainability. The now familiar adage "Think globally, act locally" addresses the idea of scale. To have an impact, to make a sustainable community, people must act locally while being aware of how their action can be felt at a broader scale, even globally. For example, many individual households recycle glass, plastics, and paper products, such as newspaper. These individual actions over time (and originally with lots of encouragement) spawned a recycling industry that in the Northeast alone is valued at $7 billion (Touart, 1998). Also, many issues can be acted on individually in your place of residence, such as protesting the development of a piece of land that contains a significant habitat for a rare butterfly. These local issues are important in the overall battle to halt species extinction due to human developments.

Sustainability is relevant at the local level for several reasons. First, the local level is where people and the natural environment interact most often and most directly. Second, local actions and strategies can often be the most effective at addressing environmental and social problems. Third, individuals live their lives in a particular place and can have an impact by altering how they consume and what they consume. Finally, in localities individuals and organizations produce things that are eventually used and consumed (Maser, 1997; Roseland 1994).

Although many actions can include political activism or organized efforts, perhaps individual actions can be considered even more important and more effective in the long run. Each person and family, through conscious choice, can simplify, self-provision to the extent possible (e.g., by gardening and canning), and recognize the impacts of actions on the local environment and surroundings. However, recognizing individual responsibility for local sustainable development does not preclude collective actions at the local level (Maser, 1997).

Though acting locally is important, so is acting for future generations. The concept of intergenerational equity is a key part of community sustainability. It means acting in a way so that the next generations are inheriting a healthy economy, environment, and society rather than the converse.

The following definition of community sustainability reflects the three E's, local scale, and to some degree intergenerational equity:

> Sustainable communities are cities and towns that prosper because people work together to produce a high quality of life that they want to sustain and constantly improve. They are communities that flourish because they build a mutually supportive, dynamic balance between social well-being, economic opportunity, and environmental quality. (President's Council on Sustainable Development, 1997, p. 3)

Case Study 10.1 shows the principles of sustainable development that one community adopted.

Because definitions of concepts can be vague, the box entitled "Sustainability" lists some characteristics of sustainability. The box also lists actions that are not sustainable. By understanding both sustainable and unsustainable activities, we can get a better handle on what sustainability is when we see it.

Daniel Mazmanian and Michael Kraft (1999) distinguished between strong and weak sustainability. Weak sustainability refers to passing on to future generations an "average capital stock." That means that the present and future generations do not further deplete resources. This type of sustainability is weak because many resources have been depleted far enough to be considered unsustainable and now need to regain vitality. Under this weak view, it is assumed that technological and other innovations can maintain sustainability. Thus, measures have been taken, for example, to control cod fishing in the ocean off New England because the cod fishery has been depleted to such an extent that the cod cannot reproduce themselves in large enough numbers to maintain a healthy population and be fished for human consumption. In contrast, strong sustainability refers to restoring certain critical ecological resources to higher levels

---

CASE STUDY 10.1

Burlington, Vermont: Principles of Sustainable Community Development

In Burlington, decision makers have embraced six principles of sustainable community development. They are:

1. Encourage economic self-sufficiency through local ownership and the maximum use of local resources.

2. Equalize the benefits and burdens of growth.

3. Leverage and recycle scarce public funds.

4. Protect and preserve fragile environmental resources.

5. Ensure full participation by populations normally excluded from the political and economic mainstream.

6. Nurture a robust "third sector" of private, nonprofit organizations capable of working in concert with government to deliver essential goods and services.

SOURCE: President's Council on Sustainable Development (1997).

---

rather than simply keeping them from deteriorating further. In this approach, critical resources should not be "averaged" over future generations. Such natural resources as the ozone layer are too important to treat the same as others. Each asset must be evaluated, and technological and other innovations should not be relied upon to achieve sustainability.

As the concepts of sustainability and community sustainability are put into practice, the definitions are becoming more grounded in reality. The next section discusses the history of sustainability.

The History of Sustainability

Where did the idea of community sustainability come from? Some claim that the Iroquois Nation believed in sustainability because of their law that required consideration of the impact of every decision over the next seven generations (Krizek & Power, 1996, p. 8). Lamont Hempel (1999) traced the sources of the sustainable communities movement to several major and a few minor sources based in the last 100 years. The box "Major Sources Influencing Community Sustainability" provides an evolutionary picture of the major intellectual threads that have influenced community sustainability.

One of the earliest sources dates to the late 19th century with the work of Ebenezer Howard and his Garden City Movement in England. His idea was to create cities with prominent greenbelts around them connected by rail. He was reacting to the growth of

---

| BOX 10.2 | **Sustainability** |

Activities are sustainable when they

- Use materials in continuous cycles
- Use continuously reliable sources of energy
- Come mainly from the qualities of being human (i.e., creativity, communication, coordination, appreciation, and spiritual and intellectual development)

Activities are not sustainable when they

- Require continual inputs of nonrenewable resources
- Use renewable resources faster than their rate of renewal
- Cause cumulative degradation of the environment
- Require resources in quantities that undermine other people's well-being
- Lead to the extinction of other life forms

SOURCE: From "Sustainability," <www.cyberus.ca/choose.sustain/sustain.html>, 2000. The Sustainability Project, Merriekville, Ontario, Canada. Reprinted with permission.

---

cities, particularly London, and their inability to provide adequate housing, physical infrastructure, and amenities for the people who migrated there during the period of industrialization. Others were similarly influenced. In 1915, Patrick Geddes, an architect and planner, stressed that urban design needed to integrate the natural world with how society was organized. Only a decade or so later, Lewis Mumford, another planner, founded and led the Regional Planning Association of America in the 1920s. Mumford believed in the unity of city and countryside and felt that regional planning, which for him emphasized an educative, grassroots process, was essential (Hempel, 1999). These early sources have influenced the community sustainability movement by emphasizing comprehensiveness, creating a link with the region, and stressing public participation.

The influences from the middle of the list are similar to these earlier ones in their alarm at the seemingly rapid environmental degradation occurring throughout the world, the many problems in urban areas, the trend toward more conspicuous consumption, and the decline in civic and voluntary activities. Many of these movements, such as Spaceship Earth, Limits to Growth, and deep ecology, were willing to abandon the present political, economic, and institutional frameworks within which society operates. In the more recent influences, the tone is far less alarmist and is working toward sustainability within the current political and economic system.

Before the term *sustainability* was coined, steady-state economics was pursued as an opposing paradigm to the dominant neoclassical economics paradigm. Steady-state

---

BOX 10.3   **Major Sources Influencing Community Sustainability**

- Garden City Movement, led by Ebenezer Howard
- Bioregional planning and design insights of Patrick Geddes, Ian McHarg, and the Regional Association of America
- American New Towns Movement (e.g., Reston, Virginia; Radburn, New Jersey; Columbia, Maryland) that began in the 1920s
- Grassroots communitarian movements in the late 1940s
- Great Society urban program of Lyndon Johnson in the 1960s
- The decline of faith in technological progress as a solution to urban problems
- Spaceship Earth idea
- "Limits to growth" arguments of the late 1960s and early 1970s
- Studies of the resilience of ecological communities
- Local self-reliance and appropriate technology movement of the 1970s and early 1980s
- Urban ecology and eco-city movements
- The strategic coupling of environment and development interests in the 1980s (e.g., the Brundtland Commission of 1987) and the 1990s (e.g., the Earth Summit of 1992 and Habitat II of 1996)
- The new urbanism; neotraditional towns and healthy cities
- Social capital debate of the 1990s, led by Robert Putnam and Amitai Etzioni
- Application of industrial ecology concepts, environmental audits, and sustainability indicators in the early 1990s by struggling communities attempting to recover from economic downturns and urban decay (e.g., Sustainable Chattanooga)

SOURCE: From "Conceptual and Analytical Challenges in Building Sustainable Communities," by L. C. Hempel, in *Toward Sustainable Communities: Transition and transformations in Environmental Policy,* edited by D. A. Mazmanian and M. E. Kraft, 1999 (pp. 43-74). Cambridge, MA: MIT Press. Copyright 1999 by MIT Press. Reprinted with permission.

---

economics, and its best known advocate, Herman Daly, proposed the idea that "enough is best" rather than "growth is best." In his work, Daly (1996) maintained that

> population growth and production growth must not push us beyond the sustainable environmental capacities of resource regeneration and waste absorption. There-

fore, once that point is reached, production and reproduction should be for replacement only. Physical growth should cease, while qualitative improvement continues. (p. 3)

The idea of sustainability began to gain ground and become part of mainstream thought beginning in the 1980s. But it was not until 1987, when the Brundtland Commission report, *Our Common Future,* was published, that sustainability entered the lexicon. The report focused on defining and operationalizing the idea of sustainable development (Krizek & Power, 1996, p. 10). It defined sustainable development as the ability to "meet the needs of the present without sacrificing the ability of the future to meet its needs" (Daly, 1996, p. 1). The Brundtland Commission examined two central questions: (a) Is it possible to increase the basic standard of living of the world's expanding population without unnecessarily depleting our natural resources and further degrading the environment upon which we all depend? (b) Can humanity collectively step back from the brink of environmental collapse and, at the same time, lift its poorest members up to the level of basic human health and dignity? (Krizek & Power, 1996, p. 10). This report was the first international policy document to address sustainability in a manner that linked the natural world with the human/economic world.

Several years later, at Earth Summit 1992, Agenda 21, which focused on both local and national sustainable development strategies, was conceived and agreed on by participating nations. Part of this shift was due to the problems of addressing environmental problems at a global or national scale. Agenda 21 was a plan to achieve global sustainability. The plan's goal was "to halt and reverse the environmental damage to our planet and to promote environmentally sound and sustainable development in all countries on earth" (Krizek & Power, 1996, p. 11). The plan focused on six themes— quality of life on Earth, efficient use of the Earth's natural resources, the protection of our global commons (air and water resources), the management of human settlements, chemicals and the management of waste, and sustainable economic growth— and proposed many means for their implementation.

Following the Earth Summit in 1992, Habitat II was convened in 1996 in Istanbul. Known as "The City Summit," it aimed to make the world's cities, towns, and villages healthy, safe, equitable, and sustainable (Krizek & Power, 1996). A total of 6,000 delegates attended, with 2,400 from nongovernmental organizations (NGOs). At the same time, 6,000 delegates attended a parallel NGO forum.

Other movements such as "smart growth" and "the new urbanism" gained momentum. Smart growth focuses on making land use planning and decisions more attuned with regional efficiency, environmental protection, and fiscal responsibility (Hempel, 1999, p. 52). New urbanism is focused on renewing city centers, creating new centers in sprawling suburbs, and protecting the environment.

The U.S. government is also pursuing a sustainability agenda. The Environmental Protection Agency (EPA), the Department of Energy, and the President's Council on Sustainable Development are three key players.

The EPA established the Office of Sustainable Ecosystems and Communities (OSEC) in 1995 but closed its doors in 1999. Many of the programs under that office moved elsewhere within the EPA. One initiative started under OSEC is called Community-Based Environmental Protection (CBEP). Under this program, the EPA is encouraging local individuals and groups to address their own environmental concerns. To assist communities on a path toward sustainability, the EPA has pilot programs that it is pursuing to test community-level activities with a sustainability agenda. Another program is the Sustainable Development Challenge Grant Program (SDCG), which grants federal funds to communities to leverage private and other public funds to integrate programs of economic development, environmental protection, and social well-being through community partnerships, educational efforts, and voluntary action.

Measuring Sustainability

There are a number of methods to measure sustainability. One of the most popular methods, because of its ease of use, participatory approach, and accessibility, is sustainability indicators. Many organizations and Web sites promote the use of indicators to measure and evaluate community sustainability initiatives. The purpose of these techniques is to help communities gather, sort, and analyze data with the purpose of making more informed choices.

Another technique is called ecological footprint analysis. This technique, developed by Wackernagel and Rees (1996), is an accounting tool for estimating resource consumption and waste assimilation requirements of a community, region, or nation. The authors examined Vancouver, British Columbia, Canada and found that the city needs "an area 19 times larger than its 4,000 square kilometers to support food production, forestry products, and energy consumption in the region" (Holtzman, 1999, p. 42).

This chapter focuses on sustainability indicators. Indicators enable communities to measure progress toward sustainability. In Chapter 4 on the community development process, we discussed indicators and how to measure them. Similarly, sustainable community indicators need to be developed that are relevant and measurable.

There are many different frameworks within which to develop sustainable indicators: domain based, goal based, sectoral, issue based, causal, and combination (Maclaren, 1996). A domain-based framework organizes indicators into the three E's: environment, economy, and equity. It allows for and accentuates the linkages among the three dimensions. Thus, using this kind of framework, one would develop indicators under each of the three dimensions. In contrast, a goal-based framework develops goals first. Then for each goal, it develops indicators. "The strength of a goal-based framework is that it reduces the number of indicators that have to be considered to only those relating to specified sustainability goals" (Maclaren, 1996, p. 190). The sectoral framework is divided by the sectors that an institution, such as a local government, is responsible for maintaining. Typical sectors include housing, welfare, recreation, transportation, and economic development. The strength is that local government agencies and departments can be better informed on their programs. Issue-based frameworks are organized to contend with the issues of the day, such as urban sprawl, crime and safety, or job creation. The weakness of this framework is that the issues are bound to change over time so that the indicators can become irrelevant. The causal framework introduces the notion of cause and effect. However, indicators may be difficult to establish, for example, given the complexity of ecological models and the policies that might affect them. Finally, a combination framework can combine two or more of the above

---

| BOX 10.4 | **Evaluation Criteria for Potential Indicators** |

- They reflect stakeholders' concerns.
- They are measurable.
- They are understandable.
- They are comparable/meaningful.
- Data are available to construct them.
- They are targetable/interpretable.
- They have a suitable geographic/temporal scale.
- They are timely/anticipatory.
- They are results oriented.
- They have long-range reliability.
- They are flexible.

---

frameworks. The purpose is to overcome some of the weaknesses of any one framework while taking advantage of the strengths of each (Maclaren, 1996, pp. 190-194).

Using Indicators

Choosing a framework and identifying indicators can be a long and intensive process. Many communities use a visioning process to help them establish a community vision, goals, and finally indicators. One way to select indicators is by brainstorming with all interested parties to identify an ideal set. Ways to narrow down a list of possible indicators include looking at data sources, investigating sources of help, and deciding what information is most useful. It is wiser to monitor well a few key indicators that provide useful information than to monitor poorly a wide variety of indicators. Data may be available for certain indicators but not for others. An indicator that can be supported by available data may be more practical than one that requires extensive data gathering. Another way to narrow down a list of possible indicators is to use evaluation criteria. The box "Evaluation Criteria for Potential Indicators" provides a list of criteria for narrowing down an indicators list. See Case Study 10.2 on Sustainable Seattle, an indicators project. From this example, you can get a glimpse of the process that was used to select indicators, and you can get an idea of the indicators that were chosen.

Community-Based Organizations and Sustainability

Community sustainability can address many issues. Some organizations, such as the Center for Neighborhood Technology, use a sustainability agenda in their programs and projects (see Case Study 10.3). And because community sustainability is so broad a

CASE STUDY 10.2

Sustainable Seattle: Involving the Public in Selecting Indicators

Sustainable Seattle began in 1990 as a multiyear effort to make the greater Seattle region a more ecologically and economically sustainable community. Project organizers recognized that the well-being of Seattle residents would play a key role in making sound policy choices. Therefore, the organizers placed a major emphasis on development of indicators that could measure community well-being.

The Sustainable Seattle group used a multistep process that emphasized community involvement to develop indicators. A core group of 25 trustees defined the scope of the project and served as advisers in the indicator development process. A task team then was formed to generate an initial set of draft indicators in preparation for community participation. A final set of indicators was chosen at a series of civic forums where over 250 members of the community participated. At the first meeting, community members were introduced to the project, reviewed the task team's initial indicator suggestions, and identified additional indicators. Four more meetings were held over a period of 5 months, leading to the identification of nearly 100 sustainability indicators. Of these, 40 were selected for publication in two groups. The first set of 20 indicators included

1. Environment
   - Wild salmon runs through local streams
   - Number of good air quality days per year
2. Population and Resources
   - Total population of King County
   - Gallons of water consumed per capita
   - Tons of solid waste generated and recycled per capita
3. Economy
   - Percentage of children living in poverty
   - Housing affordability for medium- and low-income households
4. Culture and Society
   - Percentage of infants with low birth weight
   - Juvenile crime rate
   - Percentage of youths participating

Each indicator was classified as moving toward, away from, or neither toward nor away from sustainability. Sustainable Seattle is now using the indicators and the development process to influence urban planning and implement programs that promote sustainable homes and businesses.

SOURCE: Sustainable Seattle (2001).

CASE STUDY 10.3

Sustainable Calumet

The Center for Neighborhood Technology (CNT), located in Chicago, is a nonprofit organization that focuses on building "prosperous, sustainable communities by linking economic and community development with ecological improvement." CNT works in the Chicago region but has recently expanded to projects that are national in scope. One of its key projects is called "Sustainable Calumet," which is aimed at a single geographic area in southeastern and northwestern Indiana. The area has been actively and intensely used for industry, primarily steel and chemicals, for a long time. The intensive use has resulted in over 300 toxic waste sites and a dozen landfills. In conjunction with this industrial activity are important and valuable habitats for about 17 threatened or endangered species. CNT has worked in the region for about a decade working on brownfield restoration, wetlands conservation, and the organizing of opposition to large-scale public works projects.

The most recent project is a planning process that is focusing strategically on five topics: transportation, air quality and economic development, open lands and water, materials and energy efficiency, and environmental recovery and ecological restoration. The planning process is covering basic research, sponsoring issue forums, creating working groups on aspects of transportation, for example, and distributing information to citizens.

SOURCE: From "Sustainable Calumet," <www.cnt.org/calumet/>, 2000. Center for Neighborhood Technology. Copyright 2000 by the Center for Neighborhood Technology, Chicago. Reprinted with permission.

concept, many types of CBOs (see list in box entitled "Organizations Addressing Community Sustainability Issues") are addressing some aspects of it. Shuman (1998) provided a list of issues relevant to community sustainability that includes such topics as barter, carbohydrate economy, community-friendly trade, green taxes, livable wages, permaculture, and time dollars. His list is long and diverse in its topics, but it underscores the many types of organizations that are involved in addressing these issues in a sustainable manner.

Krizek and Power (1996) noted that creating an institutional environment that fosters sustainability at the local level is critical. They identified three types of institutions whose involvement is necessary for sustainability to work: government, businesses, and community. Community is identified as citizens, CBOs, and others, such as local interest groups and churches. The authors used transportation as an example of how a sustainable focus can be fostered. They identified four organizations that can assist in making transportation more sustainable: The local school district can "schedule bus

---

BOX 10.5   **Organizations Addressing Community Sustainability Issues**

- Business incubators
- Community corporations
- Community development credit unions
- Community development financial institutions
- Community land trusts
- Cooperatives
- Nonprofits
- Official action (government)
- Producer cooperatives
- Productivity banks
- Regional think tanks
- Seed banks
- Water-efficiency service companies

SOURCE: Shuman (1998).

---

routing assignments that complement one another," a large employer can "create parking pricing programs that encourage transit patronage," the chamber of commerce can implement parking pricing strategies and help to facilitate attractive downtown transit stops, and an artist community can "encourage tasteful and attractive art in transit stop locations" (Krizek & Power, 1996, p. 29). (See Case Study 10.4.)

CBOs are becoming more involved in projects that can be considered sustainable development. Such organizations as the Dudley Street Neighborhood Initiative have worked on projects to improve the community's environment while creating wealth and jobs and job training. CBOs and Community development corporations (CDCs) especially have worked on projects such as weatherizing homes for energy efficiency, removing lead-based paint or asbestos, retrofitting plumbing systems, "deconstructing" unused buildings, and reusing valuable components in new construction. They also are beginning to work on transit-oriented development, brownfields redevelopment, waste cleanup, pollution prevention, remanufacturing, open space preservation, natural resource conservation, rural-urban market connections, ecoindustrial parks, and urban gardens.

Summary and Conclusions

It is important to understand the concept of sustainability because it has become and will continue to be important, infiltrating all aspects of political, social, and economic

Nos Quedamos/We Stay

Nos Quedamos is a nonprofit organization located in the heart of the South Bronx. It represents a broad-based, grassroots coalition of residents and groups who have a long-standing commitment to their community, Melrose Commons. This organization created a sustainable plan for its community and developed an effective and productive collaboration with public agencies to implement it.

Melrose Commons is a 35-contiguous-block area east of Yankee Stadium that for roughly 30 years was largely neglected by the city and suffered from the traditional housing, infrastructure, and unemployment problems associated with urban decay. Its 6,000 residents were primarily Latinos and African Americans, and their median annual household income was less than $12,000.

In 1992, community residents came together to respond to the city's proposed Urban Renewal Plan, which could have displaced almost all the local residents and many local businesses. Citizens who wanted to stay decided to undertake a planning process to put forward some of their own recommendations for the design of their neighborhood.

By 1994, Nos Quedamos had succeeded in postponing the certification of the proposed city urban renewal plan and had obtained a 6-month extension granted by the borough president to continue to develop an alternative proposal, the new Melrose Commons Urban Renewal Plan. Since that time, the community initiative set up Studio 811, the Nos Quedamos office, where city officials came to work with the residents on the initiative.

This effort attracted the assistance of many professionals—planners, architects, lawyers, and others who, with community members, established a set of planning principles for the new Melrose Commons Urban Renewal Plan that became further refined as planning continued. They addressed social, environmental, housing, design, infrastructure, and many other community issues.

The plan focused on the following topics: parks, public transportation, especially increasing transportation links, mass transit and "friendly" sidewalks, water use, ways to capture and recycle it through rainwater systems, community gardens, and housing.

Throughout the process, Nos Quedamos emphasized the importance of using local contractors to implement the plan and met with local labor coalitions. A job completed by the middle of 1995 as a joint venture of a local contracting company with one of the largest construction companies in the city employed 80% of the workers locally.

Nos Quedamos gained wide recognition both nationally and internationally for negotiating the Urban Renewal Plan. Los Angeles and Chicago city planners visited them to discuss strategy. Groups from around the world have come to talk about empowerment and community development.

SOURCE: Sustainable Communities Network (1998).

life. At the same time, it is important to recognize that there are formidable challenges in making the sustainability concept operational. Many communities are charting a path toward sustainability through visioning processes and by establishing indicators or benchmarks for monitoring progress.

As yet, the term *sustainability* and the strategies and actions to achieve a sustainable community still seem vague and unrealizable. Also, without support from the local political structure and the local business community in addition to a large proportion of community residents willing to work at sustainability at a household and individual level, it is hard to imagine that we will see sustainable communities in the near future.

However, given the motivation of sustainability advocates, the extent of the literature on the topic, and the increasing number of community organizations and local governments involved in sustainability projects, it is a certainty that we will see more communities attempting to adopt a sustainability agenda.

CBOs of many kinds (see box titled "Organizations Addressing Community Sustainability Issues") have an opportunity to continue with their primary focus but to adjust their strategies and actions to include sustainability. Sustainability in many respects represents a new way to live, work, and recreate. Sustainability ideas need to be integrated into the work that CBOs do. For example, a CDC that focuses on housing could begin to construct affordable housing using "green" building techniques. The same CDC might work on economic development and could focus on bringing "green" industries into a neighborhood industrial area or assist in developing an ecoindustrial park. The possibilities are as diverse and broad as the society in which we live. CBOs and the communities with which they work will need to be creative and thoughtful about how they can fully integrate sustainability into their everyday operations.

KEY CONCEPTS

Agenda 21	Intergenerational equity	Steady-state economics
Domain-based framework	New urbanism	Strong sustainability
Ecological footprint analysis	Regional Planning Association of America	Three E's
Garden City Movement		Weak sustainability
Habitat II	Smart growth	

QUESTIONS

1. What is your definition of community sustainability?

2. Why is sustainability important at the local level, and why is it relevant at the local level?

3. Name three people or movements that have influenced the current sustainability movement, and discuss how.

4. Why are sustainability indicators important?

5. Of the five frameworks for establishing indicators, which one would make sense for your community? Why?

EXERCISE

1. Find out if your community is pursuing a sustainability agenda. If it is, what organizations are most involved? Find out what they are doing by interviewing appropriate and key actors. If your community is not pursuing sustainability, find out why it is not by interviewing the mayor, city manager, or planner from the local government and someone from a CBO, like a CDC.

REFERENCES

Beatley, T., & Manning, K. (1997). *The ecology of place: Planning for environment, economy, and community.* Washington, DC: Island.

Berke, P. R., & Kartez, J. (1995). *Sustainable development as a guide to community land use.* Cambridge, MA: Lincoln Institute of Land Policy.

Daly, H. (1996). *Beyond growth: The economics of sustainable development.* Boston: Beacon.

Hempel, L. C. (1999). Conceptual and analytical challenges in building sustainable communities. In D. A. Mazmanian & M. E. Kraft (Eds.), *Toward sustainable communities: Transition and transformations in environmental policy* (pp. 43-74). Cambridge: MIT Press.

Holtzman, D. (1999, July/August). Economy in numbers: Ecological footprints. *Dollars and Sense,* p. 42.

James, S., Power, J., & Forrest, C. (2000, February 28). APA policy guide on planning for sustainability. <www.planning.org/govt/sustdvpg.htm>

Kinsley, M. J. (1997). *Economic renewal guide: A collaborative process for sustainable community development.* Snowmass, CO: Rocky Mountain Institute.

Krizek, K. J., & Power, J. (1996). *A planner's guide to sustainable development.* Chicago: American Planning Association.

Maclaren, V. W. (1996). Urban sustainability reporting. *Journal of the American Planning Association, 62,* 184-202.

Maser, C. (1997). *Sustainable community development: Principles and concepts.* Boca Rotan, FL: St. Lucie.

Mazmanian, D. A., & Kraft, M. E. (1999). The three epochs of the environmental movement. In D. A. Mazmanian & M. E. Kraft (Eds.), *Toward sustainable communities: Transition and transformations in environmental policy* (pp. 3-41). Cambridge: MIT Press.

President's Council on Sustainable Development. (1997). *Sustainable communities: Task force report.* Washington, DC: Government Printing Office.

Rainforest Site. (2000, November). About rainforests. <www.therainforestsite.com/cgi-bin/WebObjects/CTDSites>

Roelofs, J. (1996). *Greening cities: Building just and sustainable communities.* New York: Bootstrap.

Roseland, M. (1994). Ecological planning for sustainable communities. In D. Aberley (Ed.), *Futures by design: The practice of ecological planning.* Gabriola Island, BC, Canada: New Society.

Sargent, F. O., Lusk, P., Rivera, J. A., & Varela, M. (1991). *Rural environmental planning for sustainable communities.* Washington, DC: Island.

Shuman, M. H. (1998). *Going local: Creating self-reliant communities in a global age.* New York: Free Press.

Sustainable Communities Network. (1998). Case studies: Nos Quesdamos/We Stay, Melrose Commons, South Bronx, New York. <www.sustainable.org/casestudies/newyork/NY_epa_nosquedamos.html>

Sustainable Seattle. (2001). The history of Sustainable Seattle. <www.scn.org/sustainable/about.htm>

Touart, A. (1998). New partnership to gather economic data on recycling industry. *BioCycle, 39*(10), 6.

Van der Ryn, S., & Calthorpe, P. (1986). *Sustainable communities: A new design synthesis for cities, suburbs, and towns.* San Francisco: Sierra Club Books.

Wackernagel, M., & Rees, W. (1996). *Our ecological footprint: Reducing human impact on the earth.* Gabriola Island, BC, Canada: New Society.

World Wildlife Fund. (2000, November 21). Living planet report 2000. <www.livingplanet.org/livingplanet/lpr00>

World Wildlife Fund. (2001, February 12). Endangered species. <www.worldwildlife.org/species/species.cfm>

ADDITIONAL SUGGESTED READINGS

Readings ■

Beaton, R., & Maser, C. (1999). *Reuniting economy and ecology in sustainable development.* Boca Raton, FL: Lewis.

Daly, H. E., & Cobb, J. B., Jr. (1989). *For the common good: Redirecting the economy toward community, the environment, and a sustainable future.* Boston: Beacon.

Daly, H. E., & Townsend, K. N. (1993). *Valuing the earth: Economics, ecology, ethics.* Cambridge, MA: MIT Press.

Elkington, J. (1998). *Cannibals with forks: The triple bottom line of 21st century business.* Gabriola Island, BC, Canada: New Society.

Maser, C. (1996). *Resolving environmental conflict: Towards sustainable community development.* Delray Beach, FL: St. Lucie.

Maser, C. (1999). *Vision and leadership in sustainable development.* New York: Lewis.

Web Sites ■

APA Policy Guide on Planning for Sustainability. <www.planning.org/govt/sustdvpg.htm>. This page provides explanations of unsustainability as well as a guide to achieve community sustainability.

Center of Excellence for Sustainable Development: Case Stories. <www.sustainable.doe.gov/management/sstoc.shtml>. This site provides success stories on a variety of topics, of which land use is one. It is useful for the range of case studies it provides.

Center for Neighborhood Technology. <www.cnt.org>. This organization links economic and community development with ecological improvement in an effort to build prosperous and sustainable communities.

Center for Rural Affairs. <www.cfra.org>. This organization focuses on working to build sustainable rural communities through social and economic justice with environmental stewardship.

Community-Based Environmental Protection. <www.epa.gov/ecocommunity>. This site focuses on communities and the initiatives they can take to protect their environment.

Ecoforestry Institute. <ecoforestry.ca/default.htm>. This site is dedicated to teaching and certifying holistic, ecologically sound forestry practices that protect and restore the sustainability of forests while harvesting forest products.

Global Action Plan. <www.globalactionplan.org>. Global Action Plan for the Earth (GAP), founded in 1989, is an environmental education, nonprofit organization that promotes and supports the development of environmentally sustainable lifestyles in America.

Institute for Local Self-Reliance (ISLR). <www.ilsr.org>. ISLR is a nonprofit research and educational organization that provides technical assistance and information on environmentally sound economic development strategies.

Resource Renewal Institute (RRI). <www.rri.org/home.html>. RRI is a nonprofit organization founded in 1985 to support innovative environmental management in the United States and worldwide. Its main role is to promote the implementation of green plans: long-term, comprehensive strategies designed to achieve sustainability.

Rocky Mountain Institute. <www.rmi.org>. The mission of this organization is to foster efficient and sustainable use of resources as a path to global security. You can find information on resource-efficient buildings, sustainable economic development, and more general topics such as water and transportation.

Sustainable America (SA). <www.sustainableamerica.org>. SA is a national membership organization that rejects destructive consumption and development patterns and promotes public policies and private actions that support sustainable development.

Sustainable Jobs Fund (SJF). <www.sjfund.com>. SJF is a community development venture capital fund and a certified community development financial institution (CDFI) that makes investments in growth enterprises that create quality jobs in economically distressed regions in the eastern United States.

Videos ■

Affluenza (1997), produced and directed by John de Graaf and Vivia Boe. "A scathingly funny historical documentation of America's consumer society that has won acclaim as 'a film that could change your life.'" Available from Bullfrog Films, P.O. Box 149, Oley, PA 19547, phone (800) 543-FROG.

Bullfrog Films, P.O. Box 149, Oley, PA 19547; Internet, <www.bullfrogfilms.com>. This company distributes about 600 titles for school and community use on a wide range of topics in a variety of film styles: animation, drama, personal essay, and documentary. To order a catalogue, call (800) 543-3764.

Ecological Design: Re-Inventing the Future (1995), produced by Brian Danitz and Chris Zelov. A video collection about "what imaginative people in this country are doing, including one of the most effective urban planners in the world." Available from Genius Loci Gallery, 1259 Northampton Street, #340, Easton, PA 18042.

CHAPTER 11

The Role of Community-Based Organizations in International Development

Community development practice is rooted largely in the U.S. experience. Most other developed and underdeveloped countries tend to be much more centralized and have less history with community-based organizations (CBOs) and locality development. Yet there has been tremendous growth in nongovernmental organizations (NGOs) and grassroots efforts in developing countries over the past 40 years. In this chapter, we explore community-based efforts in international settings, especially in developing countries. Although there is not much of a history of local control in most developing countries, there is a growing dissatisfaction in many countries with the role of large international development organizations. NGOs have provided an alternative approach to promoting development in these settings. Although there are many differences between NGOs in developing countries and CBOs in the United States, we focus on some of the similarities between the two.

Context for International Development

Many problems confront developing countries throughout the world. The rapid pace of urbanization has been a trend for about 40 years in developing countries. Poverty continues to be a problem, with many people in both urban and rural areas suffering from lack of basic necessities of food, water, and shelter. Environmental degradation has become a key concern of many organizations, countries, and people. Below, we discuss some of these problems so as to understand the context for the activities of NGOs in these settings.

Urbanization

For most of recorded human history, the vast majority of people have lived and worked in rural areas. As late as 1920, the world was only 14.3% urban (Renaud, 1981). In the United States, industrialization spurred rapid urbanization and transformed cities of mercantilism into cities of industry with high densities and many of the social problems associated with this transformation.

International Development and the Role of Nongovernmental Organizations: Some Facts

- The global GDP in 1993 was U.S.$23 trillion, with U.S.$18 trillion being the GDP of industrial countries, and U.S.$5 trillion being the GDP of developing countries.

- As of 1995, developing countries were home to 80% of world population.

- In 1995, assets of the richest 358 people in the world exceeded the combined annual incomes of countries with 45% of the world population.

- Between 1965 and 1995, the ratio of shares of global income between the richest 20% and poorest 20% of people doubled from 30:1 to 61:1.

- In 1992, the Organization for Economic Cooperation and Development estimated that 13% of all development assistance (U.S. $8.3 billion) was channeled through NGOs.

- The amount of U.S. overseas development assistance passing through private groups doubled from 1993 to 1996.

- In 1993, there were over 200,000 Grassroots Organizations (GROs) in Asia, Africa, and Latin America.

- In 1993, there were over 50,000 Grassroots Support Organizations (GRSOs) in the Third World.

- It was estimated that in 1996 these GRSOs were reaching about 300 million people throughout the Third World.

SOURCE: Krut (1997), Fisher (1998).

In a span of about 80 years, from 1920 to 2000, the world became more than 50% urban (Renaud, 1981). The urban share of total population tends to understate the number of people who will live in cities. Renaud (1981) predicted that the worldwide urban population would exceed 3.3 billion by the year 2000, which is about on target. The growth rate of urban areas since 1950 has been about 4% per annum. The World Bank (2000) predicted that urban populations will increase by another 1.5 billion by 2020 and that by 2025 two thirds of the total population will live in urban areas (p. 16). In addition, it has been estimated that of the total urban population, at least one quarter, or 330 million people, lived in poverty in 1990 (International Bank for Reconstruction and Development, 1991). The number of people in poverty has increased in urban areas along with the increase in urban populations. If about one quarter of urban populations remain in poverty, by 2020 over 1 billion people will live in poverty in urban areas.

In 1990, there were 21 megacities (cities with more than 10 million people), 17 of which were in developing countries. Many cities in developing countries had populations over 10 million in population in 1995, including Seoul (11.6 million), Buenos

FIGURE 11.1
Growing Urbaniza-
tion in Developing
Countries

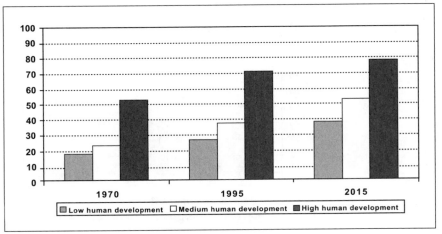

SOURCE: United Nations Development Programme (1999).

Aires (11.8 million), Mexico City (16.5 million), Sao Paolo (16.5 million), Shanghai (13.6 million), and Lagos (10.3 million). By 2015, some of these cities, such as Sao Paolo, are predicted to exceed 20 million people. These cities face some of the most intense pressures on their countries' environment and economies.

Because of rapid population growth in urban areas, cities of both developed and developing countries have had to deal with the problems that come with it: surplus labor supply, inadequate services (both social and physical), and environmental degradation (Figure 11.1). Analysts often accuse governments and others of exacerbating the problems of cities and the internal lagging regions of developing countries through their urban-biased policies (Pugh, 1996). Urban-biased policies are those that keep food prices low in urban areas and provide health and education services in urban areas while ignoring rural areas. In part, these policies were put in place to maintain political support of the current regime and keep wages down (McMichael, 2000, p. 71). These policies also tended to spur migration into cities from the countryside. Different policy responses then aimed at trying to slow down or halt urbanization, but they did little to halt the flow of rural people into cities.

Poverty

With millions of people living in poverty in both urban and rural areas, how to reduce poverty has been a difficult conundrum. One of the problems has been how to define and measure poverty.

According to the World Bank (2000), poverty is defined as an inadequate diet leading to malnutrition, inadequate shelter, inadequate health care, inadequate education, illiteracy, exposure to environmental risks, and powerlessness. There has been a shift in measurement focus from income and material wealth (e.g., TVs and radios) to illiteracy rates, underweight children, and average life span, among other indicators (Kanbur & Squire, 1999). Figure 11.2 shows the differences between countries high, medium, and low in human development (a UN-created index) in terms of access to safe water and sanitation. In the poorest developing countries—those with low human development—access to safe water and sanitation is very low. Figure 11.3 shows differences

FIGURE 11.2
Population Without
Access to Safe Water
and Sanitation

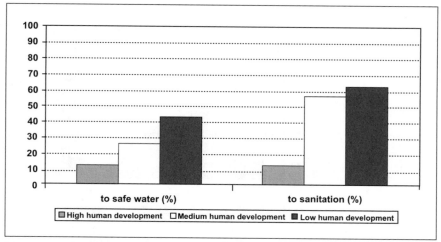

SOURCE: United Nations Development Programme (1999).

FIGURE 11.3
Poverty Indicators in
Developing Countries

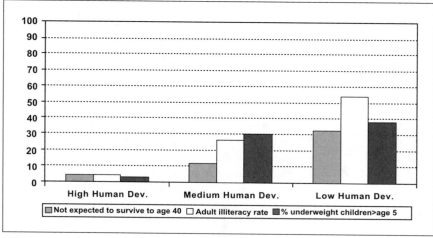

SOURCE: United Nations Development Programme (1999).

between these categories in terms of survival rate, illiteracy, and underweight children, all indicators of poverty. The figure shows how developing countries, categorized as low human development, have the highest measures of poverty.

The Environment

Part of the concern over population growth and urbanization is environmental degradation. It is the poor who are most affected by environmental degradation. The poor often do not have access to clean drinking water. Many families use coal to heat and cook with, which results in air pollution and high rates of respiratory illnesses. In addition, many families live in undesirable areas subject to natural disasters (flooding) or near garbage dumps infested with rats. However, some undesirable places also provide a means of employment. Many families recycle garbage and eke out some income from this activity.

Environmental degradation consists of the loss of biological diversity, ozone depletion, an emerging water crisis, desertification, deforestation, loss of wetlands, and
marine environment and resource degradation. These various forms of environmental
degradation have various causes and effects, but what is important to note is that these
global environmental issues are intricately related also at the local level and will have
devastating local effects.

The Informal Sector

Many people in poverty do have formal jobs. In 1972, the International Labour Organization (ILO) recognized a trend in developing countries that they called the informal
sector. The ILO (2000) defined the informal sector as consisting of

> small-scale, self-employed activities (with or without hired workers), typically at a
> low level of organization and technology, with the primary objective of generating
> employment and incomes. The activities are usually conducted without proper rec-
> ognition from the authorities and escape the attention of the administrative ma-
> chinery responsible for enforcing laws and regulations.

The ILO estimates that 50% to 60% of the workforce in urban areas of developing
countries are employed in this sector. Activities range from hawking vegetables to selling recycled materials. The informal sector is the only form of work that many people
know and provides the only source of income for many households. The informal sector
is important because it is not likely that formal labor markets would be able to absorb
the large number of labor force participants in many developing countries. NGOs in
many countries work to develop the skills and resources necessary for residents to maintain their level of living through the informal sector.

Decentralization

Urbanization, poverty, environmental degradation, and the informal sector are concerns of the international aid community. Another trend in many Third World countries
that has the blessing of aid organizations is the introduction of decentralization as a
process of government reform. Reasons for decentralizing government programs and
other aspects of government are complex. Some reasons include "encouraging local
involvement in the provision of government services" to make them "more relevant
and responsive to local needs and conditions," "improving the planning and implementation of national development," and "facilitating effective popular participation"
(Conyers, 1983, p. 99).

There are two types of decentralization: devolution and deconcentration. Devolution refers to a situation in which a central authority devolves power and responsibility
down to lower or subnational levels of government. Deconcentration, in contrast, refers
to a situation in which decision-making power remains at the central or highest level of
government but an implementation role is granted to lower levels of government
(Conyers, 1983, p. 102).

Decentralization has been advocated by many development organizations because
it is seen as a mechanism for promoting democracy in the Third World. It is assumed

that if governmental responsibilities and powers are shifted to lower levels, local residents will have greater access to decision making. It is unclear at this time whether decentralization has been able to stimulate democratic decision making in developing countries.

Concepts, Theories, and Debates

In the previous section, we have used terms such as *development, developing country,* and *underdevelopment.* In this section, we define these terms and discuss theories that inform how international development is carried out and some of the debates over these theories and concepts.

It is useful to think about the term development as a goal and as a process. As a goal, *development* refers to an end state. For example, a developing country will aim to achieve a level of economic growth that makes outside aid unnecessary. For a community, development may entail a high quality of life that includes every child getting a good education, a healthful and safe environment, full employment, and little or no poverty. As a process, *development* refers to "progressive change in the society's status quo" (Weitz, 1986, pp. 20-21). The process orientation is much more akin to community development efforts in the United States.

In the past, many theories of international development have assumed that the developing countries of the Third World would strive for a level of development similar to that of First World countries such as the United States, Canada, and the European nations. The primary forces driving this development are technology and economic growth, although many theories address the importance of culture and values in achieving this transformation. Most of the international organizations involved in international development have worked primarily to promote economic growth in developing countries.

To understand why countries were considered underdeveloped or not achieving the same level of economic growth as the First World, explanations have focused on deficiencies of natural resources, of capital and economic infrastructure, and of social and cultural factors. These factors, however, did not completely explain the causes of underdevelopment. In contrast to *development, underdevelopment* came to mean "lacking in capital, knowledge, and technology" (Fowler, 1996, p. 170). But underdevelopment can also be interpreted more radically as being caused by an outside force, usually First World countries. An unequal power relationship is maintained by keeping Third World countries indebted to the First World through loans and other aid (Conyers & Hills, 1984).

According to many development theories that are often referred to as *modernization theory,* countries should progress through a similar set of economic stages. Economic growth has been considered the key indicator of change (Conyers & Hills, 1984). One theory that influenced how development was carried out and general thinking about development was the work done by Rostow in *The Stages of Economic Growth* (1971). He identified five stages of economic growth: (a) the traditional society, (b) the precondition for take-off, (c) the take-off, (d) the drive to maturity, and (e) the age of high mass consumption. The key to moving from one stage to another was to increase the rate of productive investment, which meant the need for capital. Thus, part of the development agenda on the part of multilateral and bilateral agencies has been to

BOX 11.2	**Acronyms for Types of NGOs and Related Organizations**

PINGOs	Public interest NGOs
BINGOs	Business and industry NGOs
INGOs	Individual-based or international NGOs
QuNGOs	Quasi-government NGOs
ENGOs	Environment NGOs
GONGOs	Government-organized NGOs
GRINGOs	Government-run NGOs
DONGOs	Donor-organized NGOs
CONGOs	Congress of NGOs
ANGOs	Advocacy NGOs
NNGOs	National NGOs
ONGOs	Operational NGOs
DINGOs	Australian NGOs
CBOs	Community-based organizations
CSOs	Civil society NGOs
POs	Private organizations or people's organizations
PVOs	Private voluntary organizations
SHOs	Self-help organizations
GROs	Grassroots organizations
GRSOs	Grassroots support organizations that incite and support GROs
SHPOs	Self-help support organizations
GSCOs	Global social change organizations
ECOs	Ecological citizens organizations or environmental community organizations
SMOs	Social movement organizations

SOURCE: Krut (1997, pp. 13-14).

inject capital into underdeveloped countries to push them to a point where "take-off" would be possible (Brookfield, 1975; Malecki, 1991).

This theory was not reflective of the conditions in developing countries. A spatial division of labor was evident between developed and developing countries that seemed to create and reinforce uneven development. Global capital production within multinational firms is very flexible in terms of both products and markets, which means firms can make products where they find the cheapest labor and sell those products across the globe. The spatial division of labor is the split between corporate headquarters and research and development facilities, generally located in developed countries, and production facilities located in developing countries. For example, Nike, a company that produces athletic shoes, is headquartered in Oregon, but manufacturers (over 700 factories) of their shoes are located in 50 countries around the world. This spatial inequality across nations presents obstacles for development in the Third World because the profits over most of the economic activity in these countries are still controlled in the developed countries.

A core/periphery theory emerged that explained economic inequalities between regions within a country and then between countries. This idea led to viewing the process of development as a dominance-dependence relationship, and a new theory was proposed—dependency theory. Under dependency theory, it was argued that trade relationships were unequal between core and periphery areas, both internal and external to nations, and would remain so unless an alternative development strategy was followed. This new strategy involved "industrialization through import substitution, the promotion of exports of manufactures, and institutional changes in favor of underdeveloped countries at the international level" (Muñoz, 1981, p. 2).

Most development theories focus on national, and even international, forces. Rarely do they help inform the activities of NGOs. Certainly, some NGOs would view their activities as supporting one theory of development or another, but the link between theory and practice is generally not very strong.

The Aid Community: A Brief History

The story of the aid community begins during World War II. The war had been raging for several years, and the U.S. government had not yet stepped into the fray, but individuals in the U.S. Treasury and elsewhere foresaw the need for reconstructing Europe after the war was over (Mason, 1973). The people in the Treasury particularly realized that the U.S. economy was connected with the vitality and strength of the economies of Europe. They realized it was important to help reestablish these economies to avert another economic disaster. The Great Depression was still fresh in everyone's minds, and at all costs people wanted to avert another one. In 1941, a special adviser to the U.S. Secretary of the Treasury drafted a proposal for a stabilization fund (Mason, 1973).

After discussions with many of the Allied countries in 1942, the Secretary of the Treasury invited 37 nations to discuss a stabilization fund and an another idea from the United Kingdom proposed by John Maynard Keynes, an economist (Mason, 1973). In July 1944, the Bretton Woods Conference was held to discuss and set up a framework for establishing two international organizations, the International Monetary Fund (IMF) and the World Bank. The IMF would provide balance-of-payments support; the World Bank would first provide reconstruction for war damage, and only after this was completed would it provide development loans (Mason, 1973).

Another attempt at development assistance was science based rather than financial. The idea of the Green Revolution was to bring plant-breeding agriculture technologies

FIGURE 11.4
Aid Flows Net Official Development Assistance

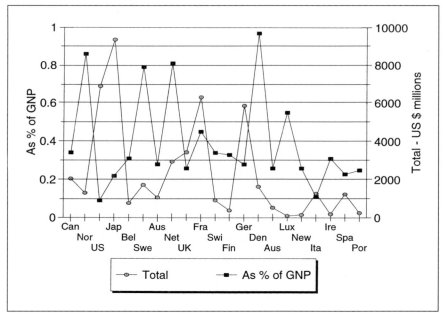

SOURCE: United Nations Development Programme (1999).

to Third World countries in an attempt to increase yields of various crops. These technologies were very successful in their goal, and many Third World countries grew these new hybrids. Africa, however, was largely bypassed in these efforts.

Unfortunately, the Green Revolution increased rural income inequalities because wealthier households were able to afford to buy hybrid seeds while poor households and women were left behind. Thus, wealthier households tended to get more wealthy because of their advantage in growing and selling their high-yield crops (McMichael, 2000, pp. 69-71).

The perceived failure of the Green Revolution had several consequences in academic and policy circles and broadened the target of criticisms to the entire international aid enterprise. Many people became critical of large aid-funded government projects that were intended to promote development. Government bureaucracies were accused of skimming off the aid for their own use. In addition, critics charged that there was little evidence that the poor actually benefited from the projects. As important as aid is to specific communities and to a country, it represents a small proportion of the flow of capital and other resources into a country (Fowler, 1996, p. 173). Thus, aid works at the margin.

In Figure 11.4, we show the amount of aid that flows from First World countries and the percentage of GNP (Gross National Product) that this amount of aid represents. On one end of the spectrum is the U.S. government with almost $7 billion, which represents about 0.1% of its GNP. On the other end of the spectrum is Denmark, with assistance that amounts to about $2 billion, which represents almost 1% of its GNP.

A relatively new trend in the aid community is to form partnerships directly with CBOs and bypass national governments entirely. "In 1992 the OECD estimated that 13% of all development assistance (U.S.$8.3 billion) was channeled through CBOs, and this amount is increasing. The amount of US overseas development assistance passing through private groups doubled from 1993 to 1996" (Krut, 1997, p. 12). Edwards and Hulme (1996) found more NGOs working on development throughout the world, multilateral and bilateral aid organizations using NGOs to channel aid, and governments seeing NGOs as effective providers of a variety of services. They found that "the proportion of total aid from OECD countries channeled through NGOs increased from 0.7 percent in 1975 to 3.6 percent in 1985 to at least 5.0 percent in 1993-94 (US$2.3 billion in absolute terms)" (p. 3). Thus, NGOs represent an alternative institutional approach to development (Riker, 1995). "The rise of the NGO as a strong institutional alternative reflects the growing recognition that the central government and the private sector lack sufficient capacity 'to respond to the challenge of poverty alleviation'" (Riker, 1995, p. 15).

In contrast, Uphoff (1996) argued that NGOs do not represent an alternative institutional form or a third sector but are actually a subsector of the private sector. He stated that people's associations and membership organizations represent the real third sector because they operate between the public and private sectors (p. 23). Nevertheless, NGOs represent an important force within the aid community.

Organizations Involved in International Development

At the highest level, multilateral aid organizations such as the World Bank and IMF focus on central government financing and very large infrastructure projects. In the past, the World Bank has funded dams, ports, and rail and road projects, for example. Bilateral aid organizations, such as the U.S. Agency for International Development (USAID), focus on programmatic areas, such as agriculture, on a countrywide basis for the most part. Current projects in Sub-Saharan Africa include agriculture, private sector development, income-generating programs, democracy and governance, environmental programs, education, and workforce development, among many others.

Large international relief agencies, such as CARE, focus on disaster relief from war, droughts, and other natural and manmade disasters. These organizations also target community development projects that aim to help communities raise their quality of life. CARE has programs in agriculture and natural resources; child, reproductive, and other health; education; environment; infrastructure; nutritional support; small business development; and water and sanitation. In 1994, CARE responded to the Rwandan refugees who were crossing the border into Tanzania by the thousands. CARE Tanzania provided food, water, sanitation, shelter, and health care to 500,000 refugees. It has many other projects in Tanzania as well that are aimed at community development rather than relief.

Of the international NGOs, the "big eight" control half the U.S.$8 billion market for NGOs (Krut, 1997, p. 13). Those eight are CARE, World Vision International, Oxfam, Médecins sans Frontières, Save the Children Federation, Coopération Internationale pour le Développement et la Solidarité, the Coalition of Catholic NGOs, Association of Protestant Development Organizations in Europe, and Eurostep (Secular European NGOs) (Krut, 1997).

Regional NGOs work on specific areas, such as East and Central Africa. Countrywide NGOs, such as Solidarios of the Dominican Republic or the Bangladesh Rural Advancement Committee (BRAC), often have a topical focus, such as primary education or

FIGURE 11.5
NGOs in the Aid Chain

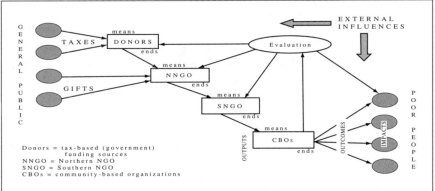

SOURCE: From "Assessing NGO Performance: Difficulties, Dilemmas, and a Way Ahead," by A. F. Fowler, in *Beyond the Magic Bullet: NGO Performance and Accountability in the Post-Cold War World,* edited by M. Edwards and D. Hulme, 1996 (pp. 169-186). West Hartford, CT: Kumarian Press, Inc. Copyright 1996 by Kumarian Press, Inc. Reprinted with permission.

health care. Many grassroots organizations as well work in individual communities on an ad hoc, project-by-project basis. For example, the Aasthan Latif Welfare Society, an NGO in the rural region of Sindh, Pakistan, focuses on basic education for girls and women. This NGO has assisted in constructing community girls' schools; trained village members about water, health, and sanitation; and carried out health awareness, training, and a polio vaccine program.

Figure 11.5 shows how NGOs are linked to the general public both directly through gifts and indirectly through donors. You can see that there is a long chain through different kinds of NGOs before aid reaches poor people through locally based CBOs.

Nongovernment Organizations: Their Role at the Community Level

As the previous sections demonstrate, NGOs are increasingly playing a key role in development assistance from working with multilateral agencies such as the World Bank and bilateral agencies such as USAID. But we have yet to define what these entities are, how they function, and what they do. In this section, we turn to the role of NGOs in development.

Riva Krut (1997) defined an NGO as

a category of organizational entities [that] were created at the founding of the United Nations. The category was invented in order to describe a specific relationship between civil organizations and the intergovernmental process, and since then the term has been loosely applied to any organization that is not public. (p. 11)

Edwards and Hulme (1996) made a distinction between NGOs that "are intermediary organizations engaged in funding or offering other forms of support to communities and other organizations" and grassroots organizations (GROs) that "are membership organizations of various kinds" (p. 15). Fisher (1998) offered a similar definition. She defined two types of NGOs in the Third World: grassroots organizations (GROs) and grassroots supporting organizations (GRSOs). GROs are located in communities and have a local membership. GRSOs are located at the national or regional level, are staffed by professionals, and channel international funds to GROs (p. 4). Fisher recognized that there are many different definitions of NGOs. By focusing only on NGOs in the Third World, she defined NGOs as "organizations involved in development, broadly defined." However, she preferred to recognize GROs as the NGOs of preference because they have "locally based memberships" and "work to develop their own communities" (p. 6). Grassroots organizations come closest to the CBOs that we find in the United States.

We should make a distinction between Northern and Southern Hemisphere NGOs. Many northern NGOs emerged after World War II to assist in providing aid to European communities devastated by the war. In contrast, some southern NGOs survived colonialism while others have been formed only recently and for many different reasons (Nelson, 1995, p. 38). Northern NGOs are located in developed or First World countries, whereas southern NGOs are located in developing or Third World countries. One criticism of northern NGOs is that they have relied on the easy availability of funding for humanitarian assistance rather than keeping a focus on the longer term capacity building and institutional development that is necessary to assist people out of poverty (Edwards & Hulme, 1996, p. 6).

NGOs, like most CBOs in the United States, are embedded in a large network of organizations and institutions involved in aid and development. In the next section, we briefly describe some of these networks.

NGO-Aid Relations

Fisher (1998) identified two types of horizontal NGO networks in the Third World. One type is made up of GROs that link up with one another. The other type is made up of GRSOs that link up with other GRSOs (p. 4). According to Fisher, the networks between GROs work in three different ways:

> First are the formal umbrella networks that link individual GROs. . . . Second are the informal economic networks tied together by barter arrangements that can widen local markets and build a vested interest in regional collaboration. Third are the amorphous grassroots social movements that increasingly focus on environmental concerns. (p. 6)

GRSOs network vertically with GROs, assisting them with funding, projects, and other issues. Also, GRSOs, like GROs, network horizontally. Formal networks usually include an umbrella organization that assists GRSOs with training and bulk purchases and represents them in negotiations with governments and donors. The relations between and among NGOs can appear cordial and supportive, but financial and political support needed from aid agencies, donors, and the government can take its toll in promoting rivalries (Riker, 1995, p. 49). (See Case Studies 11.1 and 11.2.)

CASE STUDY 11.1

Partnering With Local NGOs

Bangladesh is a country of over 115 million people. Despite a decreasing fertility rate, declining food import requirements, and a consistent rate of agricultural production, nearly half of all Bangladeshis live in poverty, and more than two thirds of all children under age 5 are malnourished. The country is situated in a delta at the convergence of three major rivers, where the land rises to only a few feet above sea level. Bangladesh is subject to floods on an annual basis.

Oxfam America partnered with two local NGOs to work on a variety of projects. With the Bangladesh Rural Advancement Committee (BRAC), the partnership has worked on a comprehensive relief and rehabilitation program stressing disaster preparedness. BRAC recognizes that relief aid alone will never improve the economic condition of the Bangladeshi people and that Bangladeshis do not want to depend on charity. BRAC designs and builds cyclone shelters that are also used as primary schools.

With Thengamara Women's Cooperative (TMSS), the partnership provides services ranging from emergency relief and disaster recovery to long-term community development. In one community, after heavy rains and flooding, TMSS helped to house refugees and then built 200 houses above flood levels on government-leased land. It also helped the village get access to clean water and latrines and small plots for gardens. One of TMSS's primary programs is providing women with access to credit. Through this program, women are provided with business training. TMSS has an almost 100% repayment rate. Since 1985, over 250,000 women have received training in various educational and economic programs, such as health and sanitation, agriculture, family planning, fisheries, environmental management, human rights, and disaster management assistance.

SOURCE: From "Bangladesh: Emergency Relief and Rehabilitation Programs and Long-Term Community Development," <www.oxfamamerica.org/global/ft/bang/globangtr.html>, 2000. Oxfam America. Copyright 2000 by Oxfam America. Reprinted with permission.

NGO-Government Relations

Government policy toward NGOs is wide-ranging and depends largely on political factors within a country. Such factors include degree of democratization, stability of the government, strength of political culture and tradition, and ability to implement policy (Fisher, 1998, p. 39). Fisher identified five general responses or approaches to NGOs that represent a spectrum from most to least repressive governments. At the most repressive, governments fear NGOs and their activities. These governments can make it diffi-

---

Somaliland Partnership Project

The purpose of this project was to build the capacity of indigenous NGOs and find support for identifying and mobilizing resources required for sustained community development. CARE launched the Somaliland Partnership Project (SPP), which operates in Somaliland, a comparatively stable part of the country. Through its SPP, CARE helps Somaliland communities overcome critical gaps in health, water supply, agricultural production, and other areas by building the capacity of 18 local development organizations to implement high-quality rehabilitation and development programs. The SPP follows a successful 5-year program that CARE implemented in conjunction with 40 indigenous NGOs throughout Somalia, 12 of which work in Somaliland.

The program's goal is to enhance the ability of communities to mobilize the resources they need to sustain long-term development initiatives. CARE emphasizes women's participation, respect for human rights, and close collaboration between communities, indigenous NGOs, and local authorities. CARE provides institutional, technical, and financial support to the dozen Somaliland NGOs that participated in CARE's earlier project and to six additional NGOs to improve their capacity to provide quality services to communities. Training subjects include ensuring meaningful community participation, designing effective development programs, and programming for sustainability. The program and its predecessor serve as models of how progress can be made within and in spite of Somalia's difficult operating environment.

SOURCE: Netaid.org Foundation (2000).

---

cult for NGOs to work because, for example, they may arbitrarily close down NGOs, arrest and imprison their leaders, keep NGOs under surveillance, subject them to harassment, or simply make laws so onerous that NGOs find it difficult to remain open. Another approach has been to ignore NGOs. This approach, according to Fisher, has been the most common one, due to many governments' inability to implement policies that would affect NGOs and their work. A favored approach by many governments is cooptation. Governments favor some NGOs and not others, give grants to NGOs in an attempt to control them, or create their own NGOs. A fourth approach is to take advantage of NGOs for financial reasons (i.e., to increase the amount of aid and foreign exchange into a country), enhancement of government legitimacy, military and security purposes (i.e., to shield the government from ethnic rivalries or guerilla movements), and help in implementing major reforms. The final approach involves cooperation and learning that can be either ad hoc or systemwide, but this is far less common than the other approaches. Governments may use this approach because of budgetary

---

CASE STUDY 11.3

ATprojects, Papua New Guinea

ATprojects is a Goroka-based NGO that works with communities, other NGOs, and the provincial government in the Eastern Highlands Province of New Guinea. The mission of this NGO is to enable rural people to develop and use skills and technologies that give them more control over their lives and that contribute to the sustainable development of their communities. The main focus of ATprojects' work is water supply projects.

SOURCE: ATprojects (2000).

---

pressures, using NGOs to implement policy by lowering costs and/or to reach more people (Fisher, 1998, pp. 40-46; Riker, 1995, pp. 28-34).

NGOs function with governments to promote development in several ways. Riker (1995) recognized five approaches: autonomous development that is independent of the central government; partnership in development to minimize duplication of efforts; competition in development; advocacy for government accountability such that NGOs serve as watchdogs and policy advocates; and bypassing of the state, which can put NGOs and their programs at risk from a hostile government (pp. 2-22). (See Case Studies 11.3 through 11.5.)

Models of NGOs

There are several ways to examine NGOs and their work. Korten (1987) provided a generational approach. The first generation of NGOs focused on relief and welfare. The second generation focused on a self-help model involving local organizations and mobilizing local resources. In the third generation, NGOs took on an advocacy role, trying to change institutions and policies at the national and subnational levels (look again at Case Study 11.5.)

Krut (1997) offered a different way to examine NGOs. She discussed two general models: the charitable model and the transformative model. The charitable model

> fails to recognize the capacity of communities for transformation, and works within the "neo-liberal paradigm of global development [that] continuously undermine[s] the activities of those NGOs which struggle against racism, gender-based oppression and marginalization of people with disabilities, children and elderly in society. (p. 18)

In contrast, the transformative model

(*text continues on page 218*)

Preserving Bolivia's Natural Beauty

In October 1995, the government of Bolivia created Amboró National Park, located in the western department of Santa Cruz. It covers an area of approximately 2,400 square miles, roughly the size of the state of Delaware. Amboró has some of the most diverse flora and fauna of any natural park anywhere in the world, including species unique to the park.

However, the park is under threat. Two major highways pass close by, bringing in people and goods and aiding encroachment. Old and new settlements surround the park. Hunters take few precautions to protect the animals. Trees are felled recklessly, and nearby farming does little to conserve soil and water. Not surprisingly, local people often see the park as an area to exploit rather than to preserve.

In response, CARE and local and national organizations together designed the Amboró Rural Development Project, which aims to reconcile conservation with sustainable development—seeking ways to enable local people to manage resources while preserving the park's beauty and biodiversity. The central areas of the park are uninhabited. CARE supports the park administration to preserve the pristine environment of the uninhabited central areas.

Additionally, CARE is focusing on the surrounding buffer zone, inhabited by approximately 4,000 poor rural families. Most are farmers, who use traditional slash-and-burn techniques, clearing and cultivating land and then moving on once it has played out. This widespread use of slash and burn is endangering Amboró. Even more destructive are the cattle and other livestock that are being introduced into some areas.

In tackling these problems, rather than making decrees on what people should or should not do, the Amboró project aims to involve local people in park management.

CARE works closely with a range of partners in Amboró. These include three local NGOs; a farmer's organization; the municipalities of Buena Vista, El Torro, and Camarapa; the park administration; and the general director for biodiversity. Initial funding of $5 million over 3 years came from the U.K. government's Department for International Development (DFID).

Each organization has a role to play. In particular, the three NGOs work directly with 900 families, developing environmentally friendly alternatives to slash-and-burn agriculture and livestock rearing. One possibility is beekeeping, with the honey being sold in nearby markets. Another is direct involvement in the park itself: maintaining trails and acting as paid and trained tourist guides. Families also are taught more sustainable ways of managing forest resources to allow them to satisfy their basic needs and improve their quality of life.

All the partners are enthusiastic about progress and have requested that the project continue for an additional 5 years when the first phase ends later in 2000. Plans are being made to extend the project area from three to eight municipalities and to include 4,000 families living in 90 communities. More local NGOs will become partners, and park management will benefit from the skills and expertise of local universities and research organizations. The estimated cost for this second 5-year phase is $11 million.

SOURCE: From "Diversity and Development in Bolivia," by Kaye Stearman, <www.care. org/info_center/field_notes/bolivia0127.html>, 2000. CARE, Atlanta, Georgia. Copyright 2000 by CARE. Reprinted with permission.

CASE STUDY 11.5

Artisans in Mali

Mali is one of Africa's poorest countries. The artisan sector includes craftspeople who make cloth, jewelry, and woodcarving and skilled tradespeople involved in carpentry, metalwork, mechanics, and electrical work. They make up about 30% of the labor force in Mali. As a sector, artisans have had to contend with a number of intractable problems on their own, such as financing, technical training, skills to run and own a business, and marketing their products. With the assistance of Oxfam America, the Federation of Malian Artisans (FNAM) was established in 1991. It has a membership of over 16,000 people in 255 associations.

FNAM began to work at addressing some of the problems that artisans were facing by setting up a series of programs. The credit program enables artisans to buy raw materials. With another organization, FNAM set up a training program and trained 600 apprentices in all different trades. Women can participate in these training programs as well as men. Part of the impetus to join FNAM was to establish fair pricing practices for goods produced and sold to wholesalers.

FNAM also worked with the central government on a number of programs. For example, FNAM worked on establishing an artisan code that requires all artisans to get certification. Another program was set up so that artisans could received medical care if injured on the job.

SOURCE: From "Artisans Skillfully Helping to Strengthen Mali Economy," <www.oxfamamerica.org/global/pr/glomalipr.html>, 2000. Oxfam America, Boston, MA. Copyright 2000 by Oxfam America. Reprinted with permission.

is collectivist at its roots. It often starts with a local focus group and the building of community assets, and may gradually extend its links to a wider community and potentially also to wider issues, without losing its original raison d'être. (p. 18)

NGOs have also been classified in five ways as identified by Nelson (1995): (a) according to level in pyramidal networks (international, national, local); (b) according to shared values or interests; (c) according to task focus; (d) according to working style (blueprint, broker, process); and (e) according to functional roles in terms of serving public or private purposes (pp. 39-44).

As the box "Acronyms for Types of NGOs and Related Organizations" shows, it has almost become a challenge to think of a new type of NGO that can have a new acronym. This list of acronyms shows the numerous ways in which NGOs—estimated at over 200,000 GROs and over 50,000 GRSOs in developing countries—have differentiated themselves. Fisher (1998) pointed out that there are two common types of GROs— those that represent an entire community or neighborhood and those that are interest based. She recognized a third type of GRO—those that make profits. This third category includes borrower groups, precooperatives, and cooperatives (p. 6). As the sheer numbers of NGOs have increased, so have individual NGOs grown in membership, staff, and the breadth of their work. For example, the Bangladesh Rural Advancement Committee (BRAC) employs over 12,000 people and expects to work with over 3 million people (Edwards & Hulme, 1996, p. 1).

What Do NGOs Do?

Part of the assumption within the aid community, including NGOs, GROs, and others, is that "there is a need for development in a particular place" (Biggs & Neame, 1996, p. 41). Another assumption is that NGOs have a "comparative advantage over the government sector in doing certain types of work" (p. 43). They also provide services to the poor who cannot afford to pay the full cost of those services (Fowler, 1996, p. 174). NGOs have several advantages over other types of aid organizations (Biggs & Neame, 1996, p. 51). They can do the following:

1. Reach the poor (i.e., target assistance to chosen groups)

2. Obtain true, meaningful participation of intended beneficiaries

3. Achieve the correct relationship between processes and outcome

4. Choose the proper mix of assistance—educational, technical, material

5. Be flexible and responsive

6. Strengthen local-level institutions

7. Achieve outcomes at less cost

8. Tailor interventions to the needs of specific situations

9. Experiment with alternative ideas and practices

10. Employ long-term strategic perspectives and time scales

11. Undertake people-centered problem identification and research

12. Use indigenous knowledge and other local resources

13. Learn from and (re)apply experience

14. Analyze and identify with the reality of the poor

15. Motivate and retain personnel

16. Promote development that is sustainable

Why would NGOs have a comparative advantage? Like CBOs in the United States, they are closer to residents than national governments and are more likely to see the needs and assets of the local region.

Impact of NGOs

A big question that NGOs face is, Who are they accountable to? If they work for and with the poor in developing countries, or at least specific constituencies in specific developing countries, are they accountable to them or are they accountable to the agency that has provided funding for their operations and projects? NGOs are accountable to a variety of institutions—"downward" to their partners, beneficiaries, staff, and supporters and "upward" to their trustees, donors, and host governments (Edwards & Hulme, 1996, p. 8).

Part of the problem that NGOs have is establishing how their performance and thus their effectiveness and impact can be measured. It is difficult to measure societal or organizational changes that may have occurred because of an NGO's efforts because of the many other influences—economic, political, social, and technological—that occur on a national and international scale.

Conclusions

In this chapter, we have provided a brief review of the international aid community in general and the role of CBOs or NGOs within that context. As we have tried to demonstrate, NGOs play an important role in providing aid to communities, and that role is growing with the recognition by multilateral and bilateral aid agencies that NGOs can deliver aid to communities often far more effectively than governments or the private sector within developing countries.

We also have shown that the international NGO community is very diverse and operates within conflicting organizational environments, including other aid organizations and governments among others. In many instances, locally based NGOs do not exist, and regional and international NGOs provide assistance to many communities. In addition, we have seen a growing trend toward partnering among NGOs at different levels, so that international NGOs, by working with local NGOs and other types of associations, make sure they are addressing the concerns and needs of a specific community.

It should be recognized that although NGOs and CBOs have several similar objectives and face some of the same issues, there still are some important differences between the two. NGOs may be operating in several communities and frequently are not initiated by local residents. In this sense, they are not "of" the communities as much as they are "for" the communities in which they work.

KEY CONCEPTS

Bilateral aid organizations
Decentralization
Deconcentration
Dependency theory
Developing countries
Development
Devolution

First World
Grassroots organizations (GROs)
Grassroots supporting organizations (GRSOs)
Green Revolution
Informal sector

Multilateral aid organizations
Nongovernmental organizations (NGOs)
Spatial division of labor
Third World
Underdevelopment

QUESTIONS

1. What are three differences between developed and developing countries?

2. What is the informal sector? Does the United States have an informal sector?

3. What is the core-periphery model? Applying it to the U.S. context, name three areas that would be considered the core and three areas that would be considered the periphery.

4. What is underdevelopment? How would you apply it to the U.S. context?

5. What is an NGO? How are NGOs differentiated?

6. What is the relationship between NGOs and multilateral and bilateral agencies?

EXERCISE

1. Through the Internet, contact one of the international aid agencies: the IMF, the World Bank, USAID, CARE, Oxfam, Save the Children, or some other. Find out what its mission is, what its current programs are, where it spends the bulk of its funds in a programmatic sense, and what the outcomes are from past projects.

REFERENCES

ATprojects. (2000). Welcome to ATprojects Inc. <www.global.net.pg/atprojects/>

Biggs, S. D., & Neame, A. D. (1996). Negotiating room to maneuver: Reflections concerning NGO autonomy and accountability within the new policy agenda. In M. Edwards & D. Hulme (Eds.), *Beyond the magic bullet: NGO performance and accountability in the post-Cold War world* (pp. 40-52). West Hartford, CT: Kumarian.

Brookfield, H. (1975). *Interdependent development.* Pittsburgh, PA: University of Pittsburgh Press.

Conyers, D. (1983). Decentralization: the latest fashion in development administration? *Public Administration and Development, 3*(2), 97-109.

Conyers, D., & Hills, P. (1984). *An introduction to development planning in the Third World.* New York: John Wiley.

Edwards, M., & Hulme, D. (1996). NGO performance and accountability. In M. Edwards & D. Hulme (Eds.), *Beyond the magic bullet: NGO performance and accountability in the post-Cold War world* (pp. 1-20). West Hartford, CT: Kumarian.

Fisher, J. (1998). *Nongovernments: NGOs and the political development of the Third World.* West Hartford, CT: Kumarian.

Fowler, A. F. (1996). Assessing NGO performance: Difficulties, dilemmas, and a way ahead. In M. Edwards & D. Hulme (Eds.), *Beyond the magic bullet: NGO performance and accountability in the post-Cold War world* (pp. 169-186). West Hartford, CT: Kumarian.

International Bank for Reconstruction and Development. (1991). *Urban policy and economic development: An agenda for the 1990s.* Washington, DC: World Bank.

International Labour Organization. (2000, July 21). The informal sector. <www.ilo.org/public/english/region/asro/bangkok/feature/inf_sect.htm>

Kanbur, K., & Squire, L. (1999). *The evolution of thinking about poverty: Exploring the interactions.* Washington, DC: World Bank. <www.worldbank.org/poverty/wdrpoverty/index.htm>

Korten, D. C. (1987). Third generation NGO strategies: A key to people-centred development. *World Development, 15*(Suppl.), 145-159.

Krut, R. (1997). *Globalization and civil society: NGO influence in international decision-making* (Discussion Paper No. 83). Geneva, Switzerland: United Nations Research Institute for Social Development.

Malecki, E. J. (1991). *Technology and economic development: The dynamics of local, regional, and national change.* Essex, UK: Longman Scientific & Technical.

Mason, E. S. (1973). *The World Bank since Bretton Woods: The origins, policies, operations, and impact of the International Bank for Reconstruction and Development and the other members of the World Bank Group.* Washington, DC: Brookings Institution.

McMichael, P. (2000). *Development and social change: A global perspective.* Thousand Oaks, CA: Pine Forge.

Muñoz, H. (Ed.). (1981). *From dependency to development.* Boulder, CO: Westview.

Nelson, P. (1995). *The World Bank and non-governmental organizations: The limits of apolitical development.* New York: St. Martin's.

Netaid.org Foundation. (2000). Governance: Building opportunity from the ground up. <http://app.netaid.org/WhatWorks//>

Pugh, C. (1996). Urban bias: the political economy of development and urban policies for developing countries. *Urban Studies, 33,* 1045-1061.

Renaud, B. (1981). *Urbanization policy in developing countries.* New York: Oxford University Press.

Riker, J. V. (1995). Contending perspectives for interpreting government-NGO relations in South and Southeast Asia: Constraints, challenges and the search for common ground in rural development. In N. Heyzer, J. V. Riker, & A. B. Quizon (Eds.), *Government-NGO relations in Asia: Prospects and challenges for people-centred development* (pp. 15-56). New York: St. Martin's.

Rostow, W. W. (1971). *The stages of economic growth: A non-communist manifesto.* Cambridge, UK: Cambridge University Press.

United Nations Development Programme. (1999). *Human development report: Globalization with a face.* New York: United Nations.

Uphoff, N. (1996). Why NGOs are not a third sector: A sectoral analysis with some thoughts on accountability, sustainability, and evaluation. In M. Edwards & D. Hulme (Eds.), *Beyond the magic bullet: NGO performance and accountability in the post-Cold War world* (pp. 23-39). West Hartford, CT: Kumarian.

Weitz, R. (1986). *New roads to development.* Westport, CT: Greenwood.

World Bank. (2000). *Understanding poverty.* Washington, DC: Author. <www.worldbank.org/poverty/mission/up1.htm>

ADDITIONAL SUGGESTED READINGS

Readings ■

Edwards, M., & Hulme, D. (1996). Beyond the magic bullet? Lessons and conclusions. In M. Edwards & D. Hulme (Eds.), *Beyond the magic bullet: NGO performance and accountability in the post-Cold War world* (pp. 254-266). West Hartford, CT: Kumarian.

Frank, A. G. (1966, September). The development of underdevelopment. *Monthly Review, 18*(9), 17-31.

Friedmann, J., & Weaver, C. (1979). *Territory and function: The evolution of regional planning.* Berkeley: University of California Press.

Hancock, G. (1989). *Lords of poverty: The power, prestige, and corruption of the international aid business.* New York: Atlantic Monthly Press.

Korten, D. C. (1990). *Getting to the 21st century: Voluntary action and the global agenda.* West Hartford, CT: Kumarian.

Perlman, J. E. (1993). Mega-cities: Global urbanization and innovation. In S. Cheema (Ed.), *Urban management: Policies and innovations in developing countries* (pp. 19-50). Westport, CT: Praeger.

Web Sites ■

Accion International. <www.accion.org>. This NGO provides small loans and training to poor people who start their own businesses so they can work their own way out of poverty. It has loaned $2.2 billion to more than 1.6 million poor business owners and has 98% of its loans paid back.

ActionAid. <www.actionaid.org/home.html>. This organization aims to work with poor and marginalized people to eradicate poverty by overcoming the injustice and inequity that cause it. It has helped about 1 million people in Africa get better access to health services.

CARE International. <www.care.org>. This private international relief and development agency focuses on improving the lives of people in over 60 countries by working at the family and community level on food, health care, shelter, education, and sustainable livelihoods.

Médecins sans Frontières. <www.msf.org>. This organization provides medical relief to victims of armed conflict, epidemics, natural and manmade disasters, and social marginalization.

Food First/Institute for Food and Development Policy. <www.foodfirst.org>. Food First is a nonprofit education-for-action center dedicated to eliminating the injustices that cause hunger.

Grameen Bank. <www.grameen.org>. This organization in Bangladesh provides collateral-free microloans for self-employment to the poorest of the poor in rural areas and technical assistance to microcredit programs around the world. It operates in over 39,000 villages in Bangladesh and has a 97% repayment rate.

InterAction. <www.interaction.org>. This organization is a coalition of U.S.-based relief, development, and refugee assistance agencies. It serves as an information clearinghouse for donors during humanitarian crises, provides forums to gather and exchange information on many issues, and leads advocacy campaigns to support disaster relief, sustainable development, and refugee protection assistance.

Netaid. <www.netaid.org>. Netaid uses an Internet-based approach to fight extreme poverty around the world. It provides links to many other organizations.

Oxfam America. <www.oxfamamerica.org>. This organization works on creating lasting solutions to hunger, poverty, and injustice with poor communities around the world.

Save the Children. <www.savethechildren.org>. This international nonprofit child-assistance organization works in 42 countries, providing health care, education, economic opportunities, and disaster relief.

World Vision. <www.worldvision.org/worldvision/master.nsf>. This Christian humanitarian organization seeks to eradicate poverty by working with the poor by providing aid and long-term assistance, from disaster relief to sustainable nutrition, health, education, and psychosocial development.

Videos ■

Vietnam's Tram Chim: Pearl of the Mekong (1999), produced by Worthwhile Films (30 min.). Tram Chim is in the Plain of Reeds, a wetland area devastated during the Vietnam War. Here we see a major conservation project that has succeeded because of the commitment of many people. Available from Worthwhile Films, 605 McMillan Road, Poynette, WI 53955, phone (608) 635-7170, fax (608) 635-7170, Internet <www.DANEnet.Wicip.org>.

Africa: Two Steps Forward (1999), produced and directed by Clayton Bailey (30 min.). Documents two successful projects in Africa: first, mills that help people rely on their own agriculture; second, a local tree-planting program created to hold back the desert and supply firewood.

African Stories Series (1999), produced by CARE International (30 min.). CARE International is known throughout the world for its relief efforts of countries in need. This series of programs takes viewers to Africa to view how members of CARE handle their humanitarian projects. Available from Chip Taylor Communications, 2 East View Drive, Derry, NH 03038, phone (800) 876-CHIP, Internet <www.chiptaylor. com/ht/srls0170.html>.

Battle of the Titans: Problems of the Global Economy (1995), produced and directed by P. Heilbuth and H. Bulow for Danmarks Radio (54 min.). Filmed in Indonesia, Venezuela, Egypt, and Nigeria, this film poses tough economic questions while showing the correlation between economic deprivation and political unrest. Available from Filmakers Library Inc., 124 East 40th Street, New York, NY 10016, e-mail info@filmakers.com, Internet <www.filmakers.com>.

The Continent That Overslept: Africa (1998), produced and directed by P. Heilbuth and H. Bulow (58 min.). Why is Africa lagging farther and farther behind the rest of the world economically? Despite a wealth of natural resources, Africa still suffers from poverty, disease, corruption, tribal warfare, and exploitive dictatorships. Available from Filmakers Library Inc., 124 East 40th Street, New York, NY 10016, e-mail info@filmakers.com, Internet <www.filmakers.com>.

Living in Africa: African Solutions to African Problems (1996), produced by South African Broadcasting (five videos, 30 min. each). A series of five films: (a) *Masai in the Modern World—Kenya;* (b) *The Survival Age—Tanzania;* (c) *The Virus That Has No Cure—Zambia;* (d) *The Riches of the Elephants—Zimbabwe;* and (e) *A Land of Immense Riches—Mozambique.* Available from Filmakers Library Inc., 124 East 40th Street, New York, NY 10016, e-mail info@filmakers.com, Internet <www. filmakers.com>.

Water for Tonoumassé (1989), produced and directed by Gary Beitel (28 min.). The film shows the efforts of a group of villagers to get clean water by drilling a well nearby. It chronicles the success of this project in which women played a key role. Available from Filmakers Library Inc., 124 East 40th Street, New York, NY 10016, e-mail info@filmakers.com, Internet <www.filmakers.com>.

CHAPTER 12

The Future of Community Development

Trends in Community-Based Development

Community-based development faces a variety of obstacles. Blakely (1989) argued that the most serious problems facing community development practice are the uncoupling of production from place, community consciousness, and community institutions. The production process is less tied to place and is now becoming global and increasingly mobile. Globalization presents obstacles because employers are less tied to their community and less willing to make investments in place. Similarly, communities have less control over their destiny because large corporations are now making decisions about when and where to move their operations, often in response to cost considerations. This position regarding the effects of globalization on community development, however, may be overstated. Most businesses are not very mobile. They are tied to their suppliers and customers in the region in many cases. Only a small percentage of businesses actually move each year. It is the threat of capital mobility that often affects local residents and policy makers. The growth of the service sector, however, may dampen the effects of globalization because these firms are unlikely to be as mobile as a garment or automobile factory.

People are less shaped by "territorial consciousness" and participate in organizations that are national and international. These processes have been taking place for decades now but may have been exacerbated in recent years by technological change (such as the Internet), globalization of the economy, and the growth of multinational corporations. These developments may make it more difficult for communities to act on their local problems for a couple of reasons. As decisions affecting communities are increasingly made in corporate headquarters, the ability of local residents to shape these decisions becomes increasingly difficult. These trends tend to incapacitate many residents because they have come to believe that they cannot effect change at the local level. Blakely also argued that these changes have made it more difficult for residents to become conscious of their community. Many people maintain social contacts and ties outside of their local community and have become much more oriented toward regional and national organizations. Thus, there are fewer inducements to become involved in local issues, and there are more inducements to become involved in national and even international issues. Also, because people now live, work, and consume in different places, their allegiance to a specific place becomes much more diffuse. Other developments such as school choice add to these problems because the quality of local schools becomes less important to individuals. All of these changes make the connection between individual well-being and the conditions of a local place much more tenuous for most residents.

We have argued in Chapter 1 of this book that there is substantial evidence that people are much more likely to develop and maintain social relationships outside their local area than they were in the past. Yet this does not mean that residents do not have social ties and relationships with their neighbors or that they cannot be motivated to act on local issues. Residents are especially likely to respond to a threat to their neighborhood, such as a zoning or school issue. Individuals who have lived in the community longer and who are home owners are more likely to respond to these local issues than are others in the community. The real issue facing community development is how to institutionalize these issue-based efforts among local residents.

Putnam (2000) has argued persuasively that there has been an erosion of civic society over the past 50 years. Much of his evidence for this claim is based on declines in the number of people belonging to and participating in local organizations. The decline of social capital has important implications for community development efforts. If local residents lack social and organizational ties, it is more difficult to mobilize them to address local problems and raise their consciousness about local issues. Putnam's thesis may be more about middle-class communities than lower-class communities. The problem in poor neighborhoods may be more that middle-class residents have moved out and that they were the major supporters of local organizations and institutions (see Wilson, 1987). Putnam's point, however, is well taken, and the decline in civic organizations certainly has had negative effects on efforts to promote community development. At the same time, a wide variety of other sources of social capital are available in poor and minority communities. Residents in poor and minority communities are more likely to rely on neighbors and kin to meet their material and emotional needs (Green, Hammer, & Tigges, 2000). Thus, there appears to be a broad base for social contacts and ties within these neighborhoods. The problem may be that residents in these neighborhoods are less likely to have social relationships with individuals outside these neighborhoods who could provide assistance and support.

Overall, we must recognize that many societal trends seem to be working against the field of community development. We are becoming a more mobile society in many ways, and individuals are less oriented toward local institutions than they used to be. But some forces are pushing for more community-based strategies for addressing local problems. Although critics are right to be concerned about the effects of global trends and capital mobility, these obstacles are not necessarily insurmountable. The asset approach that was presented here suggests that most communities have resources that can be used to help build these areas. The fact that there continue to be major social and economic problems in many communities is not necessarily an indictment of the failure of the community development movement but rather a result of the failure of national and state policies that have addressed these concerns.

Limits to Community-Based Development

The community development field has become institutionalized over the past 40 years. Most local leaders and government officials today recognize the importance of engaging residents in the decisions that will affect their community. Federal, state, and local governments have formalized public participation efforts. We may question whether local residents actually have any control over these policies and decisions, but they are asked for their input on almost all local matters. At a minimum, most public officials would acknowledge that public participation does affect the implementation of programs; when local residents have some input into the process, they are more likely to "buy in" to the program. But most public officials still want to control the process, and they rely heavily on technical experts, rather than local knowledge, for the most important advice.

Similarly, the idea of place-based development is firmly entrenched in federal and state policy, largely because politicians see it as directly affecting their constituencies. Also, most people recognize that economic development, even within a metropolitan area or rural region, may not affect neighborhoods or communities evenly within these areas. We have argued that markets and government programs have a limited capacity to address some of these problems. Community-based organizations (CBOs) appear to be a likely mechanism for carrying out place-based strategies of development.

Even some of the community-based development institutions, such as micro-enterprise loan funds, have become mainstream and are being promoted by federal agencies (e.g., the Small Business Administration). Community development corporations (CDCs) are considered the key organizational mechanism for providing affordable housing in most cities and some rural areas. But although they can receive some federal funding, these institutions cannot obtain enough funding to address the needs of low-income and poor neighborhoods. And as they become part of the mainstream, there is a danger that they will lose their local orientation and become more standardized across communities.

Although the community development field is well established, most practitioners and policy analysts recognize that community development programs have not come close to addressing the breadth and depth of problems that exist in the inner city and in underdeveloped rural areas. Even the most successful CDCs have been able to produce only a fraction of the need for affordable housing. Successful economic development efforts have not generated enough jobs to replace those that have been lost to economic restructuring and the globalization of the economy. Although CBOs have been able to provide job training to underserved populations and help job searchers make connections with employers, the level of human capital in most inner cities and underdeveloped rural areas continues to lag behind other parts of the country. New financial organizations have emerged to address the needs of poor and minority communities, but these too have only scratched the surface of the credit needs of most communities. Although many issues are at play here, one of the common problems that CBOs face is a lack of resources. This is not to say that more financial resources alone will solve the problems. In fact, in many instances CBOs have too many resources and do not have a good plan for effectively allocating them. But providing stronger infrastructure that supports CBOs could make them much more effective.

In many instances, community-based development efforts are struggling to overcome the powerful influence of policies that undermine their activities. Probably the best illustration is in the area of economic development. Although there has been continuing federal and state support for CDC activity in the area of economic development, transportation programs have facilitated the flight of the middle class out of the city, leaving areas with concentrated poverty and little hope for investment. Similarly, government programs have promoted the flight out to the suburbs by subsidizing home loans. Businesses have followed the migration out to the suburbs and have been provided incentives that often include federal tax breaks. The result has been the loss of job opportunities in the inner city. Community-based development, at least to this point, has not been able to overcome these forces. We need community-oriented policies that recognize the linkages between state and federal programs and the differential effect on places throughout the United States. Community-based development would have a much greater chance of success with these types of policies.

Some critics have expressed concern that the community development field has become too institutionalized and has lost its ability to challenge the existing structure of power. Many of the successful community development efforts of the 1960s were built on community organizing efforts. In particular, many CDCs were established as a direct result of these efforts to mobilize communities. But because many CDCs are dependent on the federal government and foundations for financial assistance, they may be reluctant to challenge the political structure too much and may be less likely to get involved in mobilizing residents, turning instead to the provision of technical assistance.

Local Versus External Initiation of Community Development

One of the recurring issues in the community development field over the past 40 years has concerned the proper role for external organizations and institutions in promoting development. On the one hand, there is plenty of evidence that external support through foundations and intermediary institutions can influence the success of community development projects. These external organizations can provide financial resources, information, technical assistance, and contacts with other communities or organizations. Intermediary organizations in community development, such as the Local Initiatives Support Corporation and the Neighborhood Reinvestment Corporation, have demonstrated their success in producing affordable housing. This model also has been used to a more limited extent in the support of human capital (training) and financial capital (lending) at the local level.

On the other hand, there is growing concern that CBOs often feel they lose control to these organizations (Rubin, 2000). Because CBOs must rely on these organizations for financial assistance, the focus of projects may be changed, and projects may not be directed at the needs of local residents.

The evidence from many programs around the country suggests that community development programs are less likely to be successful if they are initiated outside the community. Even cities that attempt to generate grassroots efforts within neighborhoods often face obstacles. One of the most recent efforts by a major city to create a grassroots effort occurred in Atlanta, Georgia, where former President Jimmy Carter attempted to build capacity in over 20 neighborhoods in Atlanta. Corporations in the region provided a great deal of support for the project. Yet most of the evaluations suggest that the project had only a minimal impact because it was never able to generate the neighborhood support that was so badly needed. This example suggests that external organizations can at best play a supportive role and are limited in their ability to actually generate grassroots efforts.

The dilemma facing CBOs is that they need institutional support from external organizations but also need to maintain control over their activities. There is a delicate balance to maintain here, and there will always be external pressures to set the agenda. Foundations, governments, and other support organizations have their own agendas that may not be at all consistent with the goals and objectives of neighborhood groups.

An Agenda for Promoting Community Development in America

Fundamental changes have occurred in the social, political, and economic systems in which our communities are embedded. How should practitioners respond to these changes? What types of policies will help promote community-based solutions to the problems of inner cities and underdeveloped rural areas? One temptation is the longing to return to the notion of community that existed in America in the 1950s. The emphasis on participation in local organizations, a strong sense of neighborliness, a common set of values, and local institutions that serve primarily local residents is very appealing in today's individualistic world. Reconstructing community along these lines, however, may be impossible and not necessarily desirable. Communities in the 1950s also were characterized by a lack of diversity, less individual freedom and choice, and limited roles for women and minorities. Decision making in communities was not necessarily any more democratic. Technological, economic, and social changes probably make it almost impossible to return to this world again anyway.

Build on Successes

So what is to be done? First, we need to build on the successes of intermediary organizations, such as the Local Initiatives Support Corporation, in areas other than housing. Similar types of organizations could be established for lending programs, training programs, conservation programs, and other areas of economic development (e.g., small business incubators, food cooperatives). The Clinton administration had initially planned to support hundreds of development banks that were built on the model of the South Shore Bank in Chicago. This type of program is an ideal model of how community-based development can be promoted by the federal government and foundations.

Create Spaces for Public Participation

Second, it may be very difficult to reconstruct the sense of community that we once had, but it may be possible to create "spaces" for community visioning and planning. These opportunities, frequently called search conferences or visioning sessions, permit local residents to identify their common values and develop a vision of what they would like their community to look like in the future. Too often, communities are simply responding to local crises and do not act in a proactive way to shape their community. Search conferences or visioning sessions are excellent opportunities for bringing together diverse interests in the community and discussing the major issues they face. Many of these programs are currently sponsored by universities and some state governments (e.g., in Oregon). A variety of models might be considered.

Provide Training for CBOs

Third, we need to provide more professional development opportunities for community development practitioners. Many of these practitioners feel that they do not have the background or training necessary to address their community's needs. There are several training programs for nonprofit organizations, but there are fewer opportunities for training of professions in other types of CBOs, such as neighborhood improvement associations, that are critical to the community development effort. Many of these other CBOs rely heavily on volunteers, and there is essentially no opportunity for training. In particular, these organizations may need some basic training on community organizing or development issues.

Form Regional CBO Consortiums/Networks

Fourth, communities are no longer self-contained entities where residents live, work, and consume. In most cases, community development efforts are influenced by regional factors. Efforts to create new jobs in an urban neighborhood may be influenced by the health of the economy in the larger metropolitan area. Efforts to plan for development can be influenced by the actions of other neighborhoods and communities in the region. Thus, it is important for community development practitioners to consider how their programs are influenced by and in turn are influencing other communities. One of the best means of accomplishing this goal is to form consortia of community development organizations that can work together on issues of common interest.

Use Meaningful Public Participation Techniques

Fifth, there is a need to seriously reconsider public participation efforts practiced by federal, state, and local governments. Most of these efforts do not grant any real decision-making authority to local residents. The emphasis that the federal government is placing on community-based decision making is often a veiled attempt to gain local support for decisions that are made elsewhere. These efforts could provide real opportunities for local residents to particulate fully in the decision making that affects their community. CBOs may have a role in facilitating these processes in the future.

Conclusions

The field of community development has undergone dramatic changes over the past 40 years. Originally conceived of as community organizing around social service delivery, it has evolved into areas such as economic development, planning, housing, and natural resources. As a result, community development has become more professionalized and dependent on external resources. These changes have produced both benefits and costs for communities and practitioners. Local organizations now need to know how to "play the game" and develop the necessary expertise. Local residents may become frustrated in dealing with external organizations, such as foundations, and the need to become more knowledgeable about the issues affecting their communities. Yet access to resources and information may ultimately improve the success of these community development efforts. The challenge is to keep the development efforts accountable to residents and based on their visions of what the community should look like in the future.

QUESTION

1. What are the benefits and costs of involving external organizations in community development programs? How can external organizations support local grassroots efforts?

EXERCISES

1. Talk with a local community development practitioner, and ask what are the major obstacles that he or she faces in his or her work. What types of things does he or she think would be most helpful in efforts to revitalize the community?

2. Talk with a city or county government official who is responsible for community development activities. Ask him or her what he or she is doing to increase the capacity of neighborhood organizations and groups. What type of relationship does he or she see as most beneficial?

REFERENCES

Blakely, E. J. (1989). Theoretical approaches for a global community. In J. A. Christenson & J. W. Robinson, Jr. (Eds.), *Community development in perspective* (pp. 307-336). Ames: Iowa State University Press.

Green, G. P., Hammer, R., & Tigges, L. M. (2000). Someone to count on: Social resources. In D. L. Sjoquist (Ed.), *The Atlanta paradox: Race, opportunity, and inequality in a new southern city* (pp. 244-263). New York: Russell Sage.

Putnam, R. D. (2000). *Bowling alone: The collapse and revival of American community.* New York: Simon & Schuster.

Rubin, H. J. (2000). *Renewing hope within neighborhoods of despair: The community-based development model.* Albany: State University of New York Press.

Wilson, W. J. (1987). *The truly disadvantaged: The inner city, the underclass, and public policy.* Chicago: University of Chicago Press.

Index

ABOUT THE AUTHORS

Gary Paul Green is Professor of Rural Sociology at the University of Wisconsin–Madison and a Community Development Specialist with the University of Wisconsin–Extension. He received his PhD from the University of Missouri–Columbia. His applied research program at the University of Wisconsin has focused on community, workforce, and economic development issues. He is author of *Finance Capital and Uneven Development* and coauthor of *Places of Consumption: Restructuring and the Growth of Nonmetropolitan Localities in the United States.* He has served as an adviser on community development issues in New Zealand and Ukraine.

Anna Haines is Assistant Professor in the College of Natural Resources at the University of Wisconsin–Stevens Point and a Land Use and Community Development Specialist with the University of Wisconsin–Extension. She received her PhD from the University of Wisconsin–Madison in the Department of Urban and Regional Planning. Her research and teaching focuses on land use planning, urban and regional planning, and community and economic development. Her current research project examines the role of workforce development networks in providing job training. She has served in the U.S. Peace Corps as an urban planner in Kenya and has worked as a consultant for the World Bank.